Christian Living

THE CHURCH'S TEACHING

I

THE HOLY SCRIPTURES

II

CHAPTERS IN CHURCH HISTORY

III

THE FAITH OF THE CHURCH

IV

THE WORSHIP OF THE CHURCH

V

CHRISTIAN LIVING

VI

THE EPISCOPAL CHURCH AND ITS WORK

VOLUME FIVE

Christian Living

STEPHEN F. BAYNE, JR.

With the assistance of the Authors' Committee
of the Department of Christian Education of
The Protestant Episcopal Church

A Crossroad Book

THE SEABURY PRESS · NEW YORK

© 1957 BY THE SEABURY PRESS, INCORPORATED
LIBRARY OF CONGRESS CARD CATALOG NUMBER: 57-5739
PRINTED IN THE UNITED STATES OF AMERICA
BY THE COLONIAL PRESS INC., CLINTON, MASSACHUSETTS
DESIGN BY STEFAN SALTER

ISBN: 0-8164-2007-6
TENTH PRINTING, 1976

Foreword

With the publication of *Christian Living* the series known as *The Church's Teaching* is complete. The entire Church owes a debt of gratitude to the several members of the Authors' Committee for the many hours of labor given to completing this task. Seldom have manuscripts received such careful scrutiny at the hands of so many competent readers representing the best scholarship and almost every shade of significant difference in the Church.

All six volumes of *The Church's Teaching* will have an increasing effect upon the belief and practice of children, young people, and adults as leaders and parents use these books in the faith, life, and worship of the Church. The existing volumes already are the best selling books ever produced by our Church, exceeded only by the Book of Common Prayer. More and more they are becoming the standard resource book in parish house and home in the Church's growing parish-wide program of Christian education.

The Church would be barren without a knowledge of the Mighty Acts of God throughout the ages, and Volume V confronts the Christian with some of the choices which are his in relating this knowledge to the saving grace of God now present in our midst. To this end all of the volumes and the Church's entire educational program speak.

David R. Hunter
John Heuss
Co-chairmen of the
Authors' Committee

Preface

Any book about Christian living is almost bound to be either a "what" book or a "how" book. This is a "what" book—that is to say, I have chosen to devote it primarily to the things most Christians agree that they should think and do, and only secondarily to the means by which those thoughts and deeds are accomplished.

This does not mean that I feel, or the Church feels, that the "what" is more important than the "how." It means simply that any book that tried to be both would be almost unmanageably long, and an author must do one or the other; and that I chose to write mainly about the duties rather than the grace which makes the duties possible.

I did so because—in my own diocese, at any rate—we feel a great need to think together more deeply about Christian moral ideals and practice. The Church is much more than merely an association of people around a common faith. It is also a company of sincere and thoughtful people who know that our life must reflect the deep truths of our faith, if it is to be truly a Christian life at all. Therefore it is natural, and seems needful, to us to think deeply and corporately about "the ensample of godly life" which our Lord gave us in His own mortal years and in His teaching.

This book is written for those people, to supply basic material for our thoughts about how we should make the decisions which life crowds on us, and how we should move ahead in the reordering of our lives and our society so that both are in better accord with God's Will. It is a quite serious book, not one to be skimmed through rapidly, but designed for thoughtful study (often common study in groups) and reflection. It does not supply easy answers for our ethical dilemmas. It does intend to supply the fundamental raw material on which Christian attitudes are based.

In examining the book, readers will notice that the first part—the Prologue—is a connected and thoughtful essay about Freedom, quite different in character from the shorter chapters on various areas of Christian living which follow. This arrangement is purposeful. There is a theme running all through the book, which is discussed fully at the beginning, then taken for granted in the body of the book, then briefly summarized in the Epilogue.

Readers, then, should note that there are three different ways of studying this book. One would be to read it straight through from beginning to end. Another, equally helpful, would be to start at the end, with the brief summary, then follow with the topical material in the three middle sections, concluding with the Prologue. The third way would be to plunge at once into those chapters which deal with specific areas of Christian concern (Six through Twenty-one), and reserve both Prologue and Epilogue for more careful study after the main body of the book has been explored.

There is probably something to be said for each of these three methods. However, whether the Prologue is deferred or not, it should be studied carefully *at some stage,* for I am sure that, if the Prologue were omitted, a reader might well be led to think of Christian living as nothing more than an assortment of miscellaneous duties that have no roots in our humanity. But the order in which you study the Prologue, whether first, last or in the middle, does not matter very much.

This, like the other Church's Teaching volumes, is the product of very extensive common thought and counsel by the members of the Authors' Committee. Whatever strength it has comes from the fact that it represents real and painstaking and sometimes quite strenuous, corporate examination and discussion; but certainly the Authors' Committee should not be held responsible for any mistakes, or for anything I have said which is untrue.

My thanks go particularly to the Reverend David R. Hunter, co-chairman of the Author's Committee, and Director of the Department of Christian Education of our Church. I am very sharply in his debt for both counsel and patience. I want also gratefully to acknowledge the immeasurable help of Mrs. Margaret Lockwood, Executive Assistant to Dr. Hunter, and also the helpful corps of readers, who read the book in manuscript and whose thoughtful suggestions were of very great assistance.

Finally, because it is a "Church" book, intended to teach only what is commonly held and taught in our Anglican moral tradition, and not at all a collection of personal opinions, readers will doubtless find many points where their own thought and practice go beyond what is outlined here. Indeed I must confess that my own attitudes are at certain points somewhat brisker than those which are here expressed. But I do not feel that the opinions of any individual are determinative in rendering the common and fundamental teaching of the Church.

It would be disturbing if there were not always an area of moral exploration beyond where our settled duties and teachings lie. In some places I have indicated where that area seemed to be. But this is not the book of moral frontiers; it means to be the book of the sober, agreed discipline of the Soldiers of the Cross and of the Prayer Book, and as such, is submitted to the glory of God and the health of His Church. It has not been our custom, in this series, to make personal dedications of the volumes. I do not alter that when I say that the Christian life of my own father, now no longer in the Church Militant, has been steadily and deeply before my eyes as this book was written; and I give thanks accordingly.

STEPHEN F. BAYNE, Jr.

Contents

EPILOGUE

PART ONE

Freedom and the Free Man

CHAPTER ONE

All Life Is Choice

THIS IS A BOOK about Christian living. It is not a textbook for experts in the theory of Christian ethics, but one written for plain people like ourselves who are concerned about our workaday Christian lives in our homes and jobs and communities. What does Christ expect of us as fathers and mothers, as employees, as citizens? What duties and responsibilities does the Church teach us? How can we be better witnesses for Christ? How are we to become stronger and happier Christians and church people? These are the questions with which this book deals.

Because it is about Christian living—about the day-by-day problems we face and the choices we have to make—this book is, inevitably, one about *freedom* and *decision,* and about the Christian as the free man who accepts and makes his choices not simply because he cannot escape them, but because he understands they are the means by which he lives in partnership with God.

RESPONSIBLE FREEDOM

In fact, the heart of this book is exactly this faith that *responsible freedom is the secret of man's existence under God.* When we use such words as *freedom, choice, purpose, responsibility,* we are using words which would not make sense if man were just a puppet or a doll. Those words presuppose a thinking person to whom freedom is not an abstraction or a theoretical possibility, but a series of necessary decisions that must be faced. These choices have real consequences, and we have to live with those consequences and be judged by them. Indeed, the choices we make and the way we make them are the way we become persons, selves. Therefore, God is also deeply involved in our freedom and the way we use it— either we will choose our way toward Him or away from Him. More than that, He has, in Christ, showed us how to use our freedom the true and right way.

THE MEANING OF THE WORD *FREEDOM*

First of all, then, we begin with the word "freedom" and its meaning. We Christians do not ask any favors in our use of words or set some private or special meaning on them at the outset. We begin where everybody else begins, with the fact of freedom of choice and decision. Like most other great words, "freedom" has grown and deepened in its meaning over the centuries as men have seen more and more deeply into the nature of human life. The word is an enormously complicated one today—the Shorter Oxford English Dictionary gives eleven principal definitions for it, and thirty-six for the root word "free," because men have so widened their understanding of the fact, the experience, that underlies it. But still we would say that the freedom the Christian talks about is the same freedom that anybody else talks about.

To the Christian as to every man, the heart of this word lies in man's universal experience and knowledge of himself. From the first moment of conscious selfhood, we have had it forced on us that to live is to choose, that our life, the very secret of being a person, consists of our response and decision in each of the myriad choices that existence poses. What shall we say? What shall we do? It is not possible for us to avoid choice; life does not stop to let us catch our breath; it keeps confronting us with issues to be decided; and even a decision not to choose is in itself a choice to be added to the cumulative record of our choices—the record that makes up so great a part of ourselves.

Further, most of our decisions are by no means morally neutral. "What shall we do?" almost always is part of a larger question "What *ought* we to do?" Most choices bring loyalties into play.

This is so despite the fact that the problems are by no means as clear, usually, as we wish they were. In fact, preachers are likely to annoy us a little because a strong sermon illustration is usually black-and-white, and real life is very rarely black-and-white. Any father, trying to follow directions as to how to put together his son's Christmas bicycle, learns pretty quickly the difference between a printed and illustrated manual and the real, stubborn, defiant, and usually incomplete, collection of parts which confronts him.

4 ·

The sermon-illustration kind of ethical problem is of the same general type.

FREEDOM AND CHOICE

Alas, no, our choices often are not very clear—black and white turn out, on examination, to be shades of grey—and to this important fact we must return to think more deeply. But, clear or not, most choices bring loyalties into play. We *care* which side we choose; there are real issues at stake; and our freedom involves the very things we care most about. It is not accidental that the birth-root of the word *free* and of the word *friend* is the same. To choose and to love are closely allied in our experience; to be free is to find some things dear and true, to give our loyalty to them as to a friend, and to turn our backs on others not deserving of that loyalty.

Marius, in Walter Pater's *Marius the Epicurean,* watched the cruel gladiatorial games in the arena in Rome and reflected on the apparent callousness of the wise and humane Emperor who saw no evil in all this great slaughterhouse. He marvelled that he, the humble seeker after truth,

was aware of a crisis in life, in this brief, obscure existence, a fierce opposition of real good and real evil around him, the issues of which he must by no means compromise or confuse; of the antagonisms of which the "wise" Marcus Aurelius was unaware.

Pagan that he was, Marius had come to know that

Those cruel amusements were, certainly, the sin of blindness, of deadness and stupidity . . . and his light had not failed him regarding it. Yes! *What was needed was the heart that would make it impossible to witness all this; and the future would be with the forces that could beget a heart like that. . . .* Surely evil was a real thing, and the wise man wanting in the sense of it, where, not to have been, by instinctive election, on the right side, was to have failed in life.[1]

The part that Christian faith has played in the history of freedom has not been to find a new meaning for the word or to dignify it with a new and special sense. What Christianity has done has been to bring new horizons into human life. The Christian sees not a

---

[1] Walter Pater, *Marius the Epicurean* (New York: The Macmillan Company, 1926), pp. 171-173. (Italics mine). Used by permission of the publisher.

different scene, but further into the familiar one. He sees not a different man, but greater dignity in every man because of Christ Jesus. The Christian's choices are not different choices; they are the same choices that man has been making from the beginning, but they are made with a greater awareness of their importance and of all that is involved in them, and with a profoundly deeper loyalty.

THE CHRISTIAN VIEW OF CHOICE

The choice of kindness or cruelty (to follow Marius' reflection for a moment more) is the same in every age in every soul. Christianity brought no new choice or new law. What Christianity gave to the pagan world, in that immense convulsion which brought the Christian Era into being, was a *new setting* for that choice, a setting which showed that the issue of kindness or cruelty was not simply a matter of good manners, or grace, or the mere acceptance of a code of noble conduct, but really the choice of life itself. Christianity showed mankind that such a choice was, in reality, a conflict in the basic material of existence itself. Life, death, and immortality hung on kindness—indeed, the clearest way to see the choice was to see it not as it affected the poor slave in the arena, but as it pronounced judgment, under the eternal laws of God, on the soul of the emperor and of the people themselves. What was at stake was not the wretched existence of a prisoner or a slave. What was at stake was nothing less than Christ Himself, who had told us that the cup of cold water given to the least of earth's children was, in truth, a gift to Him.

Therefore, the dimensions of freedom were incredibly extended in this Christian revolution, and correspondingly the loyalties involved were marvellously clarified and deepened. Freedom has always involved obedience to allegiances. Christianity did not introduce the idea of loyalty. Christianity rather awakened us to the greatness of man's loyalty—that, at heart, it was a loyalty to none other than God Himself. The words of the ancient Saxon oath by which the knight swore fealty to his lord find a profound echo in the heart of every Christian: "Before Him to Whom this shrine is holy, I will be faithful and true to my Prince; love all that he loves, shun all that he shuns, and never of my will or power do aught that may be hurtful to him."

This Christian loyalty was incomparably greater than the mere conventional code of paganism. It was what Marius had seen that mankind desperately needed: "the heart to make it impossible to witness all this." And the future, as it turned out, was "with the forces that could beget a heart like that."

SUMMARY

Thus, to sum up this first chapter, all mankind is aware of choice pressing insistently on consciousness and demanding an answer. All mankind knows that choices are not morally indifferent, whatever the standard of morality may be; decisions are "right" or "wrong" in terms of some code, and they somehow make us "right" or "wrong." These insights are as nearly universal as any human experience we know.

The peculiar Christian insight—born in our faith that when God became man, He did so completely, not evading or shirking the necessity of freedom but assuming and fulfilling it—is that this freedom itself, with all its puzzles, its costly and confusing choices, *is the very means of our communion and partnership with God.* Even the least of our human acts may be the means by which we minister to God. Even the most inconsequential of decisions and acts (as the world counts such things)—a cup of water to a stranger, a word of kindness to a casual offender—is of immense consequence to God and in our life with Him. In the picture language of the Gospel, the stranger is none other than God Himself. The unique gift, therefore, of the Christian faith was the gift of *intensity,* of the perception of the true depth and greatness of our ethical choices.

Our freedom is the same as that of every other person. But we are led to understand and see it in its deepest and loftiest perspective, in dimensions of length, breadth, depth, height no less than those of the love of God.

This gives to Christian living the soberness and reverence which is true of us at our best. No choice is really unimportant to us, no matter how unimportant we count ourselves to be, for every choice is filled with the possiblity of true service of God and our brother. No human encounter is unimportant to us, for the person we encounter, in whatever disguise, is really God Himself. All life is choice. All life is the persistent, recurring opportunity to choose God and His truth and love, and, by His power, to build our lives and our selves in His pattern.

CHAPTER TWO

The Fact of Freedom

*T*HE *Christian starts, then, where everybody else starts, with the fact of freedom.* It is important to repeat that freedom is a fact and not a theory. Most of us can remember, from school days, long debates and exhaustive questions about the very possibility of freedom. We can also remember arriving at the soul-chilling conclusion that freedom, real freedom, was simply impossible in an orderly and law-abiding universe. Man's experience in this respect is something like the familiar demonstration that, by all aero-physical science, it is impossible for a bee to fly. Theoretically the bee cannot fly, and theoretically man cannot be free. Or so, at any rate, the undergraduate argument had it.

True, we know of no way to prove the theoretical possibility of freedom in a universe such as we take ours to be. It is probable that our freedom looks a lot different to God than it does to us. Certainly the structure of the universe is vastly more complicated than man's knowledge can comprehend. And it may well be that in the infinite love of God, real freedom and a determined order of cause and effect can coexist. These are all "maybes"; they are legitimate imaginings on the frontier of man's knowledge; they are inevitable imaginings too, man being what he is.

What is important, however, is the way in which all mature thought, and particularly Christian thought, tends more and more to take the existing facts of life seriously. This is especially true of Christianity, which is supremely a religion of fact and not of conjecture. There is plenty of room within the Christian life for speculation and imagining, but these speculations do not lie at the center. At the heart of our faith is a constellation of *facts*, of events in time past, of present realities and of future hopes, around which our faith and life are built.

The Creed is an excellent instance of this. One often hears people say that they prefer the simple realities of the Beatitudes, or the Sermon on the Mount, to the complex theology of the Creed. This is a comfortable attitude mainly restricted to those who have not recently read either the Gospels or the creeds. If there is anything more fantastically speculative, more wildly theoretical, than *Blessed are the meek, for they shall inherit the earth,* we do not know what it is.[1] We believe it with all our hearts because we believe Him who said it. But here, as always in Christian theology, the fact comes first.

There is nothing more homely and soberly factual than the solemn reaffirmation of the Baby's birth and the Man's death which is what the Creed is about; there is not a dime's worth of conjecture or guesswork in the Creed; indeed, from the Christian point of view, to suggest that man's salvation must depend on some theoretical truth or some abstract, speculative doctrine or on anything else save on what God has surely done among us would be the harshest blasphemy against God's love.

Man's reason must and will wrestle continually with the task of relating these central facts of the Gospel with all the other facts we know, and with the implications of those facts. But we have learned from Christ something of His superb balance in such matters. As St. Paul said long afterward, *We preach Christ crucified, a stumbling block to Jews* (because He did not fit into the conventional patterns of orthodox speculation about the Messiah), *and folly to Gentiles* (for how could God possibly victimize Himself and submit to mortality); *but to those who are called . . . Christ the power of God and the wisdom of God* (I Cor. 1:23-24).

The fact of Jesus Christ is the heart of the Gospel as it is of the Creed; indeed, as it was of the ministry in Galilee. For what St. Paul says of the Christian, that he preaches the fact of Jesus Christ and not a conjecture about Him, is no more than a flash from that splendid, blazing fire in the Gospels. Christ does not waste much time in speculation. "Why did the wall topple on some and kill

---

[1] All quotations from the Bible are set in italics. Except in a few cases where the familiar phrasing of the King James Version seemed appropriate, the quotations are from the Revised Standard Version of the Bible (Copyright 1946 and 1952).

them, and not on others?" "what will it be like when the end of the world comes?" "what is 'enough' to do for God?" "what is the 'right' relationship between God and Caesar?"—the Gospels are filled with just such speculative questions as those; and He meets them all alike, playing with them sometimes, brushing them aside always, for there is a man's work to be done and there is no profit in idle, abstract questions. Men may be tempted to dally with speculation, to put theory first; but such is not God's way when there is a life to be lived, a love to be worked out, and death to be overcome.

Let it be perfectly clear that here we are talking about conjecture and speculative theorizing, not about theology. The massive, living structure of Christian thought is the greatest single bulwark of rational life our world knows. Theology is nothing more than hard, objective, rigorous thinking about the consequences of what God has done. The precise point of all good theology is that it does not start with a guess or a wish; it starts with life as it is, and God as He has revealed Himself, and goes on from there.

Indeed, Christianity is very far from being anti-intellectual or anti-rational—quite the contrary is true. But we share Christ's impatience with "iffy" questions, with guesswork and idle dreams. We start not with what man might be or ought to be or might have been, but with what he is. And the primary fact about him seems to be this persistent, tormenting, glorious fact of freedom. He may dream and imagine, and he does; but always in the end he must face the insistent questions, "What shall I say? What ought I to do?" And do something he must, even if his decision be to say or do nothing. Theories cannot help him much here. It is little use telling him that all this experience of choice is an illusion—if it is, then so is he, and so is thought; and all is chaos. It is of no more use to tell him that in the end it is all decided by the granite laws that surround and order his life, for this present agony of choice is still, to him, the only moment of conscious apprehension of law. This is the moment when law takes hold of him. And if, afterwards, Someone out in the universe says to him, "See, I told you you couldn't do anything else than what you did," he can only reply that such a god has less humanity about him than man does—and that is ridiculous, too.

In reality, manhood is born in this awareness of the inescapable fact of choice. Sometimes we may resent it bitterly and curse the universe or the God who made us this way. We may even envy the beast and the uncomplicated, "natural" life it seems to lead, without either any apparent necessity of choice or possibility of remorse. Indeed, this comparison of ourselves with other animals often has a peculiar fascination for us humans.

At other times we make our own tentative experiments in innocence. We decide that all these complicated codes of ethical conduct and belief, all these taboos and inhibitions, are nonsense, and we simply empty our heads of them and do instead what is natural and easy to do. But is there anybody more lost and bewildered than we, when we set out to do what is "natural"? We discover that the curious nature of man is that he is the one animal who cannot simply be "natural." There is no easy, unselfconscious, instinctive law in man to guide him. It is his nature to be inescapably aware of perplexing issues of right and wrong in everything he does, to be aware of the universal necessity that he consider and choose his course.

Freedom—at least the constant danger of its misuse—is a curse to mankind. Read again the story of the Garden of Eden (Genesis 3), and see how deeply its insights go into this predicament of freedom—how we chose the knowledge of good and evil, and by that choice lost forever the innocence with which God created us. Whether the story is taken as literal truth or symbolic myth makes little difference. It is a dramatization of the "Fall of Man," whereby our freedom brings with it a curse; and the sting of that curse is precisely *the knowledge of good and evil.* It is a paradox that such knowledge should bring pain and wrong, and not blessing, to mankind. Yet so it is.

Freedom, however, is not necessarily a curse. When used aright and to the full, it may be a great dignity and blessing to mankind. Before this story ends, we shall think of Christ, the amazingly free Person, who used our freedom as it should be used, and turned it into a blessing. For the astonishing truth about Christ is the way in which He came inside our freedom and fulfilled it from inside. In this life, we human beings stand somewhere between Adam and Christ—our freedom is potentially both a curse and a blessing. Our daily task and burden is to learn how to accept and use our freedom as the primary, given fact of life on which our very selves are to be built. It is little use to spend time in idle longing for the dear, lost world of innocence; that paradise is behind us. What lies ahead is the hard road of choice, along which He has gone before, to show us how it may lead to a second and better paradise. And we are the pilgrims of freedom, somewhere along that road of life. This is what the fact of freedom, of choice, comes to.

CHAPTER THREE

The Limitations of Freedom

THE SECOND truth is that freedom has limitations. Indeed, there are moments when our rebellion against freedom centers precisely there. How unfair of God, we say, to require us to make a choice when we are without the means to make a fair choice? One of our distinguished Churchmen-philosophers, Paul Elmer More, once put it, "Man is intellectually incompetent and morally responsible." That is exactly what we feel, and it seems to us unfair; and so it would be if our pride (or some unimaginable cruelty in God) were the last word. But the nature of manhood is too complex to fit easily into earthly ideas of propriety, as the reader will see when we outline the Christian answer to this complaint.

To act toward either ourselves or others, however, as though freedom were absolute or complete, is cruel foolishness. Part of every man's education, and assuredly part of every Christian's education, ought certainly to be an education in ignorance. To illustrate this, let me give, as an example, an experience of every pastor. A penitent person comes to him, troubled and wrestling with his sins, some of which are real and grievous enough. But often the bitterest reproach and grief of this person is attached to some word or deed which cannot truly be said to be a "sin." Great, then, is his amazement and joy when the pastor can say, "Why, this is not at all what you have charged against yourself. Temptation is not sin. The involuntary act, the swift and soon-repented word born out of ignorance or circumstances, the impurity loathed and rejected as soon as recognized—these are not sins. Rather give thanks that God has saved you from sinning."

If I did not know, from my own experience as a parish priest counselling troubled people, how often individuals make such wrongful accusations against themselves simply because they do not recognize or admit the limitations of freedom, I might justly suspect a degree of "softness" in myself toward sin. But, indeed, it is no softness, nor failure to recognize the enormity and sickness of sin, to say that we as readily accuse ourselves unjustly as we fail in penitence when we have sinned.

THE DANGER OF NOT RECOGNIZING LIMITATIONS

Sacramental confession is one of the great privileges in the heritage of church people, all the greater, as we feel, because it is not a routine requirement but an opportunity and privilege. But if the Church is going to say to us that we are "on our own," so to speak, and have no obligation to take counsel of anybody else's expert help in analyzing our own sins and determining their seriousness, except when our consciences are troubled, then we must all be far more realistic and aware of the limitations of freedom than we are. The great danger of solitary self-examination, without the aid of counsellor or priest, is that we may not justly distinguish between our responsible acts and the evils into which we fall because of the inherent restrictions and limitations on our freedom of choice.[1]

This is reflected in one of the acute spiritual dangers of our time. Just as we are often tempted to complacency, so are we tempted to a generalized melancholy, a pervasive sense of guilt that we have misused our freedom, that we have made fatally bad choices or have been unable to make the right and needful ones, without being, at the same time, at all realistic about what we could have done, or known, other than what we did. God has infinitely more sense about such things than we have. If it were not so, life would be unbearable—as it is for many who do not know Him.[2]

THE MAIN TYPES OF LIMITATION

Part of our preparation for Christian living, in other words,

---

[1] Note the emphasis of the Prayer Book on this point in the Second Exhortation (p. 88) and in the fourth rubric on page 313.
[2] You may read further about this in Chapter Five of *The Faith of the Church,* volume III of THE CHURCH'S TEACHING.

should be a sensible and honest appraisal of the limitations on our freedom. There are three main types:

Limitations of Time and Space

Who are you? You are John or Mary, born of certain parents at a certain time in a certain place, child of a certain culture, inheritor of a certain tradition, brother or sister of certain others, both gifted and limited by a certain inherited genetic pattern. You are what you are, and you have no alternative save to begin there. Both Popeye and St. Paul have a healthy and basically Christian attitude toward this—"I am what I am" says one, and the second adds *By the grace of God*. Both start where surely all mature manhood starts, with the willing and glad acceptance of the given circumstances of our life.

Indeed, the Church seems almost to raise this limitation—for it is that—to the very topmost level of our intercourse with God. We may well be impressed that at the most critical juncture in an infant's life, his baptism, the characteristic act of the Church is to give him his own certain, particular name, as much as to say, "This limited, particular selfhood of yours, so much a product of your own time and place, is going to be the very means of God's deepest relationship with you—it will be as John or Mary that He will know you and love you; and your very limitation will become the means of blessing."

So it is from then on, as far as the Church is concerned. Baptism, confirmation in many instances, marriage, sickness, death—it is by our names that God knows us. Even in the Judgment, most of all in the Judgment, we pray, He will know us by name, in all our limited, time-bound, space-bound selfhood. For it is of the nature of love to be particular and individual.

At times it is easy to forget this, or, even more, to rebel against it. Sometimes it seems more respectable or "scientific" to be vague about individuals, as if groups and classes were all that really mattered, and the oblique and arbitrary individual were somehow less real, or of lesser dignity and worth, than the mass of individuals. "The scandal of particularity" is a familiar charge against the Christian faith in Jesus of Nazareth, that charge by which it is asserted that God is really too great and universal for it to be seemly for Him to become incarnate in a particular child, born to a certain woman at a specific time and place. We are not concerned with that charge at the moment save to comment on how inherently ridiculous it is to think that a generalized Messiah, a principle of Christhood, an abstract salvation, is somehow more respectable than that vivid Person, who was fully man.

But the charge is also—perhaps chiefly—levelled against ourselves, by ourselves, in our rage or despair at being ourselves. How strong are the overtones, in the Ten Commandments, of the sin of man's rebellion against being himself: *Thou shalt not covet—thou shalt not bear false witness—honor thy father and mother.* All sin, in part at least, is profoundly infected by this rebellion against our created selfhood. "If only we were somebody else, if only we had what somebody else had, if only we lived at a different time under different circumstances, how much better or easier it would be." Many waste themselves in this barren envy, eat their hearts out in this fruitless rebellion, repeating the senseless litany of "if only."

Many take another line and try to live as if they or their neighbors were not the persons they are. This deceit, or self-deceit, can be the most ruinous of spiritual disorders. Granted that it is difficult, appallingly so at times, to be sure exactly who you are, and granted also that there is a sense in which every man ought to live as if he were on the way to becoming a different person than what he now is—the truth remains that *all mental and spiritual health begins with self-acceptance.*

The balancing virtue to covetousness, in our Church's teaching, is "to learn and labour truly to earn mine own living, And to do my duty in that state of life unto which it shall please God to call me."[3] This is self-acceptance, in the deepest Christian use: to receive with grace and dignity that God has made me as I am, to live in the knowledge that He has a life for me to live and a self to be, and to rejoice that there is a place in the universe which I can fill— which I only can fill.

Such self-acceptance permits, indeed requires, the fullest self-knowledge, and steady awareness of the things I cannot do and the selves I am not and cannot be. It is pride's way to hide in anonymity; it is of the nature of love to be particular. No earthly parent loves children merely in the abstract. We love our own particular

---

[3] Prayer Book, p. 289.

and personal brood. Is not God at least that good? So would run the Christian question and argument.

Limitations of Knowledge

Even though we may, and by God's grace do, come to a deep maturity in self-acceptance, we have still to face a further limitation to our freedom, a perfectly obvious one: nobody knows enough to make perfect choices—even assuming that knowledge alone could make such choices possible, an assumption no Christian would make.

We do not know enough about people, for one thing, to permit really wise decisions about them. We are aware of this in our better moments, and we try to withhold, as far as we can, from judgment. Our Lord told us *Judge not, that ye be not judged.* We accept that principle of charity for many reasons, but perhaps chiefly because we know that we really do not know people well enough—even those closest to us—to make fair judgments about them. God alone knows the secrets of men's hearts; God alone has the right to judge.

But some kinds of judgments are matters of choice, inescapable acts of freedom. Our national security, for instance, requires that decisions be made about the wisdom of trusting this or that individual with important military or scientific information. No normal person likes to make such decisions. More, the public interest requires that such decisions be as few as possible, and that there be every possible light thrown on the whole procedure. But they must be made; and they must be made without really adequate knowledge in many cases.

In these matters we take a calculated risk, because there is no real alternative. Yet, particularly where human personality and honor and reputation are the things being risked, it is esssential for national virtue that we recognize always the humility and penitence that ought to mark such judgments. Democracy is built on the assumption that nobody has goodness or knowledge enough to be a perfect judge or ruler, and therefore we reserve the right to correct our judgments and change our rulers. But a man's reputation is hard to mend once it has been dishonored; hence the great reluctance a democracy should show in making its human judgments.

Another example might be taken from family life. How often

parents come to a despairing crossroads, realizing that their children's future may in large part depend on a choice to be made—a choice of school, friendship, allowance, car, strictness of discipline, or whatever else it might be—and that they really do not know enough to choose wisely at all. Yet choose they must, hoping and praying that the decision is not so foolish as to bring disaster, and knowing, mercifully, that the child is not just a lump of clay, but has a life of his own.

Both these instances illustrate one kind of choice, that involving persons directly. There are other kinds of choices, some less directly personal, as for example, political or social decisions, in which our freedom is sharply limited by the fact that we do not know enough about nature and the universe and the laws that govern the creation to make a wise choice. But again, choose we must. "The attitude of the spectator," Justice Holmes once said, "is the culminating frustration of man's nature." It is hard to imagine a clearer example of just such frustration than the nonparticipating citizen who drifts resentfully along on the tide of other people's decisions.

Choose we must and choose we do, aware that further knowledge may correct our choices; always watchful that the springs of knowledge and judgment be kept clear so that the truth may have free play on our decisions; and always patient and humble toward the dissenter, for it may turn out in the end that he was right and we were wrong. Are we always this way? Clearly not—yet the ideal and the duty are plain before us, and bind us.

These are limitations on our freedom, these bounds to our knowledge of people and things. Yet even perfect knowledge would not guarantee perfect choices, for our very selves are divided and impure.

Limitations of the Divided Self

One further limitation of freedom must, therefore, be added: that of the impurity of our own motives, the dividedness of our selves. God does not say to us, "You may be free as long as your freedom expresses good will." He says to us, "You are free." And our freedom may, and does, become the means of hurt and wrong quite as readily as it is the servant of love. Freedom is real; it is a freedom to choose right or wrong equally. It is real, too, in that its consequences are real; a man may hurt his brother man beyond the capacity of this world to heal.

It is this sense of the real and irrevocable consequences of human freedom which, at the start at least, makes humanity conscious of sin. The true enormity of sin does not lie here, dark as these shadows are. The depth of sin is not found until we lift our eyes, face God, and see what our sin means to that incredibly loving and holy Person. But we do not often start with God; we start with a dog we kicked in a moment of rage, or with a callous offhand deceit of a child, or a lie discovered, or an infidelity that poisons the openness husband owes to wife. We start with the recognition of pain and hurt that cannot be undone, and work back from that to the heartbreaking question, "Why did I do that?" And if there is grace and humility in our hearts, we are willing to take responsibility for it. Our freedom was real, and it was used for wrong motives.

We do not always take responsibility for it, and indeed there are times when we are not truly responsible. There are other times when we are likely to blame something else or somebody else—to deny our real freedom to have done anything else than what we did. This abdication of freedom is a dangerous road, if it means more than a child's panicky attempt to find a scapegoat. From Adam on down, we have been tempted to lay the blame on another:—*The woman whom thou gavest to be with me, she gave me fruit of the tree* . . . And Eve blamed it on the serpent.

Lincoln Steffens once suggested that if the serpent could have spoken, he would have blamed it on the fruit of the tree! The Marxist quite clearly would do so, and he would have plenty of non-Marxist company to join him in feeling that evil lies not in the will but in the things the will desires, and even in the very illusion of our freedom to desire and will them. Take away the fruit of the tree, they say, and there would have been no Fall.

Quite simply, this is nonsense to the Christian, not alone because he is a Christian, but because Christianity is built on a solid foundation of common sense about what a man is really like. After he makes all possible allowances for ignorance and irresistible pressures and all the rest of our catalog of excuses, the ordinary man knows that there are plenty of times when the choice was clear, and he made the wrong one; afterwards, looking back, he sees how

· 19

an unnoticed motive, a corruption in his very self, a confusion between what he thought he wanted and what he really wanted, was the deciding factor.

Of course, he takes responsibility for it; he must, or else quit trying to be a man at all. For any abdication of freedom is a dangerous road: it leads to the denial of the surest feeling man has about himself, that of his responsibility to make his own decisions in the questions life presents. Once a man has abdicated, there is no home for him among men any more; he is a stranger in a strange country, the language of which he cannot learn.

This may sound fanciful. I am afraid it is not fanciful at all. The world that men and women know, and the language they speak, is one of responsible freedom. We value one another, and particularly ourselves in terms of this freedom. What use does a man make of what he has? What do we do with what comes to us to be done? These are the marks of manhood among us, and the Christian takes them as such.

Therefore, the Christian is impatient with excuses, and frankly—even hopefully—accepts the fact of his bad choices, praying that thereby his knowledge of his divided and confused self may be enlarged, and his real freedom also enlarged. It is not accidental that penitence and holiness go together. Strange as it may look to the outsider who wonders at the depth of penitence in souls transparently good and strong, it is not strange from the inside. For the very penitence itself, arising from the knowledge of impure motives and of an evil and confused will, is the means whereby God has purified the will, unified the divided self, made more explicit the real motives so that choices more truly free could be made.

This corruption of the will, this ignorance of self, is the most subtle of all the limitations of freedom, for it is so clever at disguises and so quick to hide beneath the outward appearance of virtue. Therefore, it deserves the clearest and most attentive scrutiny in the daily life of the Christian.

These three limitations on our freedom are true and important. We are men and not gods; therefore, we are what we are and may make only the choices that come to us to be made. We are men and do not know enough about the people or things we deal with; therefore, our freedom to choose aright is sharply limited by our inability to foresee what the consequences may be or even to understand fully what we are actually doing. We are men and are of insecure and confused wills; therefore, our freedom may be only an unknown and involuntary servitude in disguise.

THE IMPERFECT NATURE OF POSSIBLE CHOICES

Perhaps none of the three categories touches fully on what troubles us the most. That is the confused and imperfect nature of the possible choices themselves. We mentioned earlier the frustrating grayness of most of our problems. In books this is not necessarily so; and sometimes we enjoy books because the problems there are so easily seen and solved. But the world of books is often a contrived world, a managed world; and when we turn from it to the real world, life's problems are not so clear and sharp. Our choices come to us, trailing long streamers of history behind them. They are themselves the result of other choices, made by other men. They incorporate past good and past sin. They involve other people and still other choices. They are sticky and brittle, and they cannot be molded to suit our convenience.

Either way we choose, we will likely do some harm as well as good. Either way, there is only an imperfect result to be achieved. A clear example (if one is needed) is that of a nation's choice of war or peace. In the first place the people do not want to make the choice; it was not of our doing; it is the result of precisely this stickiness of sin which will not be washed off; it sets forces loose that never afterward can be recalled; it will not accomplish what we want accomplished, except perhaps to gain time and power if we fight and win, or to avoid destruction if we do not fight; it represents the breakdown of all rational human processes.

Yet this is exactly what our freedom has to deal with, most of the time. How constricted this freedom is! It is a world where no man can start fresh, where no man can rise above the conflict of competing goods and rival values and make the simple, clear choices his mind tells him he ought to make.

In part, this is our particularity speaking—the fact that we are men, with a name and a family and a century and a world, and therefore must make our own choices and no others. But it is more than just that. It is really the result of all our particularities, all our separate selves, from the beginning until now, living together and sharing one life. We must decide for ourselves, true enough; but it is hard to say where our self stops and others begin. Like Luigi and Angelo in Mark Twain's *Those Extraordinary Twins*, we are inextricably part of one another—one man's meat is another man's poison; one man drinks and another is drunk; one man sins and another is hurt; one man's life is another man's death. In the sober words of St. Paul, we are *members one of another* (Romans 12:5).

Therefore, it is idle to wish for neat choices, tailored for us alone. We will not find them. And our freedom looks like a pretty poor thing in consequence. If human beings are free, and yet so rarely have the chance to make a clear, simple choice between right and wrong—if most of our decisions are of this imperfect kind, starting with a conglomeration of good and evil and only possibly creating a little more good and a little less evil—then what real significance does our freedom have? Would it not have been far better to have avoided all this from the outset, to have been created puppets that are managed to suit God?

The question is an agonizing one. The answer is not simple or clear or easy. In fact, Christianity makes no claim to any definitive answer to this. We start where Christian life has always started, with the facts as we have them, not with a preconceived theory about what an ideal world would look like. The central and most unmistakable of all those facts is the imperative fact of choice, no matter how limited we ourselves and our choices may be. If, many times, the fact of freedom raises questions to which we can see no final answer, then that is a fact too, to be considered along with the other facts.

THE REALITY OF OUR CHOICES

The situation, however, is not wholly confusing. Before we finish thinking about Christian living, some fundamental answers will be clear. One answer certainly is that *our problems, our choices, are always part of our common life with our fellowmen.* When we grumble that it seems to be only in textbooks that people have clear, black-and-white choices to make, we need to remember also that no single one of us lives by himself. Our use of our freedom involves everybody else with whom we share this life. So does their freedom involve us.

Therefore, the more important factor is not whether problems and decisions are as clear-cut as we wish they were—it is rather that our choices, imperfect and involved as they are with other people's choices, are the means by which the common life and interdependence of humanity are made real, and our loving intercommunion with our neighbors is made possible.

An even deeper answer comes when we find that, no matter how sharp the limitations on our freedom are, *it is always possible for us to choose, if we are prepared to pay the price.* If we swallow our pride and our wish for textbook perfection, and are willing to take the opportunities that today offers in a very imperfect world, we can make our decision, choose our side, and stick with it.

The conscientious objector, for instance, knows this well. He knows that his opinion is an unpopular one and that it will cost him misunderstanding and criticism. He knows, even more, that he represents a minority viewpoint that is going to seem futile and useless. He simply cannot get free of the world, and make his individual choices with understanding and effectiveness. Does he then abandon his conscience? Far from it. He takes the opportunity (and the challenge) that today offers; he counts the cost in advance; and he takes his stand with courage. It is always possible to choose.

The deepest answer we will find lies in *what God did with this fact of freedom when, in Christ, He came among us and lived out our humanity to the full.* Truly we would be lost in our freedom if we did not have the constant example of Christ before our eyes, who met exactly this same sticky, imperfect world as we meet, and yet made His choices. Christianity is not example alone; it is also power. But the power comes to those who are willing to follow the example.

All three of these answers come to us as we consider the manifold problems of Christian living. But they come only in proportion as we face honestly the difficulties in our idealism about freedom. Therefore it is good to start with the facts and the questions they raise.

CHAPTER FOUR

The Obligation of Freedom

THE THIRD truth about freedom is that *an awareness of it simultaneously awakens in us a sense of obligation and personal responsibility*. The conscientious person who faces the fact of inescapable choice and thinks deeply about it perceives that there is a clear and haunting sense of obligation about the choice he is to make. It is not simply that, because he is human, he must therefore choose between the alternatives life offers. It is something deeper than that. It is the discovery that, when he makes a choice, his own deepest self is somehow involved.

A common example of this is the ethical choice every one of us faces from time to time. We are a member of a group trying to arrive at common policy, and we find that our opinion is at variance with that of most of the members. We then face the ethical choice whether to express the unpopular conviction we honestly hold, or to play it safe and agree with the others if only by silence. It is tempting, under such circumstances, to be silent, to withdraw from the debate and let the decision be made without intruding our own thought on the subject. There may be times when these differences of opinion are not really important and silent agreement is the wise course. But if the issue is important and our conviction is deep, we are impelled to express it and to fight hard for its consideration, even though we know we are running counter to what the majority think and are taking the risk of disapproval. Why are we impelled to do this?

Part of the answer lies in the fact that our convictions are the reflection of truth as we see it; and truth is an absolute that cannot, and will not, be compromised. The other, and deeper, reason is the fact that *"we couldn't live with ourselves if we didn't speak."* There is somehow not only an obligation to truth but also an obligation to ourselves; if we are going to be the kind of person we ought to be (and, therefore, the kind of person fit for ourselves to associate with), we must speak the truth and stand by it.

Sometimes we discount this feeling and say to ourselves that the choice is really not as true and important as it seems. We are especially conscious, these days, of the psychological forces that play on us, and are likely to wonder whether our differing from the group is not just a reflection of our need for self-assertion or recognition, or of our fear of being ignored. We wonder, too, whether man's sense of the importance of his choices is really well founded. Perhaps our whole sense of choice and the importance of it is simply the way our own egotism works to protect us from the pain and shame of being just an echo of life, instead of life itself. Perhaps life is just something that happens to us, and our thinking we are somehow actually in charge of it a pleasant luxury.

Most sensible people, and certainly all Christian people, would feel that this was a preposterously childish explanation of a profoundly deep experience. There may be no simple, logical way to disprove this theory. It may lie beyond the realm of simple proof or disproof and ultimately be one of those matters, like some other fundamental questions in life, about which man must make the best and truest decision he can, and proceed to build his life on the foundation of these deep assumptions.

But more important is the question how adequate such a theory would be to describe and justify the experience man has of the dignity and responsibility of his choices. It may be that our whole sense of the significance and meaning of our freedom is a sham and an illusion; but if this is so, then what sense does the whole universe make? If we cannot be guided by our instincts, if our sense of what is important and unimportant, real and unreal, is not a reliable key to the nature of reality, then what hope is there for us? It is on this ground that most of us reject any theory that explains away the sense of obligation in our choices.

Another theory, or group of theories, would admit readily enough that the experience is real and important, but that it is really an experience of our own sense of importance or our need for a sense of importance. That is to say, a man may feel that the choices he has to make are important ones and that grave consequences hang on them. But this feeling, according to the theory, simply reflects his own insecurity in the universe. He knows he does not amount to very much; he knows that he will soon be dead; he knows that he is really nothing more than a meaningless fraction in a vast and senseless complexity; and, therefore, his only refuge, for warmth and dignity, is to feel that his choices are important.

Once again, there is no easy answer to this, at least in these terms. But, still, man steadily rejects these persistent attempts to belittle his choices. If it is egotism that makes us cling to this sense of ultimate value and importance, then let it be so—we shall be in no worse case than is the critic who says that our experience of freedom is an illusion, for his criticism may just as well be egotism; and in any case a man has got to live by his own lights. If we cannot trust our own sense of what life and the universe are like, then we cannot trust anything; and the sensible man says, "I will take what light I have, and I will try to live up to it."

This book is not intended to be an attempt to deal philosophically or theologically with such problems as these. All we say here is that, in this experience, the ordinary man comes before too long to the knowledge that his freedom, his choosing, is of a profound, and sometimes frightening, significance in his whole life. To most of us, it is not merely a fact of existence that we must make the decision between alternative possibilities. We accept the fact and organize our lives accordingly. But in accepting the fact, we accept also a disturbing sense that in some profound and mysterious way, the very structure of the universe is itself involved, perhaps even changed, by our choices. Our decisions do not concern us alone as we are, or our brother men as they are.

It seems almost as if a whole new world hangs in the balance in our use of our freedom. For our freedom means, really, that we are creating something new, something which did not exist before. When we choose one way as against another, we become different, and our neighbors become different, and even our relationship to reality, to God, becomes different. Surely we are not the same, after we have chosen, for our freedom is not only real, but also the way in which we write the story of our life, or build the structure which is to be our personality and our very existence.

This experience of the gravity and depth of freedom we call here a sense of "the obligation of freedom." And the phrase underlines one aspect of this profound experience—namely that, in any choice we make, there is inescapably a sense of "must" about it. We choose as we do because we "must," or because we "ought," or because we are in some way responsible to somebody or something for our choice and its consequences.

CONSCIENCE AND RIGHTEOUSNESS

In the Christian scheme of things, the "somebody" to whom we are responsible is, of course, the God who created us, who redeemed us, and who continually wills to sanctify us, whose will is known to us and is to be obeyed. But the experience of the obligation, of the "must," is by no means simply a Christian experience; it comes as close as any experience, to being a universal fact of human self-knowledge. Christianity did not invent conscience; the pagan moralists of pre-Christian days knew nearly as much about conscience and the "musts" of life as we do; and the Old Testament remains for Christians, as well as for Jews, the greatest of all textbooks on conscience.

What happened to conscience in the Christian revelation was something quite unexpected. We did not so much learn more about it, or how better to solve the problems of conscience, as we learned what it is to be a truly conscientious person. Freedom under obligation (which is a shorthand definition of conscience) ceased to be a theory in Christian practice. It became a living fact, supremely revealed in the obedient freedom, the free obedience, of Jesus of Nazareth. From that time on, new words and new attitudes and practices came into use, and they were indeed a specific Christian contribution to the continuous moral thought of mankind. But in our understanding of ourselves and our universal experience, the Christian is shoulder-to-shoulder with everyone else; and this is an important fact to remember, when it comes to giving Christian interpretation the moral dilemmas of our contemporary world and Christian leadership in facing them.

Take, for example, the concept of righteousness. The pagan moralist stressed "virtue" as the dominant word—a man's virtue lay in his due performance of his manly duties, which were commonly divided into four: prudence, fortitude, temperance, and justice. The first three related to inner qualities in the man himself. The fourth described his duties toward his brother man and toward God;

and the word which we translate as "justice" was the same word as, in Jewish terms, was translated "righteousness." In pagan ethical tradition, proper action toward others and toward God was one of the four great duties or, as we say, cardinal virtues.

In Jewish thought a significant change occurs. "Righteousness" is used not to describe one among many virtues, but rather to describe the all-inclusive virtue, for righteousness has to do with God —His is the true righteousness, and man shares in it only as he is faithful to God. Therefore righteousness must be the commanding and central quality that embraces all others.

But Christians had profound questions about the whole concept of righteousness. Christ had taught them a new way, in which they looked not at themselves and what they had achieved, but at God and the immeasurable gulf between their best and His goodness. The example of the Pharisee was in their memory, as well as the failure of a self-complacent legalism to achieve any real love of God or neighbor. More, they had seen in Christ this new way lived out—a life of deepest humility, without self-regard but with the most intense and active love for others.

It is no wonder that, in the Gospels, and especially in St. Paul, the term righteousness takes on a wholly new meaning. It is no longer simply one of many virtues, nor even a quality that the law-abiding man is privileged to win from God. To the Christian, righteousness can never be won or earned by man; it is the free gift of God's grace, given not because we have earned it (*not by works*), but because, like the Publican in the parable (St. Luke 18:10-14), we have humbly and penitently and with full faith asked for it and, even more humbly, received it.

Well, here is a word and, far more, an idea which has undergone immense changes. Yet it was at no point a new word or a new idea. A conception of *virtue,* of *righteousness,* of full and right and manly development into what God had made us to be, was in the thought of all three traditions. To the Greeks, the emphasis lay principally on what we ourselves did and became. To the Jews, the emphasis had vastly shifted to God at the center; yet it was still held that we could hoist ourselves by our own bootstraps to share with God the central virtue of all. In Christian experience, we came finally to see that all self-established, self-satisfied goodness was in the end a snare and a corruption. God alone is truly good; and He alone can give, and freely does give to humble and gentle souls, the virtue He created us all to share.

This development and change illustrates the major part Christian experience and reflection have played in enlarging and deepening man's sense of universal, ethical terms like conscience. The great gift of the Christian faith is our new sense of the gravity, the true depth, and the significance of moral life.

Nowhere is that more evident than in this unique ethical sense of obligation. The obligation is not merely that of self-development or nobility, or even of simple obedience to God. The obligation is that of an active, personal kinship with God: *You therefore must be perfect, as your heavenly Father is perfect* (St. Matthew 5:48). *Truly, I say to you, as you did it to one of the least of these my brethren, you did it to me* (St. Matthew 25:40). Christ has led us in seeing the real depth and meaning of our sense of moral obligation from which no true man has ever been free since the world began.

THE THREE AREAS OF OBLIGATION

Such a sense of obligation is usually threefold. There is not any particular order about these three areas of responsibility; it would be hard for any of us to remember which one we first encountered, and equally hard to keep them separate in our minds. We can identify them thus: we have an obligation to *ourselves,* to our *neighbors,* and to *God.*

We are likely to describe them in that order, too, chiefly because it is almost inescapable that we start with ourselves and then with those closest to us. And when we first become aware of the way in which we ourselves depend on our choices and are determined by them, it brings a profound new seriousness to life that few of us ever forget.

Our Obligation To Ourselves

We start, then, with self-awareness, with the obligation to ourselves. How does this awareness come? It may be that it comes quite simply and directly, as when we run up against a major decision to be made and realize clearly that our whole future, in some real measure, is going to depend on how we decide the particular question. Some decisions are obviously more important than others, and some are much closer to the center than others. These differences we recognize; and we should not necessarily feel that every choice we were obliged to make would necessarily be a major one as far as our future self was concerned. But, to the ordinarily conscientious person, every choice has some importance; and the more sensitive and developed our conscience is, the greater the importance we are likely to attach to choices which, in themselves, might seem to be of little importance at all.

In the kindergarten stage of conscience, we recognize few major choices, the Ten Commandments, perhaps, being the only duties regarded as really basic and determining. It is quite likely, however, that, as we grow in depth and in our understanding of Christian living, we will pay progressively more and more attention to lesser choices, and come to feel that even such minor choices, as manner of speech to one another or day-by-day duties of home or office, are really as important in the eyes of God as the more spectacular ones. Charity is always the supreme and commanding virtue, no matter how unimpressive the occasion for it.

But however we grade these choices, the element common to them all is our sense that, in making them, we are really writing a new chapter in the story of our lives. There will be no way to erase this chapter; we shall be really creating something which was not there before, and which cannot afterward be undone; and, in a real sense, all that comes afterward will be partially determined by the outcome of this particular choice. Therefore we are thoughtful about our decisions.

We look backward to make sure that the present choice is coherent and continuous with the way we have used our freedom heretofore. We look ahead, to some imagined image of the person we want to be, to see how well this choice fits in with that ideal person. This looking backward and forward is an important ingredient in conscience, for the essence of conscientious judgment is that it is self-judgment: I look at myself, both at what I am and at what I mean or "ought" to be, and in the light of that reflection I try to make the appropriate use of my present freedom.

Our Obligation to Our Neighbor

This sounds like pure egotism, and it would be, except for a second level of obligation which we come to feel—the obligation to our brother men. The reality of their lives, their needs, and their hopes has a bearing upon our own private adventure in freedom. Indeed, it is often true that we discover duty to our neighbor before we are any too clear about our duty to ourselves.

We discover at least part of our relationship with our brother man—the part that is expressed in our sense of what the group or society expects of us and wants us to do and be. A child is not very grown up when he encounters this strong corporate discipline. He finds it, first of all, in family customs and disciplines that his parents themselves accept and impose on him. Soon he discovers something of the same situation among his playmates, as well as in school, church, and wherever he encounters society. Whether he is a constitutional conformist, or a constitutional rebel, does not matter too much at this stage. In either case, his own use of his freedom is influenced profoundly by the reality of his brother men and what they think.

But this discovery of the group will not automatically do the trick. On the contrary, it may only feed egotism and lead the youngster to see his freedom simply as a means of gaining advantage over his neighbors or of exploiting their freedom. Something more than the awareness of society is needed, if he is to be rescued from egotism. Mere coexistence is not enough, for one can be just as selfish and lonely in the middle of a crowd as in the privacy of home.

The key to a true sense of obligation toward our neighbor lies in the depth and sincerity of our sense of his reality. If he is real to us, if his freedom, his hopes, his nature, his problems, his existence, are really felt and accepted by us as being as real and as important as our own, then, and to that degree, will we feel an obligation toward him in the way we use our freedom.

The man whose only guide to the right use of freedom was how that freedom affected himself would be unbearable. Polonius' advice to Laertes, in *Hamlet*, "To thine own self be true," could be a most dangerous counsel because it leads us to think of ourselves as apart from all the others with whom we share this life. If they are no more than the painted scenery of the stage on which we play our part, if they are no more than things we manipulate to gain our own ends, then there is no way to save our own personal ethical lives from pure selfishness.

If we go on to the point that the Christian hopes to reach, the

· 31

point where other people are as real and as important to him as he is to himself, then our obligation to our brother man will be a major consideration in our use of freedom. We shall understand that whatever we do has a profound influence on our neighbor. We shall understand what the Church means when it teaches that all sin is social. We shall understand fully what St. Paul teaches about the nature of the Body of Christ, and of the interdependence of each part of that Body upon the other. And when we reach this level of maturity in understanding freedom, we have indeed gone a long way.

It is not a case simply of choosing between a personal use of freedom and a social use. It is more complex than that. For we perceive that our own selfhood—the story we are writing with our choices—is inescapably involved with the selfhoods of all our brother men. What we are, and even more what we will be, is inescapably bound up with what they are and what they will and ought to be. Thus these separate obligations ultimately have a way of merging, until in the fully developed conscience it is sometimes quite hard to draw the line between one obligation and another, one "must" and another.

Our Obligation to God

Yet even these two obligations do not quite tell the tale. For running through both of them is a third: our assurance that, both in our understanding of ourselves and of what we ought to do and in our understanding of our neighbor and what he needs, *the very foundation of the universe itself is involved*. We do not say it that way, of course. What we say is that we feel that such and such an action is "right" or "wrong." When we ask ourselves what we mean by those words, we discover that we mean something far more than that our acts fit some accepted pattern or preconceived idea. We mean that there is some kind of law in the universe, quite outside of ourselves, that eternally and unchangeably gives its authority to some kinds of action and condemns other kinds. We have a good deal of respect for laws made by men. Yet our respect for those laws is really based on a law that lies behind them and makes them right and obligatory on us. And we have much the same feeling about the law we accept for ourselves in our own consciences.

CONFLICTS OF OBLIGATION

Our sense of obligation toward this basic law in the universe may actually run counter to what we feel to be our obligation to ourselves alone or, even in some way, to our neighbor's need. Self-preservation, for example, is a fundamental obligation a man owes to himself; yet we all are aware of occasions when to seek one's own preservation would be the denial of all that was true and right about one's self—when self-preservation would really be self-destruction. True courage is an ideal instance of this, for courage is not the absence of fear, but rather the deliberate, free conquest of fear for the sake of a more commanding obedience than mere self-preservation. *Courage is fear plus obligation.*

Similar conflicts arise between our duty to our neighbor and our duty to God. We sometimes vote, for example, for a law that we are convinced is right and good, even though we know that a neighbor of ours is going to be adversely affected by it, and even though our impulse might be to put his interests first.

Such conflicts as these are familiar, and they complicate for us the use of freedom. It is necessary for us, then, not simply to understand our threefold obligation but to order rightly its separate strands. Where there seems to be conflict, then the decision must be made which loyalty takes precedence. Ideally, the three areas of obligation should coincide with, and reinforce, one another; ideally, to do what is right is best for our neighbor and best for us, since then, and only then, is there complete unity within the self, and full and obedient freedom under God.

We do not live in an ideal world, however, and it will often happen that we cannot completely resolve these conflicts. The conscientious man, at such a time, chooses his highest obligation, for he knows that the adventure of freedom is not without risk and pain, yet he also knows that the event is in the hands of God—that the final accounting of freedom is not made by an adding machine but by a loving Father, who draws us to Himself through all our choices honestly and bravely made, whether or not they are clear and perfect choices. Life is not a mathematical equation. Life is a continuing, creative intercourse among persons; and even imperfect decisions and choices we do not fully understand can well be material out of which the dialogue of love can be made.

CHAPTER FIVE

Christ the Free Man

THERE is always something a little unreal about discussions like this, which attempt to give a cool, dispassionate description of freedom from the outside. This is not the way freedom looks to us. We cannot analyze it and examine its various aspects in the way a student in a laboratory dissects a frog. We are inside freedom; we are doing the choosing all the time, even while we are thinking about the experience of choice. For freedom is, like the body we live in, an inescapable and necessary condition of our existence.

Much of the time we are no more aware of it than we are of our physical body. We speak or act, without thinking much about it, by habit, impulse, or imitation. This is probably as it should be. If we had to go into an agony of choice every time we passed a friend in the street or were questioned by a child, life would be impossible—if not insane.

But there are times when, hauling out our habits and impulses, we should, and do, examine them to see how they square with our true convictions. These are serious occasions in our lives. And there will be choices examined that do not fit into our habitual patterns and require attention and thought. At such moments we become acutely aware of freedom. These important moments often come when we have heard a sermon that moved us deeply, or read a passage of Scripture, or said a prayer that seemed to bring us up short in the presence of Christ.

At such a time, we are likely to be of two minds about freedom. We see the possibility of good—or right and true choices—which is always hidden in our freedom. We see also that freedom has a tormenting and perplexing side to it. We do not always choose aright. Our choices seem, much of the time, to be infected with selfishness and fear; and freedom seems to be as much a curse as a blessing.

HUMAN FREEDOM TAINTED

Why is this so? The biblical answer to this question is cast in the form of a story about man's beginnings—the story of the Garden of Eden and the Temptation and Fall. We considered earlier how this story set forth an answer to the question of man's lost innocence: man's inability to choose automatically the true and right. The answer is that man, once having been tempted to seek the knowledge of good and evil and once having that knowledge, could nevermore return to the obedient and innocent paradise into which he was created. From then on, man was bound to a life of conscious choice of good and evil, to the self-conscious, sometimes agonizing, experience of freedom to do right or wrong. His freedom became a curse, instead of the blessing that God intended it to be.

It is a mistake to deal with this story of the Fall as an historical curiosity or an awkward bit of folk-lore. (We all have met people who have been confused, as well as hypnotized, by the question of whether Adam was a real person, as if it made a particle of difference whether the first man's name was Adam or Pat or Mike.) For the story makes no pretense to being a literal, objective, historical account. Taken as literal truth, it could be quite misleading, as, for example, it is misleading to point up to the sky and say, "God is up there." We know that God is not "up" anywhere any more than He is "down" anywhere; we know that love is not a "higher" value than hate; we know that a "warm heart" has exactly the same temperature on a thermometer as a "cold" one. In other words, we often use mythological language to describe things better described that way than any other; and we know that the language communicates something far more than literal truth.

The magnificent myth of the Garden of Eden is, obviously, a more complicated communication than our manner of speech when we speak of a "warm heart." But both metaphoric uses have one thing in common: each helps us to say vividly and clearly something which, otherwise, we find hard to describe. The danger in our use of this way of speech is that of our asking silly questions about the metaphor, like "what is the actual temperature of my friend's heart?" or "did Adam really live?"

The point is that this individual (his name might have been Adam) is recognized as the *first* man by virtue of the fact that he, unlike other beings on this earth, was mysteriously and thoughtfully aware that *good* and *evil* attached to his choices. Therefore, he was distinguished from all else as *man* in that he did not lead an instinctive life but had to choose what he should be and do. This "first man" existed somewhere, sometime, ages ago. But what is important about him is not his prehistorical "firstness," but the fact that he was, and is, *representative man:* Adam is ourselves, both blessed and cursed in his, and our, freedom.

ITS EFFECT ON OUR LIVES

As we reflect upon this tormenting truth, we discover other interesting things about ourselves. *The first is that we always know a better way than the one we follow*—we can imagine a state of affairs better than anything we have experienced. Do we just guess about this? Do we remember it from some bygone time when things were better than now? The story of the Garden gives the answer that there was a "better time" back somewhere, and a perfect place where we once lived, where our choices were always unthinking and always right. To find that place and to live in it again would be wonderful beyond words. But it is impossible, as long as we are the kind of persons we are, capable of choosing wrong as often as right. The knowledge of right and wrong, and the necessity to choose between them, and the fact that the choice itself seems often poisoned and corrupted—these are the marks of our exile. Were it not for these, we could live in paradise.

We discovered a second truth—namely, that *this knowledge of right and wrong brings us, in some strange way, into the very heart of the universe.* Matters of right and wrong, of good and evil, are, somehow, the most important matters of all. They are more important even than life and death.

In former days, man's judgment as to what specific acts were right or wrong was a primitive judgment, for standards of right and wrong change as man changes and comes to see these judgments more clearly in the light God gives. But the principle of choice does not change. The taboos and savage customs of primitive man may seem absurd to us, but so may our burial ceremonials or our tradition of national self-sufficiency seem to our descendants. One thing, however, does not change: the assurance that there are absolute principles of right and wrong at stake, which have the strongest claim on our loyalty, stronger even than self-preservation.

Such knowledge of right and wrong seems to us to be the one, central, basic knowledge because it is properly God's knowledge. He alone could make things right or wrong; He alone is qualified to judge; He alone has the perfect understanding to make a true judgment. Men rightly fear having such knowledge themselves. It is "too high" for us, as the Psalmist says. Indeed, it would be better for us if we did not have it since it carries with it pain and shame. Yet have it we do, and there is no escape from it.

These two truths are basic to the story of the Garden of Eden. It is only because it is almost impossible for us to think in terms other than those of time, of "now" and "then," that the story is cast in the form of "once upon a time." The paradise it speaks of is a place where we once lived. The knowledge of good and evil is a knowledge we once did not have, which God did not wish us to have, yet which we deliberately chose to have. To ask, "Did all this happen?" is a meaningless question, like "What was it like before time began?" or "Suppose I were somebody else?" The story is true in the only way such stories are ever true: it embodies a profound truth about human experience, like the story of the Good Samaritan or the Prodigal Son.

There is a third truth we now discover—namely, that *since we cannot give this knowledge and this freedom back, our only hope lies in somehow having the freedom purified and redeemed and the knowledge perfected.* There is no way to abdicate from our humanity. What then can give us hope? Only some miracle by which we are enabled not only to see how this freedom can bring blessing and our return to God, but also to find the power to use our freedom to that end. Whatever salvation there may be for us, it must lie in our freedom and not outside it. We have to be saved from inside, by having our freedom lived out to the full and transformed from torment into joy. This freedom—at once the mark and the means of separation—must somehow be changed into a bridge across which exiled humanity can return, in happy and willing obedience to God.

The hope that this redemption and restoration might sometime come to us is as old and deep-seated in humanity as the problem of separation itself. The story of Adam and Eve is the biblical setting of the problem. The hope runs through nearly every page of the Bible. The fulfillment of the hope is revealed to us in the New Testament.

In Christ, God comes inside our freedom and works it out before our eyes, so that we may both see what true freedom can be and also find the grace to follow in His use of it. If our salvation through Christ were only something that happened to us from outside, we might still be wrestling hopelessly with our disordered world. But the heart of the Gospel is that God came within our very nature, and redeemed and fulfilled it from inside. *By a man came death,* says St. Paul (I Cor. 15:21), thinking of Adam and the Fall; and of Christ, *by a man has come also the resurrection of the dead.*

This redemption from inside we call the doctrine of the Incarnation. God, for us men and our salvation, came down from heaven and was made Man. He did not simply take on the appearance of a man, *He became us,* living inside our perplexing experience of freedom and responsibility, with all its limitations, necessities, self-conscious choices, temptations, collisions between separate freedoms, ignorances, pain, *who in every respect has been tempted as we are, yet without sinning* (Hebrews 4:15).

It could not have been otherwise and have helped us. To quote the Epistle to the Hebrews again (2:17-18), *therefore he had to be made like his brethren in every respect . . . for because he himself has suffered and been tempted, he is able to help those who are tempted.* Man has got to be saved through his freedom, not in spite of it; his final joy must be not to lose his choice but to make the right one for all eternity. Only in this way can the curse of freedom give way to the blessing it should be. Man dreams of such a happy issue, of learning the way in which his freedom can be fulfilled and brought to serve only the good and perfect end for which we feel we were made. And the splendid claim of the Gospel is that such a way has been given us in Christ, the Pontifex, the bridge builder of man's return to God.

CHRIST'S TRIUMPH IN FREEDOM

We have talked about three aspects of freedom: the *fact* of it, the *limitations* on it, and the *obligation* it imposes. If the Incarnation is real, we should expect to see all three of these manifest in the earthly life of Jesus. We do; and we see them in precisely the same framework as we discover them in ourselves.

At the very beginning of His ministry, Christ stands exactly where we find ourselves—at the point of being tested and being obliged to choose. Nobody would suppose for a minute that our choices are as clearly seen and so starkly real as His were in the depth and purity of His experience. Yet the choices are ours to make as well as His, however much we fail to discern their true depth and awfulness. Therefore, all mankind stood with Him in the wilderness; and He showed us then, in unforgettably simple and clear terms, what freedom is like.

From that somber opening, the drama proceeds with mounting intensity to the supreme climax of Calvary. Every step of the way is marked by choice. He is faced with every test and temptation we know. To Him, as to us, life comes with its glitter and rush of invitation and opportunity; like us, He must choose what is the truest and best life offers. A false piety sometimes tells us that He must have been spared the pain of the choices we must face; but there is no evidence that He was spared anything. He knew, in His own experience, the inescapable *fact* of human freedom.

So, too, in the Gospel story, are present the *limitations* of freedom. He is Jesus of Nazareth, born at a certain time, of a certain people and place, and subject to die at a certain time. This is a scandal to those who feel that it is somehow not right for God to restrict Himself to a single, particular human personality. Yet this is precisely the Christian faith: that the Incarnate God accepted from the outset the limitations of time and space.

So, too, does He accept the limitations of knowledge. A schoolboy might ask the question, "Did Christ understand the nuclear bomb?" The answer, of course, would be "No." If, within the Incarnation, there had been no limitation of knowledge, then the Incarnation would have been, to that degree, play-acting and unreal. God asked no favors when He entered our human situation. He took manhood as it was, and showed us that the problem of freedom is more than a question of how much we know. It is good to know all we can about the universe and our brother men; yet, with all the knowledge in the world, the right use of freedom is still something to be won by arduous choices.

So also does He fully understand the corruptions of freedom, man's daily peril of a divided and uncertain mind. How often does His teaching reflect this awareness, as when He reminds us that our eye must be single, or when He speaks of the pearl of great price to gain which a man will sacrifice all he has.

And when we come to think of the *obligations* of freedom—the "musts" toward self and neighbor and God—how incredibly unified Christ is. He is no stranger to the conflicts we know. The supreme illustration of this, surely, is Christ's ordeal in Gethsemane, where He is so desperately and bitterly torn between His own interest and His obedience. Yet, even at that summit, He is a single person, making a single choice; and that choice is His highest duty.

With His whole being, He knows what He wants most to do and to be: it is to obey the deepest and most commanding of all obligations. Around that central obedience all things in His life find their proper place. When He cries, "Not my will but thine be done," He is uttering not a wail of defeated resignation but rather claiming for Himself and for us, the ultimate unity of our human condition.

This is what Christian faith finds in Christ. His life and His offering of Himself on the cross are for us not symbols of either defeat or resignation but rather of victory, power, and glorious, realized selfhood. This is puzzling and paradoxical to many who ask quite candidly, "Where is there anything positive or free about this life? A few years of patient service and quiet teaching, beginning in obscurity, marked everywhere by rejection, ending in death —it may be a life of unobtrusive gentleness, filled with the pathos of a good man misunderstood and of an idealistic way of life refused by a harsh and cynical world, but where is there triumph or freedom in it?"

Let us not mistake it—this is the crucial question for Christian living. And the Christian answer must be clear and uncompromising. The clue to that answer is found in a very simple, childlike definition of freedom: freedom means "doing what you want to do." Nobody would take this as a very complete or mature definition, for the highest freedom often seems to be a denial of self-will rather than an expression of it. Still, as a definition to begin with, it directs us toward the heart of the matter.

OUR USE OF THIS FREEDOM

To be free is to have the possibility of choice and the power to make the decision we want to make. But our problem is, usually, to know what we really want. Perplexed by imperfect knowledge and the other limitations on our freedom and torn between conflicting loyalties, every man knows the frustration of choosing what he thinks he wants, only to find out later that it was not at all what he wanted. There is something we want to have and somebody we want to be, but the heart of our human problem is that we do not really know, at least when we start, what precisely these are. We are aware of our desire, and we search to become the person God created us to be, for we feel that if we can discover that person and the way of life proper for him, we can choose him and find peace and inner integrity.

How wildly we sometimes experiment in this search! We try different jobs or different houses; we buy new clothes or furniture or silverware; we experiment with different modes of living; we examine our marriages; we tinker with our personalities; we test our diets; we join churches or resign from them; we develop new friendships or reawaken old ones—and in all this we are searching to find the elusive whatever-it-is that we want most of all.

Thus our life is really a long process of education in finding an order of values and choosing what is best and truest for us. Freedom is seen, then, to be not a matter of doing what we want to do but rather of finding out what it is that has the strongest claim on our desire and our loyalty, and then of making our choices serve that end. Finally, we discover that freedom is *a kind of obedience.*

Putting this in progressive order, we start with

A. *"Doing what we want to do."* Before long, we see that what we really mean is

B. *"Being what we want to be."* But that only begs the question. The real question is, we think,

C. *"Knowing what we want to be."* To know that, we find, we have to know what the final truth and reality is, where our most important duty lies. In other words, we come at last, to

D. *"Knowing what we want to serve,"* as the best way of saying what we mean.

Is our own self-development the final end? Is it ourselves we ought to serve? There is a kind of false humility that impels us to answer "No" to that question, for we have been brought up to feel that self-assertion is wrong or, at least, not acceptable in public. Surprisingly enough, the Christian answer would not be a simple "No"—it might even be a qualified "Yes." We would say most likely, "Well, hold on a minute; don't answer that question until you have looked at the alternatives. You are not alone in this life; you are involved with your neighbors so inescapably that it is nearly impossible to separate your duties. It may be that the best service you can render to yourself is going to include your service to your brother man as well. It might be more inclusive and realistic if you said that service to humanity, to your neighbor, is the final end, because that will include you as well."

This kind of altruism is a nobler ideal than self-service, not because it sounds more generous but because it is truer to the facts. We are members one of another; and any scheme of ethics which ignores that is simply false and misleading, for we do not have here a case of either/or—one does not choose between self and others. The wider loyalty includes the narrower.

But what is the true service of my neighbor? Is it simply to put his desires ahead of mine? Is a group-ideal necessarily any truer, or better, than our own individual ideal? Christians would say "No." We do not believe that men find the truth by counting noses. What the general run of humanity thinks it wants to have, or to be, is interesting and important, but it is not the most reliable guide. There will be many times in the life of the Christian citizen when he will find himself in the minority. Indeed, Christians develop a special concern for minority viewpoints, precisely because the voice of the people is not necessarily the voice of God.

At this point Christians, as well as many non-Christians, recognize a deeper loyalty—the loyalty to the truth as God has revealed it. This third loyalty is what, in the Christian mind, somehow cleanses and purifies the lesser loyalties, and fulfills them.

An Example from History

An example or two will help here. The American Revolution confronted the colonial American with an ethical dilemma. His own self-development seemed to dictate merely that he retain his patch of cleared ground, and get his farm organized. But this was not possible, for he was not self-sufficient economically. More than that, he had kinsmen and neighbors, some of whom, at least, had uncomfortable scruples and convictions about political independence; and he must make common cause with them.

Most of them, perhaps, were of a mind with him, wanting to be let alone. But, because they were many, they could not be let alone. They had a common interest and a common importance vastly greater than any individual importance might be. And the tides of opinion ebbed and flowed so that there was no common voice to guide him.

More than that, there was an uncomfortable, over-riding loyalty, dim and unclear enough, yet which made itself known through some of his most admirable fellow-citizens; and he was touched by it, even though he did not fully understand it. His own isolated well-being—the common cause of his community—what was demanded of him by his nature as God had made him—these were the three loyalties among which he was distressed and divided.

Many if not most of the men in his position chose one way; and we respect and admire them for it, and say that their choice was the right one to make (as far as any historical decision is "right"). It would have been better, surely, if another way than war could have been found to solve the problem. But the choice for living Americans was not some "ideal" choice; it was the real one which had to be made; and it is the "patriot" whom we admire, precisely because he did not put loyalty to himself first, or loyalty to his community narrowly-conceived, but he obeyed a higher loyalty, one far harder to discern than his own good or peace with his neighbors, and one far more important.

And even though the choice may have been an imperfect one, and war a stupid alternative, yet we can see, looking back on history, how God used these necessarily imperfect choices to bring a new light and a better hope to humanity. For the final outcome of our actions is determined not by our choices but by what God does through the lives of people who entrust themselves to Him. If history were simply the record of what men had decided in their freedom, it would be a record of disaster and wrong, for men are simply not wise enough to determine their own fate. But history is far more than the sum of our wisdom. God is the final arbiter; and where we serve Him, however imperfectly and blindly, He is able to take that obedience and work a better end than we could possibly imagine. Thus even the imperfect patriotism of the men of Revolutionary times served the purposes of God.

A Contemporary Example

Sometimes it is easier to see these things in history than in contemporary affairs. Yet the same principles are at work always. Take one of the commonest of all problems—the problem of the witness a Christian tries to bear through his daily work. Here again he is torn between loyalties. One loyalty is to himself, to gain as much as he can from his energies and skills. Yet few men would accept this as the only loyalty. What is the social usefulness of my job? How can I, through my work, best contribute to the common life of my community, my family, humanity? Most men ask those questions searchingly and with reason, for we know that no job, however selfishly gratifying, will be really satisfying to us if it does not contribute also to the general good of humanity.

But suppose, even though a particular job pays well and is socially useful and accepted, it does not really witness to the deepest things we know and care about? Many a job does not truly satisfy us because we feel it does not adequately minister to the real needs and true good of the community. And when we try to say what we mean by "the real needs and the true good of the community," we find that we are not talking about what the community thinks it needs or wants, but about what, in deeper thought, we feel humanity, including ourselves, really ought to have and to be.

There again the third loyalty comes into play. We cannot really understand or evaluate our jobs until we see them not only in terms of ourselves or our communities, but in terms of a ministry to God. No man is really satisfied with his work unless he can feel that he can truly be obedient to God and serve God in it. No matter how great the gain from a job in profit and social status, if a man feels that he cannot really offer that job to God as his ministry and service, then there is a destructive and fatal cleft in his life that no amount of psychology or piety can mend.

CHRIST, OUR EXEMPLAR IN FREEDOM

A house divided against itself cannot stand. So Christ said, and so every thoughtful man comes to see about himself. We have to be integrated—whole, single, unified—if we are to be free; we have to serve one end and that the supreme one, if we are to become the selves we really want to be. When St. Augustine said, "Thou hast made us for Thyself, O God, and our hearts are restless until they find their rest in Thee," he was not talking about an ideal or a hope; he was describing us as we really are. If we cannot work for God, there is little joy in our work. If we cannot live as citizens for the service and glory of God, then citizenship degenerates into servility or tyranny. It is highest obedience to a law beyond the will of the individual or the group, which liberates and unifies.

This is why Christ is not a symbol of pathetic defeat, but of triumph. In Him our manhood, with all its confusion of duties and loyalties, is lived out, unified and fulfilled. "Christ Jesus is God's idea of manhood," is a phrase native to Christian lips. This life of free obedience, these choices made with a single eye and a single heart, this supremely unified Person who is the free master because He is the fully obedient servant of the will of God—all this is what speaks so clearly of victory and power to those who look intently and reflectively at the Christ of the Gospel.

In truth, the Christian knows no better gift to make to the world than Christ, and no better answer to the world's incredulous question, "You think this Man is free?" The answer is the gift itself: the example of this single, splendid, shining Person, who walks like a king through all the changes and chances of this mortal life, "who bore our flesh like a king's robe," and out of the symbol of shameful death—the Cross—made a symbol of life and glory.

In Him the multiple, confusing duties in life become clear. He is not distracted by the variety of claims made on Him; His freedom does not end in indecisive confusion, as ours so often does; He knows what must be done, and He does it.

Most clearly—and this is perhaps the deepest truth about freedom—He teaches us that the final end of freedom is *offering*. To us, exiled from God and our rightful heritage, He brings both the example and the means of reconciliation. If, through freedom, men have violated the unity of the creation and created a breach between God's truth and our ways, then, through freedom only, can that breach be closed. If the creation, with all nature's wealth and man's immense resources, is alienated from God because men have misused their freedom, then it can only be reunited with God through the right use of freedom. We say again, man cannot abdicate his humanity. The Christian answer to the problem of humanity is not to be less human but to find a fulfilled and redeemed humanity, which will include our universal freedom at its truest and best.

Christ's use of freedom is such that it becomes the means of restoring the creation's lost unity, and it accomplishes that by freely offering nature and humanity back to the God who created us. God has put the creation into our hands, limiting Himself in some real way by the fact of our freedom. The reuniting of the Creator and the creation, then, is a task in which men must somehow join with God. If God were to demand it of us, as of puppets, or were to frighten it out of us, as compliance may be frightened out of a child, there would be lacking in that final consummation the very love which is at stake in this whole relationship.

God does not want the dumb obedience of the slave. If He had wanted that, He would have ordered it; He has all of that kind of obedience He wants in the servitude of animals, stars, atoms, trees, water, fire, air—they all obey because there is no option open to them; they praise God in their existence and action because in truth they know no alternative. If this were all that were at stake in the creation, there would have been no problem.

But it is not the nature of love to be satisfied with automatic obedience. Love, above all, seeks an answering love; love cannot exist save on the ground of freedom; and love is at stake, the love of God which initiated the whole process of creation and ourselves with it, and which seeks an answering love at the end of the process.

In the lovely phrase of the Fourth Gospel, Jesus said (St. John 15:15), *No longer do I call you servants; for the servant does not know what his master is doing: but I have called you friends, for all that I have heard from my Father I have made known to you.* This is the clearest statement in the Bible of the reason for freedom and the true nature of it—far clearer than the moving and picturesque myth of the Garden and the Fall. For this free love of friends is what God is after; He will not be satisfied with less; and the story of mankind is a story of man's transition from being a servant, a slave (the status into which we are born), to becoming a friend who understands the deep purposes of God and offers himself willingly and gladly for their fulfillment.

Thus the supreme moment of freedom in the Gospel is the moment of the Cross, when, "Himself the Victim and Himself the Priest," Christ offers Himself and all humanity and all the creation with Himself and in Himself to the eternal Father, in the most final and inclusive terms this life holds. The reuniting of the creation with the Creator in this free act of offering, despite the sin which entangles and corrupts our freedom and made the Cross necessary —no, rather accepting, absorbing, redeeming that sin—that reuniting offering is the ultimate secret of our redemption "from inside."

It needs hardly be said that the Cross is not simply a "once-only" transaction. The quality most clearly shown us in that terrible and wonderful offering turns out to be that familiar quality which our Lord taught us and showed us in everything He said and did. The Cross is not a frightening new factor we have not seen before; it is rather the expression, in the ultimate terms of life and death, of precisely the same elements about which we have been learning all along: Freedom is obedience, and freedom is offering; and the Cross sums up those things, once and for all, not in words but in action. Therefore, it is the supreme moment of freedom, and He reigns from the Cross.

But so has He reigned in every word and act from the beginning. This is the profound Christian certainty about Him. To the cynical, doubting question of the world, "Do you really think this Man is free?", the Christian answers an unqualified and triumphant "Yes!" And to His saving freedom we bind ourselves, body and soul.

The pages that follow deal with very work-a-day matters, of our homes and jobs and communities and of the attitudes which we feel should be expressed in our relationships with our fellow-citizens and fellow-nations. Those pages will say little about the deep things, about Christ and freedom, with which this prologue has dealt. But they will take all that we have said for granted, and in the end we will come back to this great theme once again.

It is to be hoped that as you read and think about the practical matters of Christian living, you will have always in the back of your mind the supreme example of Christ, the Free Man. He is the test and the light for all that we do. To live as a Christian is to live in daily comfort with Him, making our choices under His steady gaze, and judging those choices by the single standard of whether they are fit to be offered by Him and through Him to the Father who creates us and loves us. There is no better guide for man than that.

PART TWO

Personal Life, Family, and Work

CHAPTER SIX

Personal Religious Life

THE INTRODUCTORY section of this book sketched out a setting for our thoughts about Christian living within the framework of human freedom. We thought also about the limitations within which this freedom must be used; it is by no means a perfect freedom. Sometimes it seems that the ultimate end of it may be disaster for ourselves and our world. We simply do not feel intellectually competent or morally good enough to use this freedom rightly. It is not remarkable, therefore, that one of mankind's deepest and recurring instincts is to try to divest himself of his freedom, or to substitute for it some safer and more manageable basis for action.

Freedom is a predicament—it is the heart of the human predicament. But an equal truth is the Christian certainty that God has not abandoned us here. He does not stand off from us in some inscrutable majesty, leaving us trapped in our own devices; nor is He remote in the universe, roaring with laughter at His creatures struggling with questions which are too big for them and to which they can have no adequate answers. In His love, He comes Himself within our human framework, accepting the limitations which we must accept, and redeeming us from inside our freedom, by living it out before our eyes. Christ is the supreme pattern and example of what it is to be free. Therefore, the whole of our life should be an attempt to follow Him, and to use our freedom in such a way that He reproduces Himself in us, within our own freedom. This is Christian living, in the broadest description we can give it.

Now we begin to think about specific areas of Christian living, of specific kinds of problems which we face and of Christian ways of analyzing and solving them. We need to remind ourselves from time to time that Christian living is one, a single way of life rather than a series of little pills, formulas, and techniques. It is easy for us to want to find, and think that we do find, neat little packages of ethics or psychology that will solve the day-by-day problems. This is not really what Christian living is like at all.

Christian living is the way in which we learn to bring all of our separate activities, thoughts, impulses, and decisions into one, so that we are one and whole. Thus we can offer the whole of our life to God in the supreme act of freedom. We need to guard ourselves against too much thought of our separate problems and the separate Christian answers to them. The problem of living is one; and the Christian answer is one.

Still, we cannot talk about everything at the same time; and it is well to start with practical matters of Christian living by thinking about what is signified as our "personal religious life."

FRIENDS OF GOD

If all that we thought in our introductory pages is true, then the main element in our personal religious life must be that of growth and training in the right use of freedom. All our religious practices—our discipline, our prayers and devotions—must lead to the one end of unifying us as persons around our increasingly deep and inclusive choice of Christ and His way. If we are faithful and wise in our personal devotion to Him, then little by little our freedom will be purified, deepened, and transformed, until at the end we are remade in His image, and our freedom is redeemed in His free offering of Himself. Thus, from the start, there is something dynamic about a Christian's personal religious life, and something also quite uncomfortable. For it is a life of constant growth and change. It is not a lifelong repetition of certain prayers and disciplines and devotional habits. It is much more like a school in which, step by step, Christ leads us along the road toward the singleness and maturity of self which we see in Him.

Both St. John and St. Paul have very profound phrases in which they describe this process; and it might be worthwhile taking a minute to think about these. The first, which we thought about in the Prologue, is from the magnificent "vine" passage in the Fourth Gospel (St. John 15). Christ has been talking about our unity with Him, using the image of the vine. From that He moves on to speak of the mutual love which must bind Christians together and with Him. This love He describes in terms of the love of friends. *Greater love has no man than this, that a man lay down his life for his friends. You are my friends if you do what I command you.* Then, in wonderful simplicity, He describes in a flashing phrase what He means to accomplish in us: *No longer do I call you servants, for the servant does not know what his master is doing; but I have called you friends, for all that I have heard from my Father I have made known to you.*

In our creation we are made one with the rest of nature—obedient as all nature is to the laws of its own being and to the will of God. The world of nature does what it is commanded to do. The stars wheel in their courses, the tiny universe of the atom faithfully whirls in its incredible energy, fish swim, cells multiply and divide, life is begotten and life is destroyed—all this in obedience to the law of creation. God is well acquainted with obedience for there would be no creation without it. And man knows that automatic, unthinking obedience, too. We stand with one foot in that world of obedience. We breathe, our hearts beat, our bodies grow and die, our instincts stir within us; and in all this part of our being we are one with the rest of nature.

But we are destined for something greater than the status of the servant. This is what our Lord tries to tell us when He speaks of us not as servants but as friends. A friend does not live by obedience to fear or force. There is no way nor need to coerce friendship. Knowledge and sympathy and understanding are entrusted to the friend. And friendship is built on the hope that out of freedom, rather than merely obedience alone there may be born a will to love and to share.

When a man chooses friendship, he puts himself to some degree at its mercy. Because it cannot be commanded, we take the risk of refusal or betrayal. God takes that risk with man. So much is perfectly clear from Christ's way with us, and His endless, patient, tireless persuasion.

Friends take the risk, because the prize at stake is very dear. So, too, is the prize infinitely dear to the heart of God who deliberately withholds from commanding what He most wants, but rather seeks it through our own free choice. And because of the risk, *there is joy before the angels of God over one sinner who repents* (St. Luke 15:10).

SONS OF GOD

St. Paul refers to this same profound change in status, but substitutes another word for *friend*. In his letter to the new Christians in Galatia, he is trying to teach them the difference between their old Jewish faith and their new Christian allegiance; and in doing this, he draws the contrast between the old religion of law, in which nothing but obedience was expected of mankind, and the new religion of faith, in which the free choice of God by man and man's willing self-commitment to God are the important factors. In connection with this argument (Galatians 4), he speaks about what happens to a child, even of a wealthy family, in his infancy. Even though the child will some day be master of great power and wealth, while he is a child, he is rigidly held under a rule of obedience. So, says St. Paul, mankind was held under obedience in its infancy. But when the time came, like a young man coming of age, we were set free from that bondage and, in St. Paul's phrase, received *adoption as sons. So, through God you are no longer a slave but a son, and if a son then an heir* (Galatians 4:5-7).

Of course, words should not be pushed too far, even great and simple words like these. But they speak clearly of the immense change in status which God means to accomplish in us. He intends that we shall obey Him not because (a) we don't know what else to do; (b) we are afraid not to; (c) we are forced to; but because we know what He is like and what He intends to do, and we want more than anything else to have a share in that perfect will for good. God seeks to have us know and do His will as friends and children, not as slaves.

In less vivid language, the ideal of the Christian life is the ideal of a life in which our acts are considered, consciously and freely chosen, in obedience to God's nature and will. In our natural, created condition we have only the possibility of this kind of thoughtful, free, conscientious partnership with God. By His grace and by our own choice and discipline, we can learn, little by little, how to enter into that partnership and fulfill it. We can be—to come back to our original words—*friends* and *sons*.

This is the great transition that the Christian religion is all about. This is the grand dream which makes redeemed humanity what it is. Without this dream we should still be only a versatile, dissatisfied mediocrity among the other animals. It is the dream which makes the difference. Indeed, it is more than a dream, for we are persuaded that we have seen precisely this process worked out in Christ and can go in faith where He has led the way.

One caution is necessary. In this transformation from one status to another, we do not simply leave the old status behind. The old world of instinct and obedience, the old world of the physical universe, is not simply cast off and discarded like a snakeskin or the pupa of a butterfly. It is transformed. That is to say, we carry it along with us, continually being made over from within. A saint has exactly the same equipment as a sinner—the same instincts, the same body, the same needs, the same hungers. He is not miraculously set free from these when he approaches his new status. Rather he brings all the old with him, but it is transformed or "fulfilled" (in the word which saints most like to use), and made new, to fit the new status. It is never safe for a Christian to imagine for a minute that he has somehow escaped from the old world into a new one. He has simply learned how to be master of the old world, and to walk through it like the son of the King, rather than as a slave which the old world can command.

OUR THREE RELIGIOUS DUTIES

What are the techniques of this transition? What are the tools which the Christian uses to learn his new trade of being a friend or a child of God? From the most ancient times, the Christian community has used three great groups of techniques. They go by three very simple words—Prayer, Fasting, Almsgiving.

Neither this section nor this book can pretend to be an exhaustive treatment of these matters, for the experience of the Christian community over twenty centuries has amassed an incredible wealth of theory and practice which is a limitless treasure-house for Christians to study and explore. All that we can hope to do here is to make some elementary sub-divisions and some brief notes on the more universal and common practices which every Churchman should know.

PRAYER

The prayer of the Christian is commonly divided into two sectors—corporate and personal. Our life of corporate prayer is very fully discussed in Volume IV of THE CHURCH'S TEACHING, *The Worship of the Church,* and needs only mention here. The area of personal prayer—the private, individual prayer-life of the Churchman—is our primary concern.

It may seem odd, but it is quite important to realize at the outset that the division between corporate and personal prayer is a pretty artificial one. There is obviously a difference between the prayers we say together and the prayers we say alone; nevertheless all prayer is one because all mankind is one, and it would be fantastic to draw too sharp a line between ourselves as individuals and as members of the human family. We are carried on the shoulders of other people in our prayers, and we help to carry others.

Yet there are obvious differences in the way in which we do them. Our own private and personal prayers are part of our most intimate personal life; they are parts of our autobiography, of our continuing, life-long dialogue with God. Much of that life of prayer is quite informal and may not seem like prayer at all. For in its widest definition, prayer is not limited to formal acts or phrases of petition or thanksgiving. In its widest and most general sense, prayer is simply thinking about God, or thinking about ourselves and our neighbors in the presence of God.

Even God may be disguised at times. There are moments in our lives when we turn to a friend—a lawyer, or physician, or social-worker—to seek help; and this turning may be a form of true prayer. Actually, for the moment, this person is acting as agent for God, a surrogate. It may be that we are frightened of God, or unbelieving, and in need of a substitute. Whatever the reason, it is true that all of us pray much more than we know, particularly at times when direct prayer seems impossible. And God is quite competent to understand these indirect prayers, and answer them. The help that comes from these friends is true help, and an answer to our prayer.

But there are specific acts and disciplines of prayer which comprise the art of prayer; and it is with these that we should be chiefly concerned. For prayer is an art, to be learned and practiced like any other. It is, however, a universal art, and not the property of a few who are expert or have a peculiar gift. There is no man or woman who ever lived who was not created to pray, nor given all that is needed with which to pray.

Prayer, more strictly defined, is our conscious intercourse with God. Sometimes we speak of it as "talking with God" or "listening to God." These are good and useful images, as long as they are not understood to limit God simply to our forms of words. For there are many times when God speaks to us in words other than the ones we choose, or indeed in no words at all. God is not the victim of our prayers; our prayers are really the answer to the love of God which already has brought us into existence and is sustaining us, guiding and leading us to Himself. Therefore we ought not to be surprised that God so often finds His own ways to show us His will or to lead us to Him.

Man's normal way of converting his feelings into action is through words. Therefore verbal prayer is a necessity for us. There are plenty of things which cannot be put into words. Anybody who has ever prayed knows how many feelings we have about God which escape formulation into words. Our words are not big enough to describe how we feel about God. We would worry if this were not so, for then we would need to fear that we had so small a God that He was not God at all. It is rather the other way with us—we use the best words we can to describe Him, and our awareness of Him; we know that we owe it to ourselves and to Him to formulate our prayers into words. Yet, even as we use the words, we know they are not adequate. We know what we feel when we speak of "Almighty, everlasting God." At the same time we know that our best words are but insufficient symbols which signify a reality quite beyond our capacity to describe.

In spite of all these difficulties we have nothing else to use except our words. Our feelings must be converted into action. For freedom involves action; and the action of prayer is the heart and soul of all freedom. Prayer, therefore, is the first duty of the Christian.

The second thing we want to say about prayer concerns the balance of it. Prayer is our own, total response to God. He made us for Himself, and is trying to lead us to Him along the highroad of friendship or sonship, to use two great New Testament words. He wants us to know Him, to love Him, and to follow Him, with all of ourselves and all our interests and concerns. Because that relationship with God is so total, our prayers must likewise be total and complete. In other words, we have a prime obligation to see to it that our life of prayer is balanced.

Every Christian soon learns that some aspects of prayer are far more easy and congenial to him than others. Some people find that the language of praise and thanksgiving is the most natural to use. Others find penitence or intercession most suited to their temperament, or perhaps even simple, quiet reflection about God. But we must escape the narrowness of doing what is most congenial to us. Every Christian's life of prayer needs to reflect his whole life, with all its different needs and elements. The only way our prayer can achieve that balance is by deliberate choice on our own part, and the deliberate planning of balance, so that no single element of prayer goes unrecognized or unfulfilled in us.

Many people, for example, feel that prayer for self is somehow unworthy, or less worthy than prayer for others. It cannot be said too clearly that there is no suggestion anywhere in the New Testament that it is wrong to pray for one's self. Quite the contrary; our Lord is concerned over and over again, as in the incident of the Canaanite woman or of the importunate widow (St. Matthew 15:22-28; St. Luke 18:1-8), to teach us that we should seek and ask and knock until what we desire is given to us. Christ's secret of prayer is quite different from what we sometimes think of as "unselfishness" in prayer.

Christ's secret is one of putting first things first. Consider the supreme prayer in the Garden of Gethsemane, when in the ultimate agony of spirit He prayed that the cup of this ignominious, shameful death might pass from Him, if it were the Father's will. This was prayer for Himself with all of the intensity and passion of the greatest of all souls. Yet He sought something more than simply what He wanted for Himself. Most of all, He sought to do the will of God—*Nevertheless not my will but thine be done.* Because He wanted most of all to yield Himself to the fulfillment of the will of God, it was then possible and right for Him, within that supreme prayer, to put into words His own immediate need and desire. This is the controlling pattern for all Christian prayer. We have the right to ask anything for ourselves, so long as our own needs are included in and controlled by the supreme need and hope of mankind—that God's will be done.

Christ would have us be quite precise in our formulation of our needs, and this for two reasons. First, the more clearly and sharply we analyze our needs, the better we come to understand them. Everyone who prays soon learns how prayers change—we start off asking for one thing, and before we have done more than formulate that first request, it has given way to a second and deeper one which lay hidden beneath it. This is part of the purpose of prayer, to uncover what we really want, and to help us formulate the deeper desire.

Secondly, our true intercourse with God depends on the sharpness and clarity of the language we use. Conversation with God is like conversation with a human friend. It takes trouble to say what we really want to say; and yet we can not converse with another unless we take that trouble, and reduce our vague feelings to intelligible words. *Vagueness is not the equivalent of holiness.* If anything, we need to have in our intercourse with God a greater clarity than we can have with the closest of our human friends.

It is then part of our normal discipline of prayer that we be assiduous in seeking to know what we need at any particular stage in our progress, and in asking for that, provided always that when we ask for our needs to be met, we include that request in the greater and deeper request that God's will be done and His kingdom come.

Intercession

But we do not live in a vacuum. We live as members of the human family, with obligations toward them as well as toward ourselves. Therefore part of our prayers, and probably the major part of them, must be concerned with the needs of others. Our *intercession,* as we call it, should be a normal, regular part of our daily prayers.

Many parishes are developing groups of people who join in intercessory prayer. This is a very important help; but it is by no means a substitute for the obligation which lies on us to be mindful of the needs of others and to offer to God our own strength to help meet that need. What are we seeking to do in intercessory prayer? Surely, we are not trying to change God's mind—we ought to take it for granted at the beginning that it is God's will for us, His children, that all things should come right and that we should all have what we need. Our prayers will not change that loving purpose, nor should we think of them that way.

What we are doing in our intercession is quite different. For one thing, we are giving expression to the unity of humanity. We are members one of another; and the pain and need of one is the pain and need of all. More than that, we are giving tangible expression to the love we feel for our neighbor. Sometimes to pray for another person is the only way we have of loving them. It is always the best way.

Most of all, in our intercession we are offering something real to God, namely our own time and thought and freedom. No man has any idea what these things are worth in the eyes of God. But they are worth something; they are worth at least as much as time and space are worth. God has deliberately limited Himself in creation by making us free; and so, within the limits of time and space, has put Himself to some degree into our hands. We can deny Him, and withhold ourselves from Him; we can also offer ourselves to Him, and thereby put at His disposal words and deeds which otherwise He would not have had.

No one knows what this freedom amounts to in eternity. It is hard to imagine that God is eternally limited by His gift of freedom. But in this world He is limited by His own choice; and certainly in this world man's own thoughts, words and deeds have some relative value of their own. Whatever that value is, when we earnestly offer ourselves to Him, we have put into His hands a power which He can use.

We are familiar enough with money to know that when we put it at the disposal of God it accomplishes real ends. We ought not be surprised if the same thing is true about prayer, which is quite as real as money, although of a different order of reality. This is the mystery of intercessory prayer, and also the heart of it.

When we have spoken of these two types of prayer—for ourselves and for others—we have of course omitted to speak of other great ranges of prayer, which still need to be part of our daily discipline. At least three ought to be discussed briefly.

Praise and Thanksgiving

The first is *praise and thanksgiving*. This is born not necessarily of a sense of thankfulness for particular blessings, although it is not hard for us to find occasions for particular thanksgiving. But even if our life seems for the moment to be empty of any very dramatic, special blessing, still the duty of praise and thanksgiving remains. The main reason for praise and thanksgiving is that we are alive. Existence is the gift of God; it is always good; we came into existence as an act of love, born out of the great love of God, and it is always a blessing and never a curse.

The wordly-wise will cock an eyebrow at this and wonder whether such a statement is not the purest and dreamiest optimism. At first hand it might look so. For this is not a particularly easy world to live in, and the changes and chances of this mortal life are sometimes almost more than can be borne. Yet to say that life is a blessing is not necessarily to say that it is always pleasant. To give thanks for a pleasant life is child's play and no more than the human equivalent of a cat's purr. When the fight is hardest, and the issue seems most in doubt, and the burden and heat of the day are most intense, then it is that the full and devoted Christian takes a deeper look at himself and gives thanks that in this fight, hard as it is, he is privileged to be a friend and child of God, and His partner. The fight is not between God and us—the fight is between God and us on one side, and the pain of creation on the other. God is always on our side, and the issue is never in doubt. Therefore, our fundamental relationship with God ought always to be one of praise and thanksgiving for life, for knowing Him, for sharing with Him, and for freedom to fulfill ourselves and be fulfilled in our companionship with Him.

A far more grievous question is still unanswered. Granted that we ought thoughtfully to give thanks for our own existence, what about thanksgiving for the handicapped child, the chronically ill, the helplessly crippled? Christianity has no "Pollyanna" answer for this. Although it is certainly true that life has a multitude of instances of people who rise above their handicaps, or through them, and find deep and lasting cause for thanksgiving, yet despite these heroic conquests of handicaps, there are many who have no chance for such conquest, who are doomed to be the victims of their handicap as long as they live. Do you give thanks for the mentally defective child who will never grow up?

The Christian answer to this is still an affirmative one. To give any other answer would be to say that this life is the only one, at least the only important one. This the Christian cannot say. This world and our life in it is a practice world—as serious as the most important probation could possibly be, but still only the first act in the drama that ends with the final and absolute victory of God.

Therefore the Christian judgment about this world and its accidents is always made in the steady remembrance that God reigns, and that the harsh accidents and cruelties of life are not the final story at all. The child who lacks the minimum mental ability to cope with an adult life is still a child of God; God is not going to be finally defeated by a tragic chance of nature; and the love of God for that child is still His first and greatest gift. He did not will the accident; He is on our side and the child's side in this; and it is this certainty of God's unconquerable love which is the principal object of our thanksgiving.

Penitential Prayer

The second element of prayer which ought to be a universal one is *penitence*. Here again, it is important for us to be clear and precise. *A generalized gloom is not true penitence*. It may be nothing more than fear or pride, if all we are doing is saying to God that we are sure we must be very bad and that this must bother Him very much. True penitence is humiliating as well as humbling, for it is expressed in the clear and honest account of ourselves, of what we have done amiss and left undone, and of the reasons for this as far as we can see them.

Therefore the prayers of penitence must be more than mere periodic overhaulings. Doubtless there will be special times when we shall want to take a deep, general look at ourselves. But if we are sincere in trying to keep an honest accounting, frequent self-examinations and acts of penitence, even if brief, are more helpful than more infrequent ones covering a longer period of time.

In this, too, we need to remember that our penitence is not only for the specific acts which we have committed or failed to commit. Those acts are the illustrations of something which is continuing in us and which is profoundly deep, namely our misuse of freedom and our alienation from God. It is not simply that we have sinned; *we are sinners,* and our sins are the particular ways we can remember in which our basic separation from Him was shown.

Yet in our penitence, we need also to remember that it is not an end in itself, as God sees it. As in the parable of the Prodigal Son—which is really a story about a loving father—what He wants of us is that we shall come home, not that we shall stay in a far country mourning our lot. In that immortal tale, the father would not even let the son finish his confession, but ran to meet him and to welcome him home. This is the way God is. Our penitence is not something He values for itself; it is simply the turning-back toward God, and the first steps we take on that road.

Meditation

Finally, we must include mental prayer, *meditation*. Many Churchmen stand in a somewhat curious relationship to this part of devotional life. Actually, we do more of this kind of praying than we think, for we are often thrown off by the words. "Mental prayer" sounds far more technical than we feel capable of, and "meditation" sounds far holier than we can aspire to. The result is that we think of this activity as a specialty reserved for the experts, when, in fact, a good deal of our thinking-time is consumed in doing precisely what these words signify.

The art of mental prayer, in its basic elements, is essentially a three-fold process. We read a passage of Scripture or of some other literature, or we reflect on some truth of life revealed to us in nature or in mankind, and we try to think clearly and consecutively about it, with as much concentration as we can bring to it. This is the first stage.

The second stage is to get ourselves involved in it—in the picture or the thought which occupies our mind. If it is a picture—as, for instance, one of our Lord's parables—then our part in it may be that of a bystander or even one of the principal actors. If our reflection is on some non-biblical picture or theme, then our personal involvement may consist mainly in a thoughtful appraisal of how this truth concerns us. In any case, the heart of the second step in mental prayer is that our thinking becomes personal, and bears directly on ourselves, and in that process also involves our community and our whole society, of which we are members.

The third step grows naturally out of the second—it is the step of resolution or action. After we have reflected thoughtfully and personally about the picture or theme, we come finally to will to take some step appropriate to our thoughts and to ourselves.

Normally the third step—the resolution—is likely to be some small action which we can take fairly readily and quickly. Some spiritual directors would say that every resolution ought to be something which can be acted on the same day that it is decided. This may be unduly restrictive; but it does underline the essentially practical nature of the third step. *A meditation is supposed to issue in action.* It is not aimless reflective thinking or day-dreaming; it is disciplined day-dreaming which leads us to want to change, and to be prepared to take at least the first step toward that change.

Such a three-fold analysis is, of course, an oversimplification. Some methods of mental prayer developed by the great masters of the art seem infinitely more complicated than this; and doubtless they are; but in essence the process is the same. And many people have discovered meditation and the joy of it, without ever knowing either the names or the techniques. Many thousands read their Bibles daily, and then pause for a moment of thoughtful and devoted reflection, and find something to take with them all day long. Such is the intent of FORWARD—DAY-BY-DAY, which has been a source of inestimable value to countless Churchmen.[1]

Your own pastor can be a good guide for you in this matter; and this book must be content only to say that mental prayer should be part of the normal, daily rule of life for any Churchman who wants to move forward in his day by day Christian living. Mental prayer is the nourishment for our wills which we need if we are to grow in self-knowledge and in the knowledge of God and His ways. A life without steady meditation, and particularly meditation on the Holy Scriptures, is a life which must grow more and more shallow and purely imitative in its depth and meaning.

FASTING

The second great division of our personal religious life is that wide area of self-discipline which goes by the name of fasting. The word signifies much more than merely abstaining from food—

---

[1] These little Booklets for daily Bible reading are available in most churches, or may be ordered from The Forward Movement Publications, 412 Sycamore St., Cincinnati 2, Ohio.

it signifies the whole area of the discipline of our bodies and their appetites, which is a central concern of working Christianity.

The warrant for fasting as a Christian discipline is given to us, in the first instance, in the Prayer Book. The Prayer Book prescribes (page li) two strict fasts each year, Ash Wednesday and Good Friday, and then a series of other days of fasting "on which the Church requires such a measure of abstinence as is more especially suited to extraordinary acts and exercises of devotion." These days are: (1) the forty days of Lent, (2) the Ember Days, and (3) all the Fridays in the year except those which fall between Christmas and the Epiphany. This much fasting is the minimum which the Church requires of all who are members.

But these specific fasts presuppose a whole philosophy of fasting, which is not based merely on the Prayer Book, but primarily on the teaching of Holy Scripture, and supremely on the example and teaching of Christ. In the section of the Sermon on the Mount (St. Matthew 6:16-18) where He teaches us about fasting, He takes it for granted that we will fast, as He does. He is concerned that we shall do it, but even more, that we shall do it in the right spirit— for God's knowledge and our own integrity, and not for the knowledge and applause of humanity. Unless we suppose ourselves to be very different from Him, so that He may be expected to discipline Himself in ways that are needless and irrelevant to us, we need to take a very sober and realistic view of this whole element in our religion.

There are arguments enough advanced against it. Some will say that fasting is medieval—that it is simply a hangover from primitive days, and has no place in the life of contemporary man. For this argument to be true, we would need to know a lot more about ourselves than we do. Specifically, we would have to know that human nature has changed so radically from the time of the Incarnation that much of our Lord's teaching has no significance or meaning for us any more. Any man or woman who feels that this is so is going to feel very uncomfortable in Christianity as a whole, not only in our fasting discipline.

Others will say that fasting seems somehow unworthy of a spiritual religion. This is an old argument, for man has been tormented from the beginning as to the relationship of flesh and spirit in his

· 65

nature; and we have always been tempted to deal with ourselves as if we were disembodied spirits, angels, who are accidently trapped in a fleshly body for the time being. It should be needless to say that this is very far from the Christian understanding of the relationship of flesh and spirit. In creation flesh and spirit are inextricably interwoven: the flesh being the means of the spirit's participation in time and space. And it is so by God's appointment. This body, with its hungers and needs, is not simply a dreadful accident that momentarily traps an immortal spirit; it is rather the will of God in order that our spirits may have *something* to be *somebody* with here and now.

Therefore the Christian has a good deal of respect for his earthly body and its needs. Not too much, for he knows that in the course of time he is going to leave the flesh behind and learn how to live in another kind of body. But during this lifetime his flesh is going to be the indispensable outward and visible sign of whatever freedom and maturity his spirit has achieved.

He has also learned that the current flows both ways. Not only does his spirit express itself in his body, but he knows that his body equally affects and reacts on his spirit. A man is not simply courteous with his mind or spirit; he is courteous with his body. He removes his hat, he stands in the presence of a lady. Thus, when he takes off his hat or stands, the simple outward act reminds his mind and spirit of what he is and what the lady is, and of the true relationship between them.

We bow our heads for the sake of reverence at the name of Jesus or before the altar. Likewise, bowing before the altar or at the Holy Name is, to the reflective Christian, a thought-provoking reminder of an attitude of spirit which he covets for himself. Granted that there is the ever-present danger of carelessness or thoughtlessness in such matters, nonetheless the principle is sound and deep and is a central one in Christian living.

We ought to recognize, and most Christians do, that there are real dangers in fasting. We may become superficial and unthinking in our discipline, or we may let our disciplines feed our pride and self-satisfaction before God. All Christians have to cope with these dangers. But they ought not discourage us from a humble acceptance of the principle that it is part of the task of freedom to learn self-discipline. An ordered and managed life is gained only by those who are willing to pay the price in terms of fasting self-denial; and before we talk too glibly about offering ourselves, our souls and bodies, to God—to use the familiar phrase of the communion service—we had better be sure to have something to offer.

A RULE OF LIFE

The basis of fasting is the rule of life, whether this be a detailed rule or whether it be simply the thoughtful bundle of habits which we accept and by which we try to live. Written rules have the advantage of being visible and tangible symbols, and of requiring a more exact self-examination than an unwritten rule. They have the disadvantage of often trailing off into pettiness, or of perpetuating devotional customs without too much thoughtfulness as to their relevance to our actual need. This fact underscores the necessity of frequent and regular examination and change in our rules. But the rule of life, written or unwritten, is the prime element in Christian living, in the day by day performance of our duties.

By his rule of life the Christian proclaims that he is master of himself and is, under God, determined to establish a right order in what he does and how he does it. In his rule of life he sets times and places; he establishes relative values for things; he measures out his resources and tries to apportion them justly according to the needs and claims to which he is bound to respond. This discipline is one not simply of time; it includes our money, our prayers, our reading, our family recreation, and all the many other interests we have; but necessarily it is going to express itself very largely in terms of time. Our day, our week, our year are alike going to be regarded as entrusted to us by God, to be used thoughtfully and in a balanced and temperate way, in order that our time may serve us and our neighbor and God, and that we may not ourselves be simply the victims of it. This is the basic rationale of a rule of life.

The Church Year

The Church Year is quite a unique reflection of this need for balance and order. We who are accustomed to the Church's year and its changing cycle are sometimes disposed to take if for granted, or to smile at it as a bit of ecclesiastical embroidery which at the most is helpful in relieving the boredom of regular Church attendance. It deserves far more than this kind of amused tolerance at our hands.

The Church Year is a unique crystallization of centuries of deep Christian experience. In the Church Year there is given to us a very broad and general rule of life, within which we are urged to develop our own private rules. The Church's year supplies us with a balance of mood, from the quiet and thoughtful school-time of Lent to the exultant glory of Easter or Christmas. In the Church Year, there is time for breathing in and breathing out, for all the needed alternation of rhythm and direction. Where we follow the Church Year in our own private lives, and live up to it, we gain immeasurably from the help it gives, not only in avoiding monotony and the tyranny of a single mood in our religion, but far more in nourishing and deepening our knowledge of the manifold spiritual activity of mankind.

In sum, the Church Year is the Church's general and universal way of redeeming time. In proportion as we follow it, including the discipline of the week as well as of the year, we are helped to reach the balanced spiritual diet and the ordered regularity which true discipleship requires. The year will have its varying moods and seasons, if we follow the Prayer Book calendar faithfully. So will the week have its sunlight and shadows.

The Church Week

The observance of the Friday fast, for example, is primarily a way of staking out a fresh claim for Christ every week. This fast is often discussed among us; and discussed, perhaps, chiefly because of the feeling of most people that simply to substitute an elaborate fish dish for a meat dish is no real fast at all.

Of course, this is true; and no one would seriously try to defend the substitution of one kind of luxury for another, and call that substitution "fasting." It is doubtless a wise provision of our discipline that we do not require a particular form of fast for Friday. No doubt it is useful to adopt the discipline of fish, if only because it is usually easier to do it than not to do it. But the duty is not specifically a duty to eat fish—the duty is to *fast*, to mark every Friday (save the holidays in the Christmas octave) with some peculiar and special austerity, which will help us to remember that Friday is the weekly anniversary of our redemption. The Churchman may well think long thoughts about how he shall fast on Friday—whether by abstinence from food or drink or smoking, or in some other way

68 ·

—but he ought not have any question as to the duty of it, nor the reason for that duty.

Similarly, we need the reminder that Sunday, the weekly commemoration of the Resurrection, is always, in all circumstances, a day of rejoicing in the household of God. It is not a day for fasting, nor should we use it so. Nor is it a day for purely personal celebration—it is the corporate, weekly thanksgiving of the people of God. Because we are men, and not angels, we need to express in our outward lives the spiritual realities to which we are committed. Indeed it could be said that there is a duty to rejoice and give thanks on Sundays quite as strong as the duty to fast on Fridays.

When we use our weekly fast and feast this way, to mark and remember the way Christ entered into our time and used it for our salvation, we are really learning how to master time and use it as an offering shaped and fashioned by our freedom. Friday and Sunday are not the only holy days in our week. Thursday can be a weekly commemoration of the Holy Eucharist.[2] Every day from Sunday to Friday is a day associated with some part of Creation, and our intercessions and prayers can well follow such a pattern. Many schemes for the devotional use of time can be developed to help us "redeem the time" and master it for the service of God.

The Church Day

So too should the hours of the day be marked, from morning prayers when we awake, to our last prayers before retiring. Early in the morning is always a moment of special remembrance to the Christian, when he remembers that one early morning on the first day of the week, when the news of the risen Christ first burst on the world. Nine o'clock in the morning—the "third hour" of the Gospel tradition—marks the beginning of the Crucifixion. Noon and three o'clock in the afternoon—the "sixth" and "ninth" hours—are also especially associated with the Cross. Every evening meal has some of the overtones of the supper at Emmaus (St. Luke 24:13-31), when He made Himself known to us in the breaking of bread.

Obviously there can be no general rules about such hour-by-hour and day-by-day devotions. Every Christian will have his own mem-

---

[2] Thursday, for this reason, is a particularly appropriate day for a weekday celebration of the Holy Communion, although any day, or every day, is proper.

orials and thoughts, and will as well be sensitive to his need to change them from time to time. Books of devotion will often suggest helpful alternatives. But all through this kind of spiritual discipline, simple as it may be, there runs a deep and sober purpose, that by our devotional life, we may be the better able to redeem our time, which God has given us, and make it serve Him and us better. This is a profound instance of the way in which our freedom is exercised in our personal religious life.

We ought not leave this theme without a special word or two about Lent. Lent is the one great season each year which is peculiarly dedicated to this principle of fasting. As in the case of the Friday fast, it is commonplace to notice how easily our fasting can become a purely superficial observance. True fasting does not consist in simply doing things we ought to do all the year around, or omitting for forty days what ought to be cut out for good. Lent is not the time in which we can get double credit for dieting or swearing-off smoking. If we are intemperate in food or drink or smoking or any self-indulgence, then Eastertide or Advent is just as appropriate as Lent to develop the virtue of temperance.

Lent exists for other purposes than these. It is primarily a time of preparation. That was its origin, long centuries ago, when the season came into existence because of the need of the new converts for training and education in the new duties which they were to assume at their baptism and confirmation at Eastertide. Even though we no longer restrict Christian initiation to Eastertide, the Church has clung to the six weeks of the annual school, because we knew that it was needed not only by the new converts but certainly by the old-timers as well.

This is still the best way for us to approach Lent and understand it. What we do in Lent—the discipline we undertake—ought to be calculated in the light of that purpose. What do we need in order that we may be better trained, more free, more obedient to serve our Lord?

The negative aspects of Lent are incidental to this purpose. We abstain from the common amusements and pleasure of life during Lent not because there is something evil in them, but because by so abstaining *we set ourselves free for our primary concern.* If our pleasures and relaxations were evil, then we ought never to indulge in them. But they are not evil, but good; yet there are more important things; and Lent is a time for putting first things first.

Our Lord gave us the great text for Lent when He quoted the phrase *man shall not live by bread alone* (Deut. 8:3). Such was the nature of His own fast in the wilderness. It was not a penance imposed on Him, nor was it a retreat from evil involvement in this world. He fasted because He was so profoundly concerned in a more important matter: the searching out and understanding of his own vocation. Obviously man needs bread; and the realistic and provident Lord is quick to know this; but there are times when bread is not the most important concern.

Bread is, of course, a symbol for many things. It is a symbol for all that is good and normal and natural and right about life. And there is no understanding of Lent, nor of the Christian life, if there is not understanding that Christian discipleship consists in knowing the relative values of things and in being free enough to put first things first. This is precisely the nature of the Lenten discipline. We put some of our normal and good pleasures aside; we deny ourselves certain of our normal indulgences; we change our daily and weekly routines in ways that are at least a nuisance to us. And we do all this, not to try to reclaim a lost goodness, but that we may come to Eastertide better fitted to be the soldiers and servants of Christ which we were made to be by our baptism.

The toughness of Lent needs no defense in Christian circles. Twentieth-century Christians are aware of the incredible richness and, at times, the incredible softness of life. The classic hardships, the ancient and arduous cost of life, seem almost to be a thing of the past—there is almost nothing we may not command and may not have, if we have only money enough to buy it. All this richness tends sometimes to breed a softness within our spirit, to accustom us to the many things life has to give until we think we cannot get along without them. Our Lord knew all this about us; hence the sober, thoughtful injunction to remember that we do not live by bread alone.

Freedom requires self-discipline. In great measure freedom *is* self-discipline. This is the substance of that second element in Christian living which goes by the name of fasting.

ALMSGIVING

The third of the three elements is almsgiving. By this word is signified not merely a generous and charitable use of our money, but rather the whole field of what we call "Christian service." We will not say much of this here, because most of the rest of the book is concerned with various aspects of Christian service.[3] It may suffice simply to say here that all Christian service, at its best and truest, grows out of our own personal religious discipleship rather than being imposed on us by the Church or by society.

Obviously a Christian wants to do what most needs doing. We do well to pay attention to what our parish organization provides, and the needs of our community, as those needs are expressed by those who know most about them. But the initiative ought to remain ours. Our service to our parish and to our community is our offering, not a tax imposed by the Christian fellowship. Our service must be part of our rule of life, expressing our own needs and resources and the pattern of our life as we are currently trying to establish it.

For the heart of our Christian service is going to be our offering of that service with Christ to the Eternal Father. We shall come with faithful regularity to our parish altar, and there join with all of our fellow Churchmen and with our priest in the offering which is at the innermost gateway to the Holy Communion. In the name of all of us, the priest will offer the bread and wine of which we all will share. But what will our offering be? Some of it will be in the form of money no doubt, for money is the best and easiest way we have of making an offering of our time. But money alone will not do it; we want more than anything else to offer ourselves in the most real terms we can command—our time and thought and effort, our strength and our best personal resources.

If we are to make this kind of offering, then there must be a discipline running through all our week, which commands and uses our time in the direct, thoughtful and planned service of God and our brother man. For most of us Christians, our daily work and our homes must necessarily be the chief means of Christian service. Later on in this book we shall have occasion to think about our Christian service in our jobs and communities.

Our only point here is to remind us that this kind of service, through office or shop or home, does not simply happen—it must be designed, planned, and directed by free people who deliberately choose to offer their time and handiwork to the glory of God. If this is to be done, then personal values are going to rank high in

[3] Note particularly that Chapter Nine is devoted to a consideration of the right use of money.

our conception of Christian service. For Christian service is simply the expression of the love that we should have toward one another. Whatever the medium of that expression may be, the ultimate purpose of it is to express the obligations that Christians owe to the men and women whom Christ loves, and for whom He died. If your job is the kind of job which ministers directly to persons, then so much the better. If you are denied that kind of personal service, then it may well be that you need for your own soul's sake to find some particular means of personal service apart from your vocation. Perhaps we all do, no matter what our jobs are. Even the clergy are often aware of their need for the chance simply to serve their community and their brother man apart from their professional duties.

This section on personal religious life should not close without the sober reminder which all Christians need—the reminder of the constant and insistent danger of pride. What is our motive in all this personal religious discipline? Is it simply that we may appear unto men to fast? Is it simply that we shall thereby call God's attention to ourselves, and to lead Him to think that we are better than we really are? Is it that that we may pile up credit for ourselves somewhere, and climb into heaven over the backs of our brother men? These are, of course, rhetorical questions; and when we can recognize these dangers, our response to them is swift and right. Our trouble is that we often do not recognize them because they are so cleverly disguised. Pride is the hardest of all sins to identify, for it is an expert in protective coloration, and can just as easily masquerade as humility as in its own true colors. We may even assiduously develop humility in our relationship to God, only to discover that our humility is simply another way of attracting God's eyes, so that He will know how good we really are.

The sting of pride is self-consciousness before God—the attitude of self-judgment, of trying to assert and establish our own security by our own standards, as if we could play God ourselves. The true Christian spirit in all this is one of *response,* of an attempt to answer to the love of God which we deeply and gratefully know. Our only safety lies here. If we ever let ourselves get to the point of feeling that we are doing God a favor, then we are lost. If we understand that God is doing the favor, and that our only privilege is to try to fulfill and realize our response to His love, by trying to be His obedient friends and children, then we shall have found the surest defense against pride. The universal motto for faithful and humble Christian discipleship is to remember what our Lord told us (St. Luke 17:10), that when we have done all that is required of us, we still should say *We are unworthy servants; we have only done what was our duty.*

CHAPTER SEVEN

Sex in Marriage

NO AREA in life tests the underlying Christian teaching about freedom more sharply and vividly than the area of sexual relationships. To the young man or woman, awakening to the heart-breakingly sweet and exciting knowledge of physical love, the traditional Christian sexual disciplines often seem to run counter to any real freedom. Indeed, to many, Christian and non-Christian alike, Christian thought seems to be entirely negative. We seem to act as if there were no worse sin than sexual sin—as if it would have been better for all concerned if sex had never been invented—as if "No" is the general Christian attitude, punctuated by an occasional grudging "Yes" where there is no possible valid reason against it.

The Christian attitude actually is quite different from this. But it is nevertheless true that Christian moral discipline in the sexual area is tougher and more uncompromising than it is in most other areas. This is true not because the Church is afraid of sex, but because the sexual relationship is the most profound of all human relationships, intimately personal, expressive of the personality as no other relationship can be, and affecting other personalities more deeply than any other relationship.

Anyone who deals with sexual morality as unimportant or casual is not being liberal; he is merely ignorant. The basic quarrel between Christian sexual discipline and the more relaxed attitudes of many of its opponents lies exactly here; no sexual discipline, Christian or otherwise, can be true which does not recognize at the outset that a sexual relationship can never be casual or unimportant. By its very nature it is an intimate encounter between human personalities, with profound emotional consequences.

What, then, about the man or woman who has discarded the traditional disciplines and deliberately treats sexual morals as indifferent and unimportant? The answer is that the cost of such conduct is immediate and bitter, both in the violence which is done to other personalities and in the way sexual life is then ripped out of its normal setting in life. It is isolated in a capsule of self-gratification until it acts as a cancer destroying the healthy tissue surrounding it, swollen out of all proportion to the healthy relationships between persons, relationships which are the happy gifts of discipline. Such conduct is "wrong" morally, not because of some inherent evil in the act, but because the act is taken out of its context and treated as if it had no basic relationship to the rest of human personality. This is the basis of Christian sexual morality and of its judgments of sub-Christian standards.

But the tension between our traditional discipline and the impulses experienced in our sexual life is real and sometimes painful. And it is all the more strained in our society where so often normal sexual maturity comes long before marriage is possible, and where the general knowledge of contraceptive techniques and the common availability of reliable contraceptive devices have almost done away with the ancient discipline of fear. Granted that the age of marriage is moving downward, the problems are in some ways as acute for the young and immature "marrieds" as they are for the bachelors.

Add to this another highly disturbing factor, the superheated sexual climate in which even young children are caught. Pornography is doubtless as old as man. What is added in our time is a double factor—the straight, cold, commercial calculation which has demonstrated to its own satisfaction that you can sell anything better if you can associate it with a somewhat over-developed female, accented by a disordered and grotesque sense of the place sexual relationships actually are entitled to in man's whole scheme of things.

Add to this a still deeper factor, the profound discontent and resentment which many men and women feel at their fate of being robbed of many older satisfactions in their work and their place in a living community. The fascination of sexual promiscuity is often a direct reflection of the loss of satisfaction in mature work worth doing well, and in mature human relationships. This dissatisfaction does not limit itself to direct sexual outlets; almost all our fields of interest—sports cars, clothing, drinking, athletics, music—can and do become charged with sexual symbolism, expressive of this same discontent. But the discontent itself, the failure to find adequate satisfactions in the traditional balance between work, public life and home life, plays a very deep part in the unique sex-centredness of our culture.

All of this combines to make the young man or woman of our society about as confused and dissatisfied sexually as youth has ever been. Over-taught and under-educated, their sexual life and reverie bring far less joy than jitters. And at the heart of the nervousness is a sharp and bitter ethical conflict. On the one hand is a fantastically overdeveloped emphasis on sexual relations as ends in themselves, and a tempting ease in experiment. On the other hand is an inherited code (or at least a bad conscience) which in some obscure way seems to glorify denial and continence as worthy ends in themselves. And puzzled youth in the middle, knowing all about sex except what it is and what it is worth. There is no area in human relations where both Church and society have done poorer jobs than this.

Puzzled youth is not alone in this confusion. In one way or another it affects every group in society. The unmarried woman sharing an apartment with other young women as she earns her living until a hoped-for marriage—the single man or woman of mature years who has never married and has made a satisfying life for himself alone—the man in military service, forced into single loneliness for months or years at a time because of his duties—all these are caught in the same tension, face the same choices, need the same counsel and companionship.

Even more disturbing is the plight of the husband or wife who has achieved a sort of marriage and who now wrestles with a lost love and a broken home, without the help of a habitual discipline which would make divorce unthinkable. To such a man or woman, what defense can there be of the teaching to avoid the easy indulgence offered and to condemn themselves to a self-denial for the sake of a greater freedom in the making? These people are aware of the invitation of divorce as a solution to such problems; they are taught by the subtle and powerful voices of society that there is nothing worse than unhappiness, save death; that there is no greater ideal than one's own happiness. And they are indoctrinated to find in sexual relations the supreme end of the association of men and women. What defense, indeed? In most cases they will take the cash and let the credit go, hypnotized by the superstition of the age that the way to be free is to take all you can reach and do with it what you think you want to do.

All this sounds harsh and unfeeling. There is no harshness in it toward persons, but we ought be quite willing to be harsh towards silly and childish superstitions. For the heart of these sexual conflicts is a sharp collision between a doctrine of man which raised him from fear and superstition and opened the way toward a glorious new idea of manhood, and a collection of ethical soap bubbles which did not even need the prick of Christ's teaching to explode them.

Man has always known, when he thought honestly and deeply for himself, that marriage is far more than cohabitation. The need of person for person, the simple physical necessities of food, shelter and security, the sharing of hard work, the perception of the family as the fundamental unit of society—these are not Christian inventions. They are part of the common stock of humanity. Our Lord Himself refers to them as such—it was "from the beginning" that God had made men and women to live together. But it remains true that where marriage is understood as a true living together, where the whole of common life is shared, and the marriage is woven of all the various elements—food, money, work, play, children, friends, faith . . . and sex—that marriage has the optimum prospect of joy and security. It is of this kindergarten knowledge that the Christian teaching about sex and marriage is made.

THE CHRISTIAN VIEW OF MARRIAGE

What comes closest to being unique in Christian teaching is the emphasis placed by Our Lord on fidelity in marriage. *What therefore God has joined together, let no man put asunder.* Considering the gloss in St. Matthew, *except for unchastity* (19:9), and the "Pauline Privilege" (I Corinthians 7:15), which permitted the separation of husband and wife where one was not a Christian, (but only at the initiative of the non-Christian partner), the Church has never understood this teaching in a completely literal sense. But such occasional exceptions served only to underline the extra-ordinary emphasis laid on indissolubility by the Gospel and the Church wherever a true marriage of heart and mind and will was entered into. The unbeliever and the wanton adulterer might be suffered to go, for no true relationship could be built on such utter failure or refusal to bind one's self to the marital union. But for those who, with an honest and good heart, really took one another in open agreement, the requirement of lifelong and inviolable marriage was paramount.

How does this uncompromising teaching square with the obvious facts of human nature? By his sexual inclination man is not monogamous. Sexual pleasure is as natural as breathing. And where sexual pleasure in marriage dims, or flares outside of marriage, where the strains and tensions between separate persons become irksome, where there is real failure of communion and real conflict of desire and interest, what reason can possibly be urged for a man or woman to sacrifice natural inclination for the sake of an unreal loyalty?

If the whole of human life in all its breadth and length is disregarded for the sake of a part only, no reason can be urged for such sacrifice. Christian marriage is based on the entire common life of two free people who choose to make a new whole out of their separate selves. It is not based on sexual companionship alone. It is one of the most towering affirmations of human freedom we know, for it asserts that it is possible and right for a man and a woman so to give themselves to each other, "for better for worse, for richer for poorer, in sickness and in health, to love and to cherish, till death . . . ." Where courtship has been long and thoughtful enough to permit two people really to know each other, where there is liking as well as love, where there is a will to forsake all others for this one, to bet one's whole life that a marriage can be built by the grace of God, Christianity says it is according to God's will and man's nature, and it can be done.

But such a union presupposes wholeness. There is no way to hedge the bet of marriage, to withhold consent secretly by agreeing with one's self that divorce will always be a way out, or to yield only a part of one's self to the marriage. Nor is there any way to build a true relationship between two people who neither expect it nor imagine that it is possible. God is merciful in letting us learn many things after marriage, if we are prepared to do so. Otherwise, marriage would be impossible. But how tragically often the lessons go unlearned because the mind and heart are locked against any teaching. The gravest peril to marriage is not from bad people or an evil will. It comes from a failure to expect enough and to give enough; and all too often it is too late to learn that lesson.

THE MARRIAGE LAW OF THE CHURCH

Let me comment briefly on the Church's marriage law, particularly in this connection. The basic philosophy of our canon law is that of any Christian teaching. Where two free, competent people openly and rightfully take each other for man and wife, they have established a true marriage; and it is, by Christ's own words, indissoluble. Clearly, not all people are so free or competent. Children are not; bigamists are not; those mentally retarded below the level of ordinary competence are not; the insane are not. Nor could people be said to be free and competent where fraud and coercion is materially in the picture, or where there is real error as to identity. Marriages so contracted are "marriages" in name only, and are clearly null and void.

The canons also provide that a marriage is unreal if, either openly or covertly, there is agreement to hedge the bet (a "concurrent contract inconsistent with the marriage vow"). For example, to refuse to beget children (where there is no good reason save personal convenience), or to agree to resort to the divorce court if it does not work.

Further, a marriage is unreal where there are such clear and grave defects of personality in either party as to make real consent impossible. This last provision is largely new ground in Christian thinking; it was born out of the Church's concern for those who simply were unable to achieve the freedom to give themselves in marriage—emotional cripples of a hundred different categories.

Where it is apparent to the Bishop and his advisors that, for any of these reasons, valid consent could not be given and the marriage was such in name only, he may declare so.[1] He may then permit a responsible applicant to contract nuptial vows again as though they had never been taken before.[2]

---

[1] The canon permits bishops to recognize causes arising after marriage as well as those apparent before the marriage was contracted.

[2] For a fuller discussion of these canons and their interpretation read *The Episcopal Church and Its Work*, pp. 90-95.

This legislation is of interest chiefly because it is a clue to the seriousness with which the Church takes the responsible freedom of which marriage is such a vivid symbol. The admonition of the Prayer Book, that marriage is "not by any to be entered into unadvisedly or lightly; but reverently, discreetly, advisedly, soberly, and in the fear of God," is not a rhetorical gesture. It is a statement of the plain necessities of any such immense venture in free choice. And when that is coupled with the solemn phrases "forsaking all others, keep thee only unto her (or him)" of the betrothal vows, it is clear that the underlying assumption of Christian thought is an almost breath-taking one. It assumes profound and responsible freedom to make such a life-long choice linked with a corresponding necessity that we understand such a union as involving the whole of two personalities and two lives.

Sexual love provides the spur, but the union itself is far more than sexual. Whole persons are involved, with their whole range of interests—all of it raw material out of which the marriage is to be made. Where there is that entire giving and taking, then the sexual intercourse of man and wife takes its proper, joyful, unselfconscious place in a larger picture.

Certainly the common disorders of marriage seem to arise where this whole relationship between whole persons does not exist. In the experience of pastors, these disorders most commonly arise from one of four principal factors, listed more or less in the order of their importance:

First, *"reserved areas,"* serious enough in their extent to limit or prevent the real union of the parties. Husbands and wives begin marriage with many such reserved areas. We have lived alone up until our marriage, with an independent status of our own, managing our own money, making our own friends, ordering our own lives, dependent on our own resources, thinking our own thoughts. When we come to marriage, we come with all these separatenesses; the work of marriage is to join them so that they disappear in new mutuality. "Mine" becomes *our;* "I" becomes *We.* The process is not always an easy one; it does not happen without effort; but it is usually a joyful one, and the end result is that two separate people "become one flesh."

What destroys this unity, or prevents it from coming into existence, is a deliberate will to reserve certain areas of life, or certain

· 81

levels, for one's own and to refuse to share them with the partner. If those things so held back are important ones, then marriage is impossible. A man might agree to physical fidelity, but reserve his sexual imagination and thoughts as his own private domain. A woman might consent to her marriage vows but privately reserve, in her mind, the determination to seek a divorce if her husband is not adequately successful financially. A husband might marry with a private reservation that his duty to his parents must come ahead of his duty to his wife. A wife might marry for the sake of children whom she intends to bring up for herself and not for the father or with him. These are examples, distressingly frequent, of reserved areas. If they are grave and material enough, they will effectively prevent a marriage from being created.

Second, *a disordered, confused understanding of sexual relations.* People tend to act the same sexually as they do any other way. It is not likely that a selfish man or woman tormented by fear is going to be any different sexually; and this is the more evident as people make an idol of sexual satisfaction. Many marriages are haunted and destroyed because husband or wife do not know that satisfaction refers to a whole relationship between persons, not simply to momentary pleasure.

Trust, friendship, mutuality, relaxation, common interest and common life, these all enter into the making of satisfaction, and are of greater importance than the physiological elements. The fear that dogs the conscientious spouse that the partner be unsatisfied can be a dreadful torment, and destroy the marriage altogether. It arises, usually, from a disordered sense of the part the sexual act plays in this total relationship between two persons.

This is not to plead for thoughtlessness or carelessness in the physical relationship. Husbands and wives have a duty to each other to learn what an intelligent and sensitive person ought to know about the sexual acts, to understand one another's physical and emotional patterns, and to make of their sexual relationship a relaxed and happy intimacy which seals and cements their life-long partnership. The use of marriage manuals before marriage is a helpful preliminary, and every man or woman ought to gain whatever preparation is possible from such books or from talking with qualified counsellors.

Yet, doubtless every husband and wife comes to marriage with real uncertainty and profound questions born out of inexperience, questions to which the only possible answer can come after marriage —perhaps after long months and years. Marriage itself is the only adequate school for marriage. Husbands and wives should take it so, and understand that they will grow in mutual knowledge and in the happiness of their sexual life as they grow in maturity and grace. They will where there is confidence and thoughtfulness and relaxedness. The last quality is perhaps the hardest to come by in an age as sex-conscious as ours. We are so filled with information and so over-sensitive in the area of the physical art of love that we find it hard to remember that the sexual act is a natural, free expression of the whole partnership between two people; that it need not be elaborately contrived or engaged in as if it were something quite apart from the normal relationships between persons; and, above all, that it is only one of many relationships depending, for its satisfaction and joy, on the place it has in the whole constellation of married life.

Third, *a failure to accept tensions and differences as the stuff out of which the marriage is to be made.* There are many who think of marriage as something that happens to them—either it takes or it does not. A Christian would want to say to a bride and groom that they are going to come out of the church exactly the same people temperamentally that they were when they went in. Nothing is going to happen to them. Society has altered their condition and made it possible for them to start, with God's help, in the long adventure of becoming one flesh and building their marriage. That is all anybody can do outside the marriage; the rest is up to these free people. Will they realize from the start that each of them is a unique and separate person? Will they accept the common fact that any marriage is constructed out of incompatibilities? Will they rejoice that it is possible to be so free, under God, as to make this life-wide and life-long gift of themselves to each other? Will they *expect* enough? Will they be prepared to give up small freedoms, small liberties, for the sake of the greater freedom of a successful home and a realized and mature love? Will they remember the secret of keeping in touch with each other, each going 51% of the way, so there is real meeting and exchange instead of egocentric sparring at a distance? These are the questions that may be in the mind of a Christian as he reflects on marriage, and each one points the way toward that massive assertion of wholeness and freedom which is the axis on which all true marriage turns.

Finally, *the limitations on freedom itself:* ignorance, emotional distortions, underdevelopment, and the like. There is no perfect marriage, for no person is perfectly free. Fortunately, marriage is a natural state which does not depend upon perfection. All of us fall short to some degree. Some seem unable to sustain even the minimum demands. This is only part of the wider mystery of evil, and needs no special comment beyond the recognition of the fact itself. But once again it underlines tragically one of the fundamental truths about marriage.

SUMMARY OF THE CHURCH'S TEACHING ON SEX AND MARRIAGE

Now what, in contrast to these, are the positive affirmations of Christian teaching about sex and marriage? Let us list them as simply and directly as possible.

1. *Sexual experience and pleasure are not ends in themselves.* In the natural order, at the animal level, the sexual drive serves the immediate and obvious purpose of procreation. It is a clear means toward a necessary end. So, too, is it in man. But the end is far more complicated in the case of man than with the animals, because man himself is infinitely more complicated. The sexual experience is still instrumental to some other purpose, and defeats itself when it tries to be self-sufficient.

Sex for its own sake—this barren attempt to be self-sufficient—finds its most common instance in masturbation. In children, first exploring and experimenting with their own sexuality, such eroticism is doubtless an inescapable part of that experimentation. The vast majority of people grow naturally out of that stage, guided by their normal discovery that it is profoundly unsatisfying and unreal because it is so self-centered, and is not what they were really made for. The wrongfulness of it, where it is accepted and continued in adult life, is precisely that it *is* egotism—usually born out of fear and a sense of inability to cope with real life—fostering a lonely attempt to live by one's self for one's self. In responsible adults it becomes a sin because of the tacit assumption, which is consented to, that one is one's self at the center of the stage and other persons are only background, scenery, against which this lonely posturing goes on. It is a symbol of a fruitless refusal to trust God and engage in the real community of real persons in the real world.

This same sinful nature of self-centredness appears equally in hetero-sexual relationships, where the dominant aim of one party or the other is self-gratification, regardless of the mutual nature and obligations of the sexual act. Many a husband or wife has known little else but masturbation even in so-called normal marital relations because of a lack of understanding and of right intention in this respect.

Our sexual drive, in other words, does not exist for itself alone. In its very nature it requires mutuality and involves complex human personalities. Our whole selves are involved; and satisfaction means, necessarily, the full meeting and interchange between whole selves. Therefore,

2. *The end or purpose of sex in man is a complex one.* Presumably, animals are not troubled by our human necessity to choose in this matter. Instinct supplies the necessary drive to meet the biological necessity of procreation. It is certainly not possible for man to be so direct and simple. Here is a clear instance of what we spoke of in the first section: the impossibility for man of being natural. His sex urge has become amazingly complicated; it has involved him in personal relationships of dependence and communion. It has created family obligations, has become a language of self-expression and communication, lent warmth and color to all human activities. It has begotten poetry and beauty in a thousand forms; it has become infected with man's own complex personality, and it has learned how to adopt a legion of masks and to play myriad roles. To speak of this infinitely rich activity as if it were simply the urge to procreation would be fantastic nonsense.

We left original innocence behind in the Garden. It is the nature of man no longer to be able to live unselfconsciously and without choice. It is man's nature to be *obliged* to choose, to order his desires and to select and shape the ends he will serve. Meaningful human activity requires such ordering of purposes; our sexual life is no exception.

In this process, the Church helps specifically by setting forth the complex ends of our sexual life as follows: "We believe marriage is for the purpose of mutual fellowship, encouragement, and understanding, for the procreation (if it may be) of children, and their physical and spiritual nurture, for the safeguarding and benefit of society." [3] This is part of the pledge which men and women preparing for marriage in the Church are required to sign. It is significant because it is the official doctrine of the Church defining the varied purposes and goals of our sexual activity. It is important to note the place that the procreation of children occupies; it is not the first goal in order of importance, even though it is one of the necessary ends to be served.

The first end which sexual life serves is that of the relationship between the parties to marriage. This is a commanding purpose. The need of human society for the stability and integrity of the family is also a commanding purpose. All three purposes merge in a happy marriage; yet this merging is not accidental, it is the result of purposive ordering, and of free dedication of a husband and wife to the loyal fulfillment of God's will.

Joy as well as order results from such thoughtful and reverent obedience, a joy which is the intent and gift of God and which is immeasurably deeper than simply the excitement and release of the sex act itself. This joy is not something added to God's will; it is part of God's will and ought to be received and accepted as freely and thankfully as any other gift of God, and as a necessary balance to fill out the pattern of married life.

Parents would want to add to joy and order a third element; and that is the mysterious sense of sharing in God's creative love. The conception, birth and nurture of children is a profoundly stirring and moving experience, perhaps mostly so because we feel ourselves to be so close to the eternal well-spring of life.

But all these blessings come to us in proportion as we recognize the complex, rich, varied character of the sexual relationship; and recognize a further truth; namely that

3. *Sexual relationships are worth whatever their purposes are.* Like any other form of communication, sex relationships have value in proportion to what they communicate and how they do it. They are perhaps the deepest and most dynamic expression of personality. The marital love of a mature, faithful, balanced husband and wife is rich and satisfying because it speaks clearly and fully of a self-giving and receiving at all levels. By contrast, the furtive, fright-

---

[3] Canon 17; Sec. 3.

ened intercourse of experimenting youngsters may have nothing more to say than the urgent demand for physical release, because they really have nothing more to say to each other than that; and their relationship is correspondingly unsatisfactory and barren.

Part of the sinfulness in pre-marital or extra-marital sex intercourse lies just here—it is an intercourse, a communication, between persons who cannot give themselves fully to each other, but can only give a part of themselves and share a fragment of common life. Therefore the sexual communication is deformed and untrue, and disturbs rather than releases. The bad conscience which ensues is only partly that; it is also a reflection of a sexual release which released nothing of significance because the partners could give nothing of significance to each other.

At its best and richest, sexual intercourse in marriage is a true expression of two people who trust each other, who have staked their lives on faithful and mutual self-giving "for keeps," and who rejoice in the exhilarating freedom to make a marriage out of their separatenesses. Such intercourse becomes, in the deepest sense, sacramental—both an expression of the love between them and also the means by which that love speaks tenderly and fully. It is then, a means of grace by which God knits them together and makes them one.

It is, of course, this deep experience of sexual love which leads men and women to a new reverence for the ideal of purity. When St. Paul says (I Corinthians 6:19), *Do you not know that your body is a temple of the Holy Spirit within you, which you have from God? You are not your own; you were bought with a price . . .* , he is speaking to this deepest of all discoveries, that the love of husband and wife can speak of even the most holy things, of God's sacramental love and grace, if we will have it so. Marital love can speak that profoundly; therefore it is to be received like any other sacramental gift, kneeling.

4. *Sex love, therefore, is one of man's chief ways to true freedom.* The disciplining and shaping of desires to serve the best ends is nowhere more critically important than in human sexual life. Taken by itself, the sexual drive is a poor guide and a bad master. But it is a good servant where it is absorbed into a larger and fuller personal intercourse and set in a greater framework of value. This

task is complicated by the very wealth of values themselves, and by the problems posed as man becomes more and more insulated from the natural and instinctive correctives.

The use of contraceptives in marriage, for example, raises new and sharp ethical problems, because it makes a matter of choice what once was accepted as a natural consequence—the conception of children. "How many children should we have, and when should we have them?" is still a new question for most Christian consciences. It is a question to which the Church gives us no simple, clear answer.

The only statement which could be called a "Church answer" is the resolution of the 1930 Lambeth Conference (Resolution 15) that, while abstinence is "the primary and obvious method" of limiting parenthood, still, "where there is such a clearly-felt moral obligation to limit or prevent parenthood, and where there is a morally sound reason for avoiding complete abstinence, the Conference agrees that other methods may be used, provided that this is done in the light of the same Christian principles." The Conference also recorded "its strong condemnation of the use of any methods of conception-control from motives of selfishness, luxury, or mere convenience."

A generation afterward, this statement could probably be accepted as a minimum statement of contemporary Christian judgment. As the devoted Anglican, Mr. T. S. Eliot, observed at the time, the statement was not a concession to current opinion but "a courageous facing of the facts of life." But he went on to point out the weakness which it shares equally with Roman Catholic statements on the same subject. It leaves unanswered the really difficult questions as to when it is right to limit a family at all, and specifically when it is right to limit one by contraception.

The passing years have brought no greater clarity to the Church's moral guidance in this; and the sharp questions must still be answered by conscientious individuals, guided as they may be by their own judgment.

What has changed in the intervening time has been the attitude of the Church toward the right order of the ends, the purposes, of marriage. No longer would it be taken for granted that the procreation of children was the primary purpose of sexual love. As is evidenced by the careful statement of our own Church, the procreation of children is only one, and not necessarily the chief, of the purposes of marriage. Thus it may rightly be said that new dimensions and new possibilities of marital life, as well as new problems, are opened to husbands and wives.

The possibilities are those of tender, free, unfearing companionship between husband and wife which was unknown perhaps to most of our ancestors. The supreme acts of love are good in themselves where they serve to deepen and express the loyal, faithful comradeship of a man and a woman. Yet they must not nourish selfishness, nor deny the duty of parenthood. Thus husband and wife must accept the responsibility of a new discipline, that of the decision about the number of children it is right for them to have, that of the place to be allotted to sexual intercourse deliberately engaged in without the expectation of issue. In this we are going through a profound revolution in marital relationships, filled with very great possibilities of deeper and happier fulfillment; filled also with the possibilities of selfishness and hardness of heart.

On this new moral frontier, the principles are secure and clear enough. But the practical application of them—the problems of the deliberate choice of ends and the self-discipline needed to achieve them—is not nearly so simple. Yet the problems themselves illuminate vividly the way in which greater use of freedom, while bringing greater hazard, may also open the way to a finer discipline and a more mature and satisfying selfhood.

What becomes ever clearer in cases like this is the fact that there is no joy without cost, and no selfhood without discipline. True love, person-to-person, and true enrichment of personality as God intends, are there to be had. But they must be won and held by those who are willing to think longer thoughts and become more masters of themselves by disciplining their impulses to serve greater ends. Thus, once again, the way to freedom is first of all a way of obedience.

Our Lord was not speaking particularly of marriage when He said (St. Luke 17:33), *Whoever seeks to gain his life will lose it, but whoever loses his life will preserve it.* But there is no area in life where this principle is more true than in marriage. Sex life begins as an overmastering, dumb, unreasoned, animal urge for one purpose only. It becomes more and more a rich and joyful language—poetry, play, tenderness, seeking, taking—by means of which free spirits become more truly themselves, more deeply one another's, and more fully God's. But this does not just happen. It is deliberately chosen by those who are willing to say "No" sometimes in order that their "Yes" may be truer to themselves and to God. The husband and wife who learn to subordinate lesser things to greater, the young men and women who learn how to offer all the warmth and loveliness of physical desire at God's altar, so that their love may be in truth a sacrament of God's love, have learned that it is the lot and prize of humanity to choose what we want in life. We must pay for it. But Christ told us that a man will sell all he has to buy one pearl of great price. And so it is.

One final suggestion—this is not a marriage manual, and much is necessarily omitted—but it must be said that the common religious life of husband and wife is of consummate importance in building the ideal marriage, indeed any real marriage at all. For the prayers said together, the Bible read, the companionship in public worship, and supremely the offering and receiving of the Holy Communion together and for one another—these are the ways in which our marriages are lifted above the strains and separateness of our lives to the level of their highest possibility and their highest meaning.

The next chapter deals with family religious life. Let this chapter close with the thought of husband and wife together, engaged in the richest and most venturesome of all human relationships. If they pray together, then unintended hurts and accidental misunderstandings will not persist and fester. If they can make common cause in learning and following the Christian way, they will find what countless millions of couples have found—how the deeper, eternal fellowship within Christ's Church adds to the strength and sweetness of their marriage. If they can join together in the Blessed Sacrament, bringing and offering their marriage to their Lord, they will have the greatest gift of all, in the steady transformation of their earthly bond into the eternal love which the Prayer Book calls "the mystical union which is betwixt Christ and his Church."

This is not to say that marriages between people of different religious allegiances cannot succeed. Of course they can and they do, where the separation in prayer and sacrament is frankly faced ahead of time and where there is mutual respect of convictions and of practise and an underlying awareness that both are intent and sincere in following the one God as best they know. But this is precisely the point; their fundamental unity in God and the things of God is what makes their separation in worship and allegiance bearable.

Bearable, yes, but not desirable. Parents and counsellors do well when they face this matter head-on and early enough—before attachments are made—and help youngsters to see that unity in religion is a cardinal factor in successful marriage, and that there is nothing romantic in disregarding fundamental convictions.

A popular slogan runs, "Families that pray together stay together." Doubtless this is true and there is ample statistical evidence for it. But this should not be read as if religion were a kind of emergency treatment brought in to heal and revive a failing marriage. Religion may be helpful to marriage, true enough; but the deeper truth is that marriage is intended by God to be helpful to religion. Marriage is a way of life which makes it possible for men and women, through their differences, to serve God and their neighbor and to establish a full and rich companionship for themselves and their children. Marriage is a ministry and a vocation as well as a holy state of life. Let husbands and wives, then, so receive one another and share their lives that their marriage may be, in the words of the Prayer Book, a true picture—a representation—of "the spiritual marriage and unity betwixt Christ and his Church."

CHAPTER EIGHT

Children and the Home

L O, CHILDREN, and the fruit of the womb, are an heritage and gift that cometh of the Lord. (Ps. 127) So the
psalmist; and so we say, too, at times. But it would be idle to pretend that this seems always to be so. How many different moments
there are in our lives when children seem to be anything save a *gift
that cometh of the Lord.* How many times we feel frustration, or
anger, or hurt pride, or a deep sense of alienation which make any
thankfulness for children hopelessly unreal—when they seem
scarcely to be children at all, but strangers and foreigners, not sharing our life or our ideals, all cost and no joy.

The Churchman has no special insight into this, nor any private
medicine for it. The church family is exposed to precisely the same
tensions and problems, and must make the same choices as any
other family. What is unique in the church family is a constellation
of practices and attitudes which we shall presently examine. But it
is important to start with the family itself, as it exists with all its
joy and its pain.

The biblical writer who exults in the heritage of children is expressing, above all other things, the sense of pride in progeny which
is certainly one of the most primitive and deep-seated of all parental
feelings. To watch a cat with her new-born kittens or a doe with
her fawn is to see something of what the last verse of Psalm 127
describes . . . *happy is the man that hath his quiver full of them;
they shall not be ashamed when they speak with their enemy in
the gate.* The oriental father in this psalm rejoices in more than
parental pride. Stalwart sons are a protection and a strength to him,
like arrows in a quiver; they stand with him *in the gate* where
the legal decisions of the community are given; and their presence,

surrounding and guarding him, is a guarantee of fair dealing. But the pride is there. "These sons are mine; and I may be judged by them."

THE INDIVIDUAL LOVE OF PARENT FOR CHILD

Mixed with this is an equally ancient, perhaps far less self-regarding emotion—the particular, possessive, turbulent, unreasoning and individual love of parent for child. It would not be true to say that this love is the property of motherhood alone, while the pride of progeny belongs to fathers. Fathers and mothers feel both kinds of ties with their children, and there is no man who is all father nor any woman who is all mother. But the two strains need to be distinguished; and it is surely true that the very physical fact of motherhood itself and the nursing care of young children establishes in mothers the unique tie with their offspring, now possessive, now sacrificial, always particular and individual, which is always something of a mystery to fathers. It was to a woman that Simeon said of her Son, *Yea, a sword shall pierce through thy own soul also,* a word that could have been said to most mothers then as it could today.

The father may project himself in his children. To a great degree he judges himself and expects judgment in his children; he realizes his unfulfilled ambitions, hopes, dreams in his children. It is always difficult for him to give them the unquestioning, uncritical devotion which his wife freely gives. In fact, it is hard for him even to understand that attitude wholly; and not infrequently that failure to understand—on her part as well as his—is a knot around which the most complicated marital tangles gather.

Yet the father does know that love in part, as the woman may understand the way in which the father is continually identifying himself with his children, and inevitably judging himself by them. It is hard for him to love them for themselves alone (as it may also be hard for a mother not to do so). It is hard for him not to make unfair comparisons as it may also be hard for her to see them objectively at all. And in these imperfect comparisons, I do not mean to judge or suggest anything save that there are two quite separate emotions at work, both deep in our nature and both involved in the family situation.

THE CHILD AS IMAGE OF THE PARENT

A third element is that curiously deep sense of need, which every parent who has ever done any thoughtful soul-searching knows. It is an infection that attacks impartially both parental pride and love. The father or mother, who beams with gratification at praise of his child, is not surprised when it is discovered that part of the gratification is quite selfish. Praise of the child is praise of them, too. Indeed, a twinge of jealousy may remind the father that his own self-esteem is far more at stake in his children than he likes. His son may be a rival to him, and pride may be a knife that cuts two ways. "I am proud of you, my son," may be a way of saying, "You have shown how praiseworthy I am," or "Except for me you would be nothing," or even, "God will know that it is really I who am to be praised, but I will be unselfish about it."

Alternatively, harsh judgment of the child also attacks the parent's self. The parent is endangered when the child fails. Our need of our children is real and may be a dominant and possessive usurper of the place of love.

These three elements in the parent-child relationship are not the only ones that need to be identified in any thorough analysis. There is a lot more to be said about family relationships than merely to observe these three common strains.[1] These three are cited, however, because they are universal danger areas in the complex relationship of parent and child. The Christian recognizes these in himself and knows that he must come to terms with them in his own self-discipline as a parent.

THE WHOLENESS OF THE CHILD

These are danger areas because, like all our given, instinctive responses, they may cease to be good servants and become very bad masters. When they take their natural place in the scheme of things, they serve to sweeten and deepen the family and enrich the common life of the home. But when they grow, as they can, into monstrous

---

[1] If this were a major study of family relationships, and not simply a brief chapter, note would have to be taken of the way different cultures and civilizations affect these primary bonds. There are sometimes quite profound variations in the family patterns of one culture or another. It is not felt, however, that it is particularly to the point to discuss them in this book.

and over-weening cancers of personality, they destroy the true family relationships altogether. What keeps this from happening? What prevents the cancers from forming? What surgery can heal us and our families when they come?

There is an inclusive answer to these questions which may be a deceptively simple answer. What keeps parental pride from becoming a crushing obligation on the child—what keeps parental love from degenerating into possessiveness—what keeps our proper need of one another from becoming an exhausting and dragging emotional necessity—is *the primary awareness of parents of the clear and separate wholeness of each child*. As long as our basic attitude toward our children is that of respect for their separate identity, then we are protected against the degeneration of our natural impulses; and they stay in their right and natural balance. Contrariwise, whenever the separate identity and dignity of the child is forgotten or ignored, we are at once exposed to the danger of the cancerous growth which stifles the sweet and good relationships between parents and children.

This is a somewhat deceptively simple answer. There are not many who would disagree with the value of this sense of respect and gentleness in dealing with the personality of a child. The question would be, however, "How do you maintain this attitude? What are its roots in the day-by-day life of the family?"

The suggestions which follow are not by any means intended to be a manual on family life. They claim to be no more than a summary of what Christian living implies in the setting of the family. If they are understood that way, and are thought of as supplementary to all else that we know to be true about good family relationships, they will be valuable guides toward establishing our families on a sound, Christian foundation.

SIX CHRISTIAN PRINCIPLES OF FAMILY RELATIONSHIP

In brief, Christian living would seem to establish six principles which ought to govern the relationships of parents and children within a family.

The first, in logical sequence, is that *the family itself is the Church*. It is the first church that a child knows, just as it is the first community that he knows. God seems to have His own purposes quite clearly in mind in so ordaining the manner of our birth. Long before a child is called on to confront the larger communities, he is born into a tiny world, with just enough people in it so that he is not overwhelmed by them, yet enough to guarantee him the practice he needs in learning what human society is like and how to share it. This community is not only a natural community; it is also a supernatural one. It is the first church; and it remains, through all our adult life, the basic church, or at least the basic unit of the Church, just as it is the basic unit of all human society.

It is not a complete church any more than the world of the family is a complete world. Both of them are to some degree "practice" worlds, with most of the important elements of the real world, yet without its overwhelming complexity. In this family church, there are, potentially, most of the elements which will later be found fully developed in the church of one's maturity.

There is a ministry. The mother normally carries the heart of that ministry in the early years; this is as it should be. There is no substitute in the experience of the tiny child for the assurance and the sense of reality which comes from his knowledge that his religious life is of a piece with all the rest of his life; and to the infant this sense of reality and oneness is necessarily mediated through his mother.

But it would be hopelessly wrong to suppose that the ministry remains the mother's. The sooner fathers can take their normal place as ministers within the family, the better. One of the minor annoyances of some of us in the clergy is to be asked to say grace when we are invited to dine with our parishioners. This is not a serious thing, but such an act belongs to the shared ministry of the family—father, mother or children. So, too, with family prayers— if your clergyman seems loath to lead you in your common devotion, it is not because he is embarrassed to pray in a private home! He is embarrassed at invading a ministry which is properly that of the family itself.

The Church in the family has its ministry, and it has also its corporate observances. The place of family prayer is central in this, even if the speed and complexity of our life makes only the briefest of corporate devotions possible. It may be that we do no more than read a section of Holy Scripture at the supper table. Family prayers do not depend on lengthy elaboration to be real and deep. But it is certainly a basic element in the life of the healthy Christian family to share a continuing, common tradition of prayer. Notably this would be true about the great fasts and feasts of the Church Year. All Saints' Day, Thanksgiving, Advent, Christmas, Epiphany, Lent, Easter, Whitsunday—each one of these great turning-points in our calendar offers to a family the chance to develop and to deepen their understanding of the fact that they are a church.

And all this apparatus of family prayer does not exist for itself alone, or for some imaginary time in the future "when the children will be glad they had this training." It is a present and living reality, even in the life of the youngest member of the family. Where family relationships are understood as basically religious relationships—where the great dimensions of Christianity are applied even to the routine day-by-day duties of the household— where to every common task there is attached the sacredness and dignity of a religious rite—then both parents and children learn from the very outset to understand and accept their relationship to each other with respect and gravity. And this understanding is the indispensable prerequisite of the free individuality which is the crown and blessing of childhood in a balanced and mature family.

It is also deeply true that this common religious life is a massive safeguard against the worldliness which attacks us all. A child alone, or a parent alone, is always in danger of being swamped by the pressures of the world—the invitation to possessions for their own sake, to covetousness, to self-indulgence, to carelessness about religious duties, to lust, or bitterness at one's lot, or envy of others. Our salvation in this is the warmth and serenity of the common Christian family life we share. Together in a household of faith, we remind one another, and are reminded, of the greater realities, and are helped to be more stedfast in our devotion to Christ.

The second element can be stated very simply—*it is necessary for true and right family relationships that there be one God, and the same God, for all alike.* How often we are guilty of the mistake of "talking down" to our children. And this is not far from being a sin. To talk down to them religiously is no less wrong than it is to condescend to them in any other way. We need to remember always that there is nothing the matter with a child's intelligence or ability; he thinks about the same things that adults do, and he is, within his limits, just as well equipped as adults to do that thinking. The child's two great lacks are words and experience. He can handle very big ideas, and do it very well, as long as he is given tools to use which are suited to him. Words are such tools; and no one is quicker than a child to recognize that he has not yet got the words he needs, and that he needs help in understanding those tools. Human experience is another element which he quite well understands he does not yet have. He looks eagerly and somewhat pathetically to his parents to supply this need for him. He wants from his parents, almost as much as he wants anything, that they shall tell him what really happens, what people are really like, and what the ending of it all is.

Words and experience are lacking to the child; but, when they are supplied him, he is quite capable of understanding the fundamental realities of life. We might take it from our Lord's words that children are rather better than their elders in understanding these fundamental realities . . . *Truly, I say to you, whoever does not receive the kingdom of God like a child shall not enter it* (St. Luke 18:17). The quality He refers to here is not some superior moral achievement; He is talking about the unselfconscious simplicity of a child in seeing elemental spiritual truths directly and simply, where adults have grown so complicated and involved in their minds that it is hard for them to see and hear the plain truth.

The child himself is peculiarly sensitive to this element of being talked down to, religiously. "Children's corners" in churches, designed to provide a nice, child-sized God, with pretty pictures, are notoriously unpopular with children. If there are books they can read, or pictures they can meditate about, they will be delighted; but the suggestion that it is somehow better for them to say their prayers in such a corner meets with a very cold reception. Children make a bee-line for the high altar in a church; and they do it with a perfectly sound instinct, for they know that the real God, the big God, is connected with the high altar and not with any miniature imitation. The child wants what the adults have.

Few things please a child more than the chance to play and learn with other children. His instinct in that direction is sound—he is perfectly aware that he has a lot to learn. But when it comes to worship, and to a deep sharing of the fundamental realities of life, he seeks no greater pleasure than the chance to share these with his parents. The joy of the ordinary child when he is privileged to pray with his father and mother, or to sit in church with them, exploring the mystery of existence and of love, is a very moving and beautiful thing to behold. For he knows, even if his parents have forgotten, that if there is a God at all, there can only be one, and he must be the same God for the old and the young alike.

The third principle is really an extension of the second. *If there is only one God for both parents and children, then there must also be a common law for both, and a common judgment, and a common standard of life, and a common love.* There are few principles better attested than this in the experience of mature and happy men and women. The finest claim that I can make about my own father is that I can never remember a time when he asked anything of me which I did not clearly know he also asked of himself. From my earliest youth I can never remember any time when I resented an exaction of discipline or duty, on the ground that there was a double standard. I quite understood that the *mode* of our obedience might be different, for I was a child and he a man. But the *law* for both was one, just as the God was one. I dare say that some such observation could be made by every man or woman privileged to have a happy childhood and to grow to maturity with a real sense of freedom.

What are our common violations of this principle? Doubtless one of the most common is the odious practice of "sending" the children to Sunday school. It need hardly be said that the attitude of this volume is positive and favorable toward good Sunday schools! Yet there is a kind of parental frame of mind, distressingly common in many communities, which seems to hold that religion is something that children need as part of their education, but from which adults have graduated.

The child is sent off dutifully to Sunday school under this theory; and where family discipline is strong, the child's attendance and participation may be quite satisfactory. But underneath the obedience, there is a sometimes-quite-profound resentment on the part of the child; and there is also a corrosive and ultimately destructive certainty that God is of concern only for children—and a corresponding desire to reach the point when the child can graduate from God as soon as possible. The child often comes to feel that religion is like the multiplication table, appropriate to a certain stage in his education, but only rarely to be used in later life, and generally to be allowed to fall into the background of half-remembered things. He may even gain a deeper cynicism than that, a feeling that he is being used as a kind of vicarious sacrifice to the gods of respectability—that his parents are simply easing their own conscience by "doing the right thing by their children." At the very least, the child may suspect that his being sent to Sunday school is simply a way of gaining for his parents an hour's respite and a chance to read the paper in peace.

This may have its slightly comic aspect, but it is desperately serious at bottom. If the child is to be saved from resentment and rebellion against his parents and all that his parents pretend to stand for, it is necessary for him to understand from the outset that his parents ask nothing of him to which they are not themselves obedient. We may well be grateful that in these latter years the Church has shown an increasing and healthy awareness of this and has provided more opportunities for common worship and common instruction for parents and children alike.

But the principle is at stake in much wider areas than simply the matters of Church attendance and the like. The explosive father, who roars ill-temperedly at his children that they must at once stop losing their tempers, is again a slightly comic illustration of the principle. If fathers are bad-tempered, then the child has an initial predisposition to understand that that is the way adult men ought to behave; and when he is told that he must not do that, his first and most obvious question is "Why is there a double standard in this?" Or the mother, who is a perpetual complainer, whose lot in life is hard and whose work is long and wearisome, and yet who expects cheerful and instant help and obedience from her youngsters, is likewise a somewhat comic figure, yet not really comic at all. For she will succeed, in the most remarkable way, in inculcating in her offspring exactly the qualities she least wants to see in them. One God, one law—this is the secret of the relaxed and mature Christian family.

The fourth and fifth principles have to do directly with freedom. The fourth is that *childhood is a school of freedom*. Our first concern is likely to be about the freedom of the child, for in this area lie many of the heartaches as well as the small pleasures of family life. Practically from the beginning of a child's life, we are concerned with his ever-growing area of responsible freedom. His earliest training is in that direction. As he grows in understanding, we enlarge the area of his free choices.

This is by no means an easy task. With the little child, there is often some pain connected with it which we do everything we can to avoid, yet which we more or less deliberately accept because we understand that in no other way can the child learn how to use freedom. We would not let him come to any real harm. But all parents have to learn a certain degree of inner toughness with their children, even though it must be balanced with an instant and understanding love. If a child is going to walk, we have got to be content to watch him experiment; if a child is going to learn to find his way around the kitchen, we must take the calculated risk, even at the cost of bumps and wounds.

It gets more complicated as children grow older. Nothing is more agonizing than a child's first money allowance—he gets his coin and off he dashes into the wonderful world of bubble-gum and comic books. Within an hour he has spent his money, chewed the gum, read the books, and then stands facing the indescribable wilderness of six days and twenty-three hours before more largesse comes his way. It would be a lot easier on our nervous systems if we bought him the gum or the comic books, if our tastes run to such commodities. But we have sense enough to learn that he never will gain in freedom or responsibility as long as other people are doing the deciding for him. He must experiment himself; and while we must be prepared to catch him when he bounces, at the same time we must also provide the firm and sometimes stern framework of reality within which he can practice his freedom. There are many times when "it hurts us more than it hurts you"; yet there is no help for it, and all parents understand this.

Still more fundamental and costly are the choices which lead a boy or girl into maturity—choices of college, of vocation, of marriage. Here the part of the discreet parent is almost immeasurably difficult, for the choices are so nearly parallel to our own. Furthermore the child has come to share so fully our understanding and our words, that our ability to keep our hands off is tested to the utmost. But, if we have done our work well in the earlier years, we can come to these choices with a real confidence that they are going to be made about as well as such choices ever are made. And we are going to learn something even deeper and more satisfactory than that; we are going to learn the mature joy of parents whose children have burst out of the cocoon of childhood and have become what God intended them to become—thoughtful and mature adults, carrying on into another generation the best that we could give them.

If this happy end is to be accomplished, the preparation for it must run far back into the childhood years. It is always dangerous to postpone the experiments with freedom, for fear that the child will hurt himself. Hurt himself he will; and such pain seems to be the inescapable cost of knowledge. But this can be borne if the pain is held in an unvarying matrix of love, which meets and even anticipates the pain. A major part of this swift and imaginative love is the quick willingness of the parent to help the child to understand not only the nature of the experiment he is making and the cost of it, but also the fact that the parent has known and shared this experience. Love is not simply sponge rubber around a child. Love is a meeting which brings the child to a deeper understanding of what has happened and, concurrently, a clearer sense that this experience with freedom is a universal one, and the common property of mankind.

If the parent is to do this job well, then the fifth principle must come into play, namely that *the parent also needs practice in freedom quite as much as the child does.* It is perhaps here, more than anywhere else, that the inordinate need of some parents for their children takes its toll. Parents have no right to be dependent on children or to let their children feel that there is such dependence. There is no worse burden to load on a child's shoulders than the unspoken sense that his parents are dependent on him, must possess him, and must continually sap and draw his strength to meet their necessities. It is necessary for the child's exercise of freedom that he understand that his parents are free from him, and are, therefore, competent to lead him truly and dispassionately into the ever wider world of his increasingly mature choices. No one is quicker than a child to sense a wrong interpretation of freedom, or a guidance which is misleading because it is egocentric on the parent's part.

The goal for the child is not to remain a child; it is to be independent of his parents. In order to reach that independence, he needs to know from the outset that he can give and receive exactly as much as he is prepared to give and receive, no more and no less. His question always is "Do they really want me to be a grown-up person?" And the answer to that question will not come in easy words or professions. It will come in the manner in which parents exercise their own freedom in relationship to him and his.

Let us examine one or two typical instances, again. One is certainly the very vexing area of the extent to which parents demand the physical companionship and attention of their children. Most parents are likely to be sensitive to this, for we crave for ourselves the reassurance that our children like us and like to be with us. In general I should suppose that we could take this for granted; certainly God gives to children every eager expectancy and desire to love their parents. Yet it is part of the wisdom of parents to know that children cannot grow up tied to their apron strings and to realize that there are fewer resentments sharper in the heart of adolescent boys and girls than the despairing realization that their parents "need them" and are dependent on them. The surest help that parents can give in this matter is to look carefully at their own freedom of action—to see to it that they preserve and develop their own independent social life, so that the child wants more of his parents' society than he gets.

Ideally, we will always hit the happy mean in this; practically, we never can. If we must lean anywhere, is it not better to lean away from the child rather than toward him? For there is little in a child's life which bothers and torments him more than the feeling that he is the center of his parents' world. He has no business being father and mother to them—he is going to have children of his own, sometime, to love and guide; and it is for the coming generation that God gave him his own parental instincts. Therefore, every child responds well and happily in the knowledge that his parents have their own life, and are pleased and successful in living it. Then he can copy and admire, which are two of the things most dear to his heart when he thinks about his parents.

Another instance is the child's unspoken desire that his parents be interested and well versed in other activities, and at a maturer level than he is. Sometimes we speak of this as the child's need to respect his parents. No doubt the element of respect enters into it. But the emotional situation is a little deeper than that. It is not simply that a child wants to feel that his parents have interests of their own, which he will sometime share and which, in the meantime, he feels are worthy of his respect. It is also a positive resentment when he feels that his parents are invading his world. His question then is "Why do they not have a life of their own?" Why are they so sentimental, or else so poverty-stricken, that they must continually seek for themselves what is only good enough for the teen-ager. The vocabulary may not be teen-age, but the thought is. For he is quite able to understand that the pleasures of his 'teens are not going to be the pleasures and interests of his mature years. And when he observes his parents seeming to develop a kind of second childhood of their own, there is more than lack of respect involved; there is also a sense of something unnatural, a reversal in nature, a refusal to accept the reality of mature freedom. Here as in all things, fathers and mothers need a delicacy and understanding which is well-nigh supernatural. Indeed, it is supernatural, which is the main point of talking about a Christian family in the first place.

The last of the six principles is *the need of both parents and children for a continual sense of the reality of one another.* Steady prayer for one another is doubtless the principal instrument in this, for it is in prayer that we become most real to one another. Our intercessions for our children, or theirs for us, are not simply religious duties imposed from outside. They are rather the principal ways we have in which to lay aside the carelessness and egotism of our daily life, and enter into real communion with one another in the presence of God.

"To love is to listen," in the familiar phrase. The trouble with most of us is that we do not really listen to one another—listen enough to hear the unspoken appeals and experiments in which our true selfhood is expressed. We remain simply scenery to one another. The careless and thoughtless child, if he is not helped by wise discipline at home, can very easily come to take his home for granted and as furnishing a background for his own adventuring. In like manner, our children can become simple conversation-pieces in our lives, to be trotted out upon occasion when it serves our vanity or our boredom, and otherwise to remain simply in the background like porcelain figurines on a shelf. These twin dangers are alike real and profound. And it is principally in our prayers that we shall find the answer to them.

But there is more than prayer involved. We all would do well to examine our mealtimes, occasionally, to see how our conversation is balanced and shared. Who does the talking? What do we talk about? Is there an unwitting monopolist in our conversation?

What about the discipline of our leisure time? There is no temptation more insidious than the temptation to busyness, to find easy excuses for not providing for our children (or in the case of children, for their parents) the golden hours of free and relaxed enjoyment. They may be somewhat energetic hours of games or hiking; they may be quite sober and reflective hours of music or reading. But the life of any family which does not make regular and disciplined allowance for this kind of companionship is a deformed life.

What about our letters to one another when we are separated? What about our factual discussions of books, televised plays, and radio programs? What about our sharing from time to time of one another's duties—the boy perhaps to drive his father on an errand, or the father to share the boy's paper route?

These are simple and unromantic suggestions. But it is in precisely such elementary ways that children and parents do become real to one another. There must be a definite effort, and a discipline of life, which provides both time and opportunity. It is important to emphasize the need of families for planned choice in this matter. The competition for the attention and interest of children (and of parents, as well), is too keen to let us safely neglect the need for deliberate selection of our activities. Schools, community groups and activities, even church groups, can easily monopolize family time, unless families are willing to make hard choices for the sake of their common life. The family which is not willing to invest this much in such discipline does not deserve to have the blessing of such mutual knowledge.

Those then are the six principles which seem to have a special Christian significance in family life. It may well be understood that any parent reading these principles and reflecting about them, is likely to cry despairingly, "Who, then, can be saved?" They seem to presuppose a standard of thoughtfulness and understanding far beyond the reach of most of us.

A SEVENTH PRINCIPLE

Perhaps, then, we should add a seventh principle, that *all parents need to remember that their children belong to God as well as to them;* that God caused them to be born, and that God is quite capable of taking care of His own, despite our failures and shortcomings. This ought not be taken as a counsel of desperation, as if it were God's work to intervene only when we had brought our families to the brink of disaster. It is rather a reminder that God is at work at every stage in the proceedings, from the birth of the love which brought the children into existence through to the time when, in their turn, the same eternal current of love crests again.

For His children are never really ours, but always His. He is infinitely more concerned with them than even we who bear them. His love is far more searching and enduring than ours. His freedom is inconceivably greater than ours, and so is His unflagging determination that they shall be free, *and in their freedom shall choose Him.* The Christian parent weighs these things, and they bring a sense of balance and maturity to him which no other knowledge can possibly do. He does not thereby abdicate his own responsibilities, nor does he desire to. He understands that he is privileged to be not only an instrument of, but a co-worker with, God in the family enterprise. But he knows that God is always at work, by his side, correcting what he has done amiss, fulfilling what has been left incomplete, and proceeding in His own way to evoke real and free selfhood in these children of ours.

Perhaps it would not be amiss to add that children seek and need a parallel understanding of their parents and God. "Father is not himself today" is an expression not merely of human understanding and the patient tolerance of children; it is a witness to a deeper sense that there are more important, and more frequent, times when father is himself. It is also a witness to a still deeper sense that God is a partner in this, making the same kind of patient judgment of Father as the children are. Parents owe this deeper sense to their children; so should it always be hoped that children would deal likewise with their fathers and mothers.

All this is implied in what we said in the beginning about the family being a church. Yet perhaps it is well to say clearly and simply that we and our children are both created and called to be the children of God. In this equal childlikeness and discipleship, it is possible for both generations to make common cause under the judgment and love of the God who loves them both, created them both, and is redeeming them both.

All this is suggested by the thought of the family as a little church. Yet it suggests a still deeper truth—that, in the last analysis, the Church is the only complete family. The blood-kinship of parents and children in a family seems to lead us to a still deeper kinship, which binds not only members of the same family together but members of the same humanity. The kinship which is established in Holy Baptism is the deepest and truest of all relationships; and it is to this deep bond that family life and love seem to lead us.

Just as marriage is a ministry, so is a family. It is God's way of introducing us to the interdependence and common life of all mankind, and preparing us to take our dutiful part in that greater whole. It is of this that our Lord was speaking, when they brought word to Him that His mother and brothers were kept back from talking to Him because of the crowd, and He looked around at the crowd and said *Who is my mother, and who are my brothers?* Then, stretching forth His hand to His disciples, He said *Here are my mother and my brothers! For whoever does the will of my Father in heaven is my brother, and sister, and mother.* (St. Matthew 12:48-50).

Is this saying harsh or unfeeling? It could be so interpreted by one who put the narrow loyalties of family above all others. But to the one who has thought deeply about family life, such a saying rings true. It suggests the greater loyalties, to which our first loyalties should lead us. It suggests the wider kinships and the greater duties and the higher vocation to which we are called and for which the healthy life of a family prepares us.

Parents who look reflectively at their children and realize what their children's ultimate vocation is know this. They know that their children's vocation is not merely to be sons and daughters, but to be persons in their own right, taking their full part in the life of humanity. Children know this, who understand that the test of their family life and training will be the way in which they live their adult lives. And when family life is interpenetrated and lighted by the awareness of the greatest of all families, the household of God, then the tensions and difficulties of the first family are resolved in the knowledge of the wider implications of the other.

The family is, in some measure, a church. But the Church, in infinitely deeper measure, is the truest of all families, where the children of the One Father, joined in the profound common life of the baptized brotherhood, find their own nature and their true relationships one with another.

CHAPTER NINE

Money and Stewardship

THERE CAN BE no adequate discussion of Christian living without thoughtfully considering the nature of money and our stewardship of it. For the way we use our money and the accounting we are prepared to give to God of this stewardship is, for every Christian, a test of discipleship. Our jobs differ; our family situations vary; our share in the life of the community is ours alone; but there is scarcely a person who does not express, in an important manner, his Christian living by the way he handles and uses his money.

Some may feel that it is out of place to discuss money and stewardship in a book on Christian living. These people believe that religion is concerned with "spiritual" things only, and that it is somehow wrong to introduce, in the present discussion, so material a reality as money and the way we manage it.

Others—perhaps a good many more than in the first class—will consider a discussion of money out of place in a book that is primarily about freedom. They believe that while it is necessary to think about money and stewardship, there is certainly no connection between money and freedom, for freedom implies an absence of compulsion, and money is the very symbol of compulsion. Freedom implies the ability to choose at one's will, money implies necessity.

Money, to be sure, has always been at the heart of two knotty human problems. One is the problem of covetousness, of selfishness, about which the Bible says, *The love of money is the root of all evil.* And while this saying comes of a sad, and somewhat disillusioned, wisdom, most people recognize the truth in it. For most of us know that we have an impulse to selfishness, a leaning toward covetousness, which feeds and fattens on whatever wealth we have. Our Lord suggests, in the saying about the camel and the needle's eye, that this danger increases with increasing wealth. But covetousness can be a problem for those of modest income—and for the very poor, too. Because we know this and are aware how greediness imprisons the human spirit (as in the case of "poor" King Midas with his gold), we are likely to think that there is no connection between money and freedom.

But, even if we are not particularly impressed with this problem, there is nobody who is not very sharply impressed with the other problem, of money as both the symbol and the tool of the universal human necessity which bears on us all. There may have been a time in human history when men could live in a first-hand relationship with the earth and its fruits and could meet their family needs by the work of their own hands, without need of more than a handful of money. Indeed, we grow homesick, at times, for those days and wish ourselves back in that uncomplicated world.

But that world is not ours. So enmeshed are we in a complicated and highly specialized society, that money has become all but universal as the very means itself of our life. There are not many left who could be self-sufficient any more; we live by selling our own specialized skills in the common market of humanity, and gaining thereby a currency which will buy for us the skills of other people. Because we are thus dependent on other men's skills (and, indeed, on skills of which we have no knowledge or experience at all), we have grown far more aware than our fathers were of the necessity which bears on every one of us. Money is the symbol of this necessity; without it we would starve and die; with it, we are permitted to share in a rich and varied life in our complex community.

It is small wonder, then, that, even leaving the idea of sin aside, there seems to be a binding and commanding necessity about money. It can buy freedom, if there is enough of it and if freedom can be bought; but the price you pay for that choice of the things you want is a thraldom to money and a need for it which is no freedom at all, but harsh and grinding necessity.

So do most of us reflect about our money, when we begin to think about it in relation to our fundamental philosophy of life and our Christian belief and practice. Almost everything that we know at the beginning about money predisposes us to be incredulous, disbelieving, about the part that money can play in our relationship with God. Yet, despite this well-nigh universal feeling, books on Christian living, like this one, continue to proclaim that our stewardship of our income and means is one of the principal areas where our sincerity is tested, where our discipleship is lived out. This book in particular, which has freedom for its central theme, would want to make that point very clearly—that our stewardship is one of the principal ways in which our freedom is established and seen.

STEWARDSHIP AS THANKSGIVING

How is this so? Our answer must begin with *the clear recognition of man's obligation of thankfulness for God's bounty.* Men do not attain mature discipleship in their lives until they become aware of both the privilege, and the obligation, of thanksgiving for the manifold blessings of God. It is only the childish person who boasts about what he has become and what he has accomplished in life. With maturity comes the humility—a mixture of gentle humor and wise perspective—that leads us to understand how much of our accomplishment has been accidental, and how much more has been due to what other people have given us.

This is not to deny human achievement or our right to feel a craftsman's pleasure at a good job done. Mature men and women know this pleasure; but they also know that the greater part of their lives and achievements was not primarily created by themselves, but was chosen and built by them out of the raw material of job and home and community and background and opportunity that life provided them.

With that realization of our dependence on friends and fortune and on the opportunities that God provided, there comes a far deeper and more thoughtful gratitude that God created us with the particular talents and opportunities which have come to us, and that He has seen fit to lead us step by step into a wiser use of these talents. Most of us, before we are very old, come truly to feel that what we have is ours only because God has been good enough to give us the stewardship of it. This sense of gratitude and thankful trust is the root of all true stewardship.

But this simple thanksgiving, true as far as it goes, does not enter too deeply into the heart of the matter. We do not reflect long about our thankfulness to God before we encounter the blunt question whether such a feeling of thankfulness is not mere sentimentality. "What possible connection can God have with money?" is the question that occurs to us. Faith, hope, love—these are the things God deals with, so this argument goes, and money is something that only men deal with. You can take love and honor and truth with you into eternity, but money you cannot take with you; it is current in this world only, and belongs to a different set of values altogether than the divine and eternal values of religion.

These are real questions, and the difficulty with them is an honest one for many people, particularly those who have been brought up to think of religion as "spiritual" in contrast to "material." Sometimes this distinction between "spiritual" and "material" is the product of a real hunger for deeper truths than some of us commonly find in this world. Sometimes, too, it is nothing more than a cloak for selfishness. Sometimes it is simply the product of shallow thinking. Sometimes it is born out of a false view of God's relationship with His creation.

Whatever its source, however, any such distinction between "spiritual" and "material" is both very suspicious and very dangerous. It is suspicious because, if not born in a total misconception of what the Christian faith is, it will certainly lead to such a misconception. It is dangerous because such a false distinction can lead to almost unbelievable cruelty and hardness of heart.

There is a proper distinction between these two words, a distinction based upon the different qualities to which they refer. It is important, for example, to distinguish between the vibrations of the strings of a violin as they are recorded by a scientific instrument, and the music which those vibrations are carrying. It is important to distinguish between a body, and the personality which expresses itself through that body. It is important to be able to distinguish between the historic life of Jesus of Nazareth, and the eternal, loving God in that Person.

But it is quite impossible to *disassociate* the music of the violin from the vibrations of the strings. Music, the spiritual quality, is inescapably bound up with music, the series of physical phenomena. The friends we like, the husbands or wives we love, are not identical with their bodies; we quite understand that their personalities are not imprisoned in their bodies and will not die with their bodies; yet we also understand that it is not disembodied spirits whom we love, but these particular flesh-and-blood persons. This is especially true in the case of the Incarnate Lord, where body and spirit are met in a perfect unity.

In Christian thought, the adjective we use to describe this unity is the word "sacramental." We recognize that there are times when we may want to think of the spiritual or material aspects of something separately; but they come to us bound up together, and this is the way we commonly know them and use them. A meal is generally far more than simply so many units of nutriment. A job is usually far more to us than simply an exchange for so much money. And money itself is just such a composite whole.

Certain instances of this interaction of spirit and matter are particularly important and vivid to us. And those we call *sacrament* are the supreme instances of spirit inhabiting matter, which Christ Himself gave to us, as the means of our membership in His Body and as the means of nourishment in our discipleship to Him. Holy Baptism and the Holy Communion rightly are the uniquely great examples of this sacramental principle. And part of the reason why God gave us those sacraments is that we might begin to see the same principle at work in other areas of life.

MONEY AS A SACRAMENTAL

The second great principle of stewardship is, then, *to know the sacramental character of money*. It may seem a far cry from the bread and wine of the Holy Communion to our salary check or our pay envelope. But this distance is simply a measure of the way in which we have let our lives become fragmented. God sees no such separation between them, nor should we. Our money can be an instrument in our hands whereby we may express the sincerity and depth of our discipleship. It may be a means of grace in God's hands, if we will submit our money to His will, and earnestly strive to be worthy trustees and stewards of His bounty.

To establish this sacramental sense of money brings us face to face with old difficulties. One is the ever-present danger of sin by reason of our innate tendency to selfishness and covetousness. A form of this is the way in which money itself can become an end

· 113

rather than a means. It can be a symbol of so many things: of a respectability we have sought, of a security we have needed and desired, of power which, in our fear, we have desperately wanted. Money does bring some of these satisfactions. But our experience generally is that the price we pay is far more than what these satisfactions are worth. For money has the power to enslave. And the man or woman who has known that servitude, who has allowed his life to be dominated by the fear of financial insecurity, has paid a price a thousand times greater than the money which buys them; and he knows it.

Yet the temptation is ever present and each of us has got to fight his way through it to the point where he can see the third great truth about money. We have learned much when we have learned the simple obligation of thankfulness. We have learned far more when we have discovered for ourselves the sacramental character of money. *But until we learn that our money either serves us or we serve it—until we get to the point of seeing that the use of our money is both the means and the great test of our freedom—we have not really mastered the lesson.*

Money is power. Money is time or its equivalent. Money is, in truth, ourselves insofar as it represents the investment of ourselves. Money is, for most of us, one of the principal tools of personality. If we are masters of our money, then we are, by the same token, able to use ourselves and give ourselves in the service of those things that are of the greatest importance to us. And if freedom means doing what we most want to do and being what we most want to be, then our use of our money is inevitably going to be either the servant of that freedom or its enemy.

Perhaps at this point, it would be well to recall one of the most familiar of our Lord's sayings about money: *Where your treasure is, there will your heart be also* (St. Luke 12:34). It is a curious fact that, often enough, when we hear that saying or use it, we really understand it to mean "Where your heart is, there will your treasure be." We understand, in other words, that money and concern generally go together; that we will pay, more or less gladly, for what we really want; that our means will gravitate in the general direction of our principal aims and desires; and that our treasure will follow our hearts.

This is true enough, so far as it goes. But it is not what Christ said. What He said was *Your heart will follow your treasure*—that, as is generally true in our moral life, what we do has a profound influence on what we are.

This is a principle so basic to moral life that it deserves a moment's thought and illustration. Marriage supplies an excellent example. A husband who loves his wife is going to have strong impulses to pamper her, to demonstrate his affection for her, to spend his time generously with her, and to share generously his money with her. These impulses are natural and are rightly taken for granted: treasure follows heart.

But most men soon discover that even a quite sincere love for wife is by no means an infallible charm against a wandering eye or a wayward thought. It is not necessarily the weak man who discovers this or who is tempted to unfaithful thoughts, although it is weakness to yield to them. Almost all men discover that their feelings—their impulses, instincts, emotions—are by no means either infallible or even trustworthy guides.

Nor does Christianity assume that they are. The promise made by husband and wife in the marriage service is not a promise about feelings. It would be quite impossible, and childishly sentimental, for men and women to promise that they would feel a certain way toward each other, "till death us do part." What they promise when they marry has to do not with their impulses or feelings but with their actions—it is a promise that they will "love, honour and cherish each other," all three of those duties being things that they do. They commit themselves, in other words, to what they can control—their actions—knowing that their feelings will generally follow along afterward and that we cannot do too much about them directly. The heart, we believe, will follow its treasure. If we invest ourselves, our acts, in our marriage, then our emotional attitudes will take care of themselves.

Indeed the Church quite well understands, as our Lord did, that the essence of the moral life is not primarily in attitudes but in action, that the attitudes usually will take care of themselves when the actions are right, that *as a man does, so will he be, as long as the doing involves not simply superficial appearances but really and deeply involves his whole will and self*. In terms of money, Christ's way of saying this was the remark about treasure and heart.

To many of us, such a principle as this sounds impossibly romantic and unrealistic. We are well acquainted with hypocrisy, both conscious and unconscious; we are altogether too aware of the ease with which a man or a woman can appear to be what he is not, can play a part that does not truly reflect what he is really thinking. Therefore, we are likely to be skeptical of this fundamental principle and to quote in response another Scripture about *Pharisees, hypocrites! For you are like whitewashed tombs, which outwardly appear beautiful, but within they are full of dead men's bones and all uncleanness* (St. Matthew 23:27). The solution for our human problem does not lie so much in what we do as the kind of person we really are within.

This is a quick and attractive answer, particularly in our own time when we are perhaps especially sensitive to hypocrisy and the danger of it. But it is not a very deep answer. If we reflect thoughtfully about this supposed opposition between two principles, we come before long to see that there really is no fundamental opposition between them at all. Our Lord would be the first one to say to us that what goes on inside is of infinitely greater importance than the outward appearance—He told us as much in countless instances, in comments on matters that range from alms-giving to fasting.

But, doubtless, He would continue to point out that what we are and what we do are so hopelessly interwoven that usually the only way we can tell what we are is by what we do. It is quite possible for a man to be divided in his own nature; and, actually, most of us are thus divided, filled with conflicting impulses, some good and some bad. The only way we can tell which ones matter the most to us is by acting on them, for the act commits us to the impulse, to the principle. Indeed, the act establishes us, for what we are, in our own eyes far more than it does in our neighbors'. The act involves our very selves; it is an investment of ourselves. The act is a decision, a choice, around which our developing self crystallizes. There may be regret and a looking-backward and a wishing that choices did not have such finality and clarity. But a man is what he chooses: *Where his treasure is, there will his heart be also.*

Thus it is that most of us think through this somewhat paradoxical relationship between the inner person and the outward act. It is not unlike the earlier distinction we saw between "spirit" and "matter." Just as it is impossible, in practice, to divorce the spiritual reality of anything from its material reality, so is it difficult to divorce the act from the person. As Pascal said, "We are what we do; we do what we are."

This principle is, of course, very broad; it is the principle on which our whole moral life is built, as well as the whole structure of our duty and obligation. If this principle were not true, then this life and this world would be an unbearable chaos of conflicting egotisms.

The pattern of duty is always the pattern of thoughtful and serious action. And nowhere does this stand out more clearly than in our stewardship. We are not simply the creatures of our impulses and our emotions; we are free and responsible agents. We make our choices, and in money as in everything else, our choices in turn mold and affect us because they are real expressions of our selves. How often a man who has pictured himself as one incapable of very generous impulses or of very deep convictions, will come to see that he is not really such a person at all. He will come to that discovery not because he has thought any differently about himself or because he has forsaken humility, but because suddenly he has done a generous act which has cost him something and been even painful, but which has also revealed to him the degree to which, by the power of the Holy Spirit, he is capable of generosity and partnership.

I can remember quite vividly the first time, in my youth, that I experienced this kind of self-discovery. It came about when an older man taught me how to manage my money. I had very little of it, and I had become obsessed with my helplessness and my inability to have or do the things I wanted to do. Thrift seemed to me not a privilege but a disagreeable and hopeless bondage. The principle of tithing, which I was ready enough to accept in my mind, seemed to me to be impossible of fulfillment because there was never enough money with which to fulfill it. My friend neither read me lectures nor counselled me at length. He only reminded me that if I were going to tithe (as he did), I ought to learn that the tithe came first; that unless I deliberately took the *first* tenth, and put it carefully away where I would not even think of spending it, I would never have it to use to fulfill my good intentions. From that day to this I have so ordered my own personal finances as to have always at least a definite, if very small, proportionate share of my income safely reserved from which I can fulfill the obligations I feel I owe to my church and to other good causes.

The importance of this experience was not that I had suddenly become generous or developed a new virtue, but that I discovered for myself, by a series of simple acts, that I had not only some thankful generosity in my system but also the means with which to fulfill those impulses. And the simple act of segregating the first tenth rather than the last tenth did the trick.

I daresay that many others have learned this same lesson; and with them, as with me, the effect of it was not to nourish pride or complacency particularly, but rather to commit one to sharing and stewardship in a way that was impossible so long as those words were simply pleasant ideals.

If we are going to be free, we have to be free with something. Freedom is not primarily an emotion or a spirit; it is the series of acts done with our time, talents, and money—the instruments of our freedom. A man does not develop freedom in a vacuum. He develops it with real acts that have a measurable market value. And when he comes to realize the necessity for this irrevocable self-investment, he has discovered a profound truth about good stewardship.

STEWARDSHIP AS OFFERING

When we have learned this, then we are ready for the final lesson—*the lesson of Offering*. We have much thinking to do and a lot of self-discovery to make before we are able to come to that final stage in our pilgrimage. The act of offering we have witnessed many times in the Communion service as we watched the priest prepare the elements for the sacrament, and perhaps tried to work out some devotional scheme of our own to help make this act significant for us. In truth, it should be real to us; for as long as it remains for us simply Christ's offering or, even more remotely, just the priest's ceremonial offering, it will have only abstract significance.

What this offering symbolizes is of profound importance. To the Christian, who tries to live consciously day by day in God's holy way and to remember that he has received his life and its opportunities as a gift from God, the deepest question always is "How may we so deal with this life entrusted to us that it may be fitly offered to Him from whom it came?" All men hunger after the privilege of offering themselves and all they have to some infinitely worthwhile end. God is that end; and all mature and healthy religion is such an offering of self. But not until we learn that self is more than just impulses or hopes, that self is *acts*, have we reached the point where the act of offering becomes real to us.

Our offering may not be very impressive in the world's scale of values. Not many of us have large means or the resources with which to make impressive offerings. Indeed, we have little money, and our abilities are no more than average. But this is of little consequence to God; He is quite able to strike a balance sheet and understand us against the background of what we are and what we had to begin with. The important thing is the wholeheartedness with which we make our offering to Him. This is the final secret of stewardship, the secret so touchingly illustrated in Christ's gentle and loving observation of the widow and her mite. It may be healthy common sense, of course, to remind ourselves that not many of us are widows, and that most of us have considerably more than a mite! But the principle involved is unchallenged; and the principle should be embedded in our practice.

SUMMARY

Stewardship is born out of *thanksgiving* for what God has done for us and in us, and for all He has given us. That stewardship is possible because the use of money has potentially a *sacramental* character—it is at least potentially a way in which the spirit can be expressed in the material. Futhermore, stewardship is a true expression of our *freedom,* and a necessary one. No man is truly free who is not the master of all that he owns. The final lesson is that our highest freedom lies in our capacity to *offer* ourselves and what we have to God to use as He will. For it is all His, and we are His; and, therefore, the fulfillment of our freedom is to recognize and live out that ultimate relationship of thankful praise.

A NOTE ON TITHING

It may be to the point here to speak a little about the much-discussed question of tithing. Most of us have heard something about tithing in the last few years, for this practice is growing quite rapidly in our Church and even more rapidly in some of our sister communions. Strictly interpreted, the tithe is a tenth. The Old

Testament law on the subject (as in Genesis 28:22, Deuteronomy 12:6,17, and Deuteronomy 14:22-28) laid down the general principles of a rather complicated system. But the law, strictly speaking, required only that the first tenth of the principal annual harvest be set aside for the service of God. The strict Jew (the Pharisee) was careful to tithe everything that could possibly be considered as coming under the law. Our Lord records that the Pharisee tithed even the unimportant garden herbs—mint, anise, and cummin; and in the parable of the Pharisee and the Publican, the Pharisee is portrayed as reporting thankfully that he tithed everything that he possessed.

In the new Christian Church, the system of tithe was not generally adopted for several centuries, although probably many of the first Christians, being Jews, carried the principle of tithing into their new Christian allegiance. Almost all early Christians felt that the new teaching of Christian freedom had supplanted the tithe; and certainly the spirit and mood of the early Church was such as to make a mere tenth, on a purely legal basis, seem wholly inadequate as an expression of their devotion.

By early medieval times the tithe had crept into both custom and law; and the tithe actually remained part of the law of the land in England, for example, until well into the twentieth century. It was a well-known fact that people who had no church allegiance resented having to pay a tithe for the Church's support.

But the system was also resented by many good church people, chiefly on the ground that, while they would gladly give their tithe and more, they felt that their offering should be the product of their devotion and faith rather than an exaction of the law, civil or ecclesiastical.

When we talk about tithing today, of course, we are not referring to tithing as imposed by civil law. We are talking about the principle which was the central principle of stewardship in Old Testament religion and which had also a prominent place in the Christian order.

The argument against tithing as a principle is twofold. The first objection is the practical one based on the vast differences between life today and in Old Testament times. Our incomes today are in money, not in produce; and our standards of life are so much higher and our wealth so much greater that a tithe of a tenth part would seem to many far too little to give to their Lord and their Church. This is particularly true of people of greater than average means, people who note that even the Internal Revenue Bureau apparently shares their understanding since it permits them a thirty percent deduction for church giving.

An allied problem to this is the one arising from the multiplicity of appeals which are made to us. The Church is by no means the only institution to which we want to give, even though it may be the most important. Community funds, colleges and schools, and many other agencies hold a rightly important place in our hearts; and it is the rare individual who does not divide his giving proportionately among many beneficiaries. The problem is further complicated by the fact that the Old Testament tithe was also, in important ways, a tax: it accomplished what our taxes accomplish, at least in some particulars.

The other argument against the system of tithing is that it is dangerously susceptible to a legalistic understanding and attitude. In this it is no different from any other duty. There is in humanity an ineradicable tendency to legalize almost anything that we do—to draw God's attention proudly to the fact that we have done all that is required of us, and to forget our Lord's stern teaching that, after we have done all that is required of us, we should say, *we are unprofitable servants*. To the person who is sensitive about legalism, tithing seems to suffer from this curse. At what point can we say that we have really and fully fulfilled our stewardship? How dangerous it would be if we were ever to reach a point at which we could say that we have "given enough" for God. All we had would still hardly be enough, at least if we measure it by our devotion.

Thus there are many to whom the appeal to tithe meets a certain resistance based either on the practical considerations or on our reluctance to commit ourselves to what seems to be legalism. This book proposes no easy answer to this dilemma. It is certainly true that any duty, accepted and performed, is susceptible to legalism. Yet it is also true that our religion has got to be expressed in terms of duties and disciplines, even though we know that, in accepting them, we are thereby opening ourselves to the insistent temptation to pride. This may be saying no more than that it is always dangerous to be a Christian. So it is; and we have no right to seek some easy, magical escape from those dangers.

Thus there is no simple program or solution to be proposed. The man who rejects the tithe needs to be careful that he then does more than the tithe, for his own soul's sake. Indeed, so ought the man who tithes, for, in the truest sense of the word, it is hard to speak of tithing as "giving"—the tithe is a share we owe, much more than it is a sacrificial gift; and, for many of us at least, it would be wrong to use the word "sacrifice" about the assignment of a mere tenth of our income to God's especial service.

Many men and women prefer not to use the old word "tithe" but to speak rather of "proportional giving," in an attempt to avoid the wooden limitations of a fixed percentage. If, by "proportionate giving," we understand that we are really trying to express our freedom and our sacrificial mastery of our means, and if we are serious and intend, in so doing, to make our offering to the glory of God, we shall have accomplished all that the tithe proposes, and more.

So this section must necessarily end on a somewhat inconclusive note, seeking neither to recommend nor to discourage tithing or any similar system of regular management of our means. The heart and secret of Christian stewardship is that it is born in thanksgiving, and that it is a free offering of God's sacramental gifts to Him from whom all things come. Such a profound impulse is likely not to be satisfied by any law, however thoughtful, but will rather seek to burst from the bondage of law into the free and filial relationship which we would feel is the true Christian one.

Yet, in this impulse toward freedom, we need to remember that measured and systematic action must be a necessary part of the process of freedom, lest we should run head on into the danger of self-deceit and unintended hypocrisy. We accept duty, in other words, in order to be sure that we are not giving God less than we want to give. But we try to transcend duty, because we do not want ever to be in danger of seeming to say to God, "Well, now I have done enough."

Does all this make stewardship seem impossibly complicated? It is not intended to do so; it is intended only to make us more aware of the spiritual danger of *any* form or system of giving, when we get too far away from either our sense of personal responsibility to God for what we have, or our awareness that true giving has got to have a bite to it—that we need to use the word "sacrifice" very sparingly, and only when we are sure we mean it.

For all giving which pretends to be called *sacrificial* must be a deliberate attempt on our part to make a proper, Christian, manly response to the love of God, who gave Himself for us in Christ. Whatever the system of stewardship we use, let us be quite clear that it is our best and most worthy attempt to answer, in terms of our money, the gift of God in terms of the Cross.

CHAPTER TEN

Vocation and Its Problems

THIS CHAPTER deals with work—our jobs—and how, as Christians, we should look upon them and do them. But it considers work in terms of a word that has a unique place in the Christian vocabulary—the word "vocation," or "calling." Some readers may feel that such a word is a rather fancy one to use about our jobs. Perhaps most of us feel that way since, on looking at our work as salesmen, or engineers, or housewives, or secretaries, we feel that to call such work a "vocation" is to dignify it far beyond its real importance. Many jobs seem to be just jobs, and nothing more.

The intent of this chapter is to say that each of us, in his whole life (including his job, whether it seems important or not) is called by God to that life and in it. This is a pretty broad statement. But it is an essential part of Christian living, and the word that expresses the idea of God's calling us—vocation—is an essential word.

We use it, generally, in one of three different senses. The first is a more or less technical sense, in which we refer to people being "called" to certain professions or fields of work. For instance, we often speak of a "vocation to the priesthood."

The second sense is a more general one, in which we refer to people's occupations in the broad sense, as when we speak of "vocational testing" or "vocational training."

The third sense is still deeper and wider; it is the sense in which St. Paul describes our whole Christian life as a "calling" (Ephesians 4:1), or when the Prayer Book speaks of "that state of life unto which it shall please God to call me" (p. 289).

We shall presently go more deeply into these three levels of meaning. Each of them holds an important sense of the word that is worth examining. But behind them all lies a simple, profoundly significant Christian proposition—*that God is the kind of God who calls us, and that it is possible, even a joyful duty, for us to hear and obey.* This dynamic conception of the love of God, who seeks us out and calls us, by name, to Himself, and who has so created us that we can hear and respond to His call—this conception of God comes close to being the very heart of the Gospel.

It also comes close to being the heart of the creative freedom of which Christians speak, the freedom to respond, in joyful self-offering, to the loving God who created us for Himself, yet who is not content simply to exact obedience from us but rather seeks from free and loving children to win it—to win from us a free willingness to obey.

Life is filled with the reality of God. He is not remote from us, separated by His creation from us. He is ever-present and ever-active, seeking to use all of His creation as a means of His love; pressing through the veil of created things to reach us and win from us, in word and deed, in prayer and action, in home, job, community, our free and loving service. All this is implied in the rich and tender word "calling."

THE MEANING OF VOCATION

A little word-study will help to make this clearer. (If you are impatient with such details, then skip to page 130).

The word "vocation" is, of course, the latinized form of the Teutonic-English word "calling." The Authorized Version uses it only once, preferring the simpler and more homely English word. Both are translations of the same Greek word. "To call" has two principal meanings: one is *to give a name* to something or somebody, the other is *to summon*. Both these meanings appear and reappear in the biblical pageant, sometimes interplayed with one another, sometimes used literally, sometimes quite figuratively. *Whatsoever Adam called every living creature, that was the name thereof* is an example of the first sense. The second appears, for instance, when *Eli called Samuel, and said, Samuel, my son. And he answered, Here am I.*

But what is to be said of such a use as this: *I have called thee by thy name, thou art mine* (Isaiah 43:1) or this: *Behold what manner of love the Father hath bestowed upon us, that we should be called the children of God?* (I John 3:1) Each use here is still bound up with the giving of a name, yet each leads us far beyond the act of naming into the relationship that the name establishes. To Isaiah, our name inescapably makes us His who has named us; to St. John, the unimaginable love of God in so naming us by His name adds the final depth to the relationship established.

Or what of this: *When Israel was a child, then I loved him, and called my son out of Egypt. . . . I drew them with cords of a man, with bands of love* (Hosea 11:1)? Here, there is still the summons, yet again we are led far from the simple, physical act to the infinitely tender and moving picture, Hosea draws, of the love of the Father, appealing to the remembrance and response of His children. Indeed, the highest of prophetic visions, as in Isaiah, begins also with this very summons: *The Lord hath called me from the womb: from the bowels of my mother hath he made mention of my name . . . and said unto me, Thou art my servant, O Israel, in whom I will be glorified* (Isaiah 49:1-3). To what enormous height does this plain word reach, even to the prophetic vision of a whole people named and called of God, from their creation, to be His servants and His witnesses!

Especially in the New Testament are both senses of this word transmuted. We have already seen an instance of this in the verse we cited from St. John; and St. Paul is using both senses of the word when he speaks, for example, of *the high calling of God in Christ Jesus* (Philippians 3:14), or of the peace of God *to the which also ye are called in one body.* (Col. 3:15). Here the summons is to nothing less than God Himself; the simple word is made to open a relationship with God beyond the capacity of words to describe.

The greatest of all examples seems to sum up all the shades and depths of meaning with the greatest simplicity: *Henceforth I call you not servants. . . . but I have called you friends* (St. John 15:15); *He goeth up into a mountain, and calleth whom he would; and they came unto Him* (St. Mark 3:13); *He called his twelve disciples together . . . and he sent them to preach the kingdom of God* (St. Luke 9:1-2). This is the *vocation with which we are called,* to be named the friends and sons of God and to be summoned by Him to follow and obey. To bear the name and to heed the summons is the pattern of the disciple.

This brief outline of the uses of the word "call" serves to underline a fundamental truth in Christian living—a truth profoundly biblical and profoundly central in the Gospel—the truth of God's call of us as individuals in a called society, a call that is by name, and a call that is to follow. The Christian God is the kind of God who calls us. Man's nature is such that it is not only possible, but a duty, to hear and obey.

OUR USE OF THE WORD

Let us turn once more to the word "vocation" and the three levels of meaning for it we noted. The first is the fairly strict "religious" sense, in which what is referred to is an assurance of a "call" and a duty to offer ourselves for the Church's ministry or to some other form of direct Christian service. Most commonly, the word applies to a call to the ordained ministry, although it is also used with reference to a call to the religious or monastic life, to that of a deaconess of a professional woman worker, or, in a wider sense still, to some other allied form of service in life. Medicine, teaching, the law, and social work are four professions quite frequently chosen by people in such a direct religious frame of reference.

The use of the word "vocation," in these instances, implies the two characteristic Christian elements: one, the relatively clear awareness that it is God's will that we offer ourselves for this ministry, whatever it is; the other, the corresponding sense of duty, the awareness that the expression of God's will is so clear and our life is so ordered that obedience is mandatory.

It ought to be said, in passing, that this use of the word by no means implies what people sometimes imagine it does—namely, a sudden and vividly clear revelation of God's will for us and an instant impulse to answer and obey. Sometimes it does happen that way, when, apparently quite out of the blue, perhaps even as if He were speaking directly to us, we are aware of a commanding obligation and are immediately confronted with a necessity to make our choice. The experience of many great religious leaders has been of this kind. St. Paul's experience on the Damascus Road is an exalted example. Even though it is possible to imagine stormy years of conflict leading up to St. Paul's vision and the voice that addressed him, still, to all conscious thought, the catastrophic experience at midday was completely unexpected, unsought, and inescapable. He is confronted by an arbitrary and uncompromising proclamation of God's will; he has no choice except to obey.

Such prodigious experiences are given to very few; but there are many who have known something like the clarity and directness of St. Paul's vision, and to whom the word "vocation" means, in an almost literal sense, a *call* of God. But this is not the only experience, nor even the common experience to which Christians apply the use of this word. More often, awareness of God's will for our lives comes slowly and somewhat painfully, perhaps even over a period of years while we are restlessly experimenting, or even rebelling against what we suspect to be His will for us. Flashes of a clear knowledge of God's will may be followed by long periods of disbelief. Self-questioning and tormenting uncertainty about our ability or worthiness to respond to such a possibility will lead us to postpone serious consideration or doubt the reality of our experience, to doubt even that God would, or could, so deal with individuals.

Such long periods of uncertainty and vacillation are far more common, in the experience of the Church, than the apparently sudden, "thunderclap" vocations. How the two types differ—whether, for instance, the former is a case where uncertainty and conflict are on the surface, so to speak, and in the latter, are buried in the unconscious mind until finally the tension is resolved in a sudden conscious experience—is not for this book to examine. One may doubt, however, whether there is any fundamental difference in character between the two, no matter how different they look. In both types the two great axioms of Christianity are present: the fact that God is the kind of God who calls the man to His service, and the fact that the man is free to hear and obey. In the more direct and immediate type of vocation, we are also commonly given an immediate satisfaction. The call is unmistakable and clear—we have heard and obeyed, by offering our lives, and there is no lingering uncertainty or questioning.

The other type of call, less vivid and unmistakable, far slower in coming to a resolution, is also far slower in leading to a settled and contented acceptance of the final decision. We have questioned and doubted so much that it is hard for us, at first at any rate, to give full confidence to the result. Not until the decision, our response to the call (as we have come to recognize it), has been woven into the fabric of our lives and has become part of ourselves do we become what we have chosen and does the serenity come for which we pray. Only then are we able to look back at the tempestuous months and years of uncertainty, skepticism, doubt, and see in those years both the patient and unflagging action of God, who was really calling us, and our own confusion, hesitation, distrust, and ignorance. How many clergymen there are who must wait until years, sometimes, of faithful ministry have gone by, before they are able to look back with confidence and tranquillity at the years of decision, and discern how God was unceasingly at work in them all that time. Yet in their creation God had equipped them for this ministry; He had made His will known in a thousand ways, some pretty indirect and childish as is clear in retrospect (but then, that was all they could understand for the time being); He had even been with them animating and guiding their self-examination and questioning, as far as it was true and conscientious; and in the end, the total experience—the created man, the call of God, the self-analysis, and the final choice—all had become part of the long dialog with God, which is their real life.

In this look backward, to many of us it seems as if there had been another person present in the debate, intent on diverting us from the real question, disguising the question so that it could not be answered, even leading us, as a last resort perhaps, to disbelieve in a God who could ask this of us or a self which could respond. How real that person is, or in what sense he is real, is a question for theologians to debate.[1]

Certain it is that evil has a part in this whole complex of vocation, blunting our capacity to hear the call of God and confusing us in our freedom to answer. "Surely God would not pay this much attention to an individual, or to me" may be simply the devil's way of keeping us from obedience. "I am not fitted for the ministry" may be true humility or simple honesty; it may also be the devil's way of keeping us from freedom. Wherever freedom is, there is

---

[1] The devil may be a real, supernatural person, or perhaps only a projection, an imaginary creature born out of our divided nature and symbolizing our evil will. This book is no place to debate this ancient issue.

also the subtle power of evil to keep us from being free or to lead us to misuse our freedom. Nowhere is this more clear than in the process of vocation in the strict sense.

OUR EXPERIENCE OF VOCATION

The purpose of dwelling as we have on the most technical and formal of the three senses of the word is to illuminate the various elements that enter into the use of the word at all three levels. It may be that only in a small minority of cases does the process of God's call and man's obedience become as conscious, deep, and free, as it does in the case of the sacred ministry. It may be that, for many, any connection God might have with their choice of a life work seems quite secondary. As they see their choice of job, it was very likely dictated by accidental circumstances. They had little freedom to choose, probably; they had to work and they took the first thing that came along, shifting occasionally, perhaps, as they came to know themselves better or as job possibilities opened up. To them, and they are perhaps the majority of people, the second sense of the word is the more appropriate.

In this second sense, *"vocation" means the mode of work a man or woman follows.* "Vocational tests," commonly, are tests of personality, temperament, interests, and aptitudes, designed to indicate what kinds of jobs we are most suited for, physically and psychologically. Such tests are helpful in expanding somewhat the horizons of freedom for the majority of young men and women coming to employment age. In their present stage, they are probably not refined enough to be fully accurate in establishing what a given person "ought to do"; but they are helpful, at least, in indicating what we are not well equipped to do, and they can point usefully in certain general directions.

Such tests have a distinct place in the Christian scheme of things. One of the major tests of vocation to the priesthood, for instance, is this: "If God really wills me to be a priest, one way I will know this is that I am equipped, physically and psychologically, for that work. If I clearly am not so equipped, then this notion of vocation I have must be wrong and not from God at all."

No adequate vocational test for the ministry has yet been devised, for the life of the ministry is so broad and adaptable that it can use almost any kind of man with almost any combination of gifts.

It is something like marriage in this respect; a husband and wife can bring to their marriage almost any pattern of skills, likes and dislikes, strength and weaknesses. Only life itself is a broader vocation.

But still, broad as the ministry may be, the need of certain abilities and aptitudes is an essential one. No bishop today would dream of accepting a man for Holy Orders who has not successfully passed the threshold both of self-testing and also of the objective examination by others, psychiatrists as well as pastors and friends, of his personality and his gifts. And, in jobs less broad and deep than the ministry, specific qualifications and disqualifications are far more sharply defined.

Vocation in this sense, need not, but commonly does, leave God out of the picture altogether, and concentrates almost wholly on the requirements of the particular job and of the person's aptness for it. Clearly this is a derivative sense; we would not use the word about a job, unless somewhere in our history we had used it more realistically about a God who called us to those jobs. But we may omit the reference to God altogether, and still speak of human vocations. In common usage, at least, the word has lost almost all of its theological reference.

Doubtless there are many reasons for this. One, certainly, is the fact that, in a secular society like ours, it is hard to talk easily and naturally about God. A job is a reality which everybody, atheist or whatever he is, shares with everybody else; whereas belief in God is a private matter, not of general acceptance or necessity. Therefore, we stick to what is universal—we talk about jobs and leave God out.

Another reason is that it is difficult to see any connection, at first-hand, between God and the process by which we actually find our jobs. On the contrary, the connection seems to be secondhand and remote: God made me, He gave me a certain family and background and certain skills and problems, He has put me in a certain town and school, and has given me a certain name and fortune. This far the ordinary man may go, for the doctrine of creation would imply all this.

But these factors have still only a remote connection with my job. More immediate are the other factors: who happened to talk to our class in high school; what the kid next door did; the firm that opened a branch store in town; the fact that I was lucky in answering the question right on the application form; my friendship with another young officer on my ship. Only an unbelievable God, a God of incredible patience and knowledge and love, would keep track of all these microscopic accidents.

So might run the thoughts of many men and women, discouraging them from any assurance that God is concerned with such petty details as their daily lives. The fact that Christians do believe in precisely such an unbelievable God never occurs to many of us; and many more have never heard it, nor of Him who said, *Are not five sparrows sold for two pennies? And not one of them is forgotten before God. Why, even the hairs of your head are all numbered. Fear not; you are of more value than many sparrows.* (St. Luke 12:6-7)

If you escape the second difficulty, you run into a still deeper one, namely, that the character of many vocations, many jobs, is such that no God of decency or love would call a child of His to take them. So much of life's work is senseless drudgery (not senseless because it is hard, but hard because it is senseless), that such an observation about God and work is inescapable. Jobs that are barren fractions of activity in an endless cycle of production, starting with uselessness and moving rapidly to obsolescence, are hard to reconcile with the plan of a provident and loving God. Many men, therefore, do not attempt any reconciliation; their vocation (as far as they would use the term) refers only to the way in which they happen to earn their living. Their real life (and here God may be a deeply true and nourishing reality to them), is in their home, their garden, their hobbies, their children, their community. Forty hours a week of exile from God—this is the way many people think of their vocation. But they are content to pay this necessary price for the sake of their real interests and their deep life with God and their neighbor, when their working day is done.

There is no simple answer to this. It may be that in this time of transition, no Christian doctrine of work can be stated in general terms at all. But it is important to note this divorce of God from the daily work of many of His children; it is a fact to which we will return; and it is perhaps the deepest reason why the word "vocation" has been so secularized as to suggest only the job, and rarely *the God who calls us to serve Him in the job.*

In part, that cautious use of the word is justifiable, where it reflects a deep sense of the majesty and purity of God and of the incongruity of any easy attempt to link Him too closely to our mean and shallow toil. But it is also dangerous, in Christian eyes, to think of any activity of man apart from God, or as if God is not concerned with it. If a man's work is incongruous with his nature as a creature and child of God, then let his work be changed—his status and dignity before God is of vastly greater significance than the size of his income or the comfort of his job. This is one clear consequence of our Christian concern about vocation. A second consequence is the related and all-important duty of reconciling those separated entities—God and work.

To achieve this reconciliation—to restore to the idea of vocation the true sense of the call of God which gave the word its meaning in the first place—we must look at the third level of meaning for the word. In the First Office of Instruction (P.B., page 289), we are taught that the Tenth Commandment means that we ought not "covet nor desire other men's goods," but "learn and labour truly to earn mine own living, and to do my duty in that state of life unto which it shall please God to call me." Here is the familiar emphasis, once again, on the calling of God and our response to it, this time in a very wide setting.

Note should be taken, in passing, of the tense of the verb "shall" —the call of God is a continuing and a dynamic relationship, rather than a one-time decree. We have sometimes read this phrase as if it were a kind of benediction of the *status quo,* as if God had established a fixed and stratified order of things into which it behooved us to fit ourselves in docile accommodation. Such is not the sense of the phrase. The call of God is the unfolding of the continuing will of God for truth and good, penetrating what was and what is with a new vision of what ought to be. It is an exciting call to discover new truth and to advance through new possibilities, *if we do our duty.*

The people of the Nineteenth Century might have read this phrase—indeed, they were sometimes taught to read it—as if it meant that some men were called to be rich and some were called to be mill-workers and that was the end of it. But God was not content with this; He clearly was continually at work, through men who did their duty in their "state of life"—thoughtful owners and managers of business, sensitive and passionate writers, imaginative and resolute workers, clergymen, politicians . . . Because these men continued to hear the call of God in their lives and were obedient to it, old injustices were seen and destroyed, and a new life for the masses of men became possible. This is not to suggest that we have reached a Utopia. It is to suggest only that God's call is a profoundly radical summons to a bold and compassionate manhood, being exactly the opposite of the smug resignation or the dumb acceptance of misery it has sometimes seemed to mean.

But for our purposes now, we need to think about another aspect of the phrase—*the wide setting of our duty*. We are not simply instructed to do our duty in whatever job God has assigned to us. Our whole life is involved: it is a "state of life" which is the theater of our duty, including our jobs, but going far beyond that to include all the circumstances of our existence. The "state" of our life is the whole pattern and condition of our life, that combination of attributes and persons and things and attitudes and events which compose the setting in which our life is being lived. Our daily work, our home, our family, our citizenship, our relaxations, all the ways in which we live and express ourselves—this is our state.

The part that a person's job may play in his state varies a good deal. A man who is a physician, for instance, is a physician all the time, and it would be hard to disentangle the man from the profession. So is a clergyman, as we say, "always on duty."

On the contrary, an assembly-line worker is not always on duty; his job monopolizes forty hours a week and, perhaps, nothing more than that. He is not likely to think of himself (whatever his job may be) in the same sense as a lawyer would describe himself as a lawyer, or as a teacher, doctor, or priest describes himself.

This distinction has both good and bad implications. The good ones are that certain kinds of work are absorbing enough, require so much preparation, and involve so much of a human personality that the person becomes the job, so to speak. It takes a big and important job to be worthy of this absorption.

The bad implications are that there are many jobs which do not seem big or important enough to claim a person's whole life. Many of them obviously are not that important. Many of them, perhaps, ought to be bigger in our eyes than they seem. A carpenter, for instance, might be very scornful of his job, thinking that it was only another way to earn a living, when we would wish that he could see his work in terms of the homes he builds where children will grow up in happiness and peace, or of the schools where they will learn God's truth. An assembly-line worker might be tempted to shrug off his job as just forty hours of drudgery a week, when, with a little interpretative imagination, he might see his work as part of the whole complex of the plant, as well as in terms of the end-product which his care and skill is giving to humanity.

Christians are concerned with these matters, for we do not believe it is right for men and women to have work which has no real value and significance in their own eyes or in the eyes of their fellows. Christians are not the only ones so concerned, either. But this concern does not affect the principle at stake. No matter what kind of job a man may have, the "state" of his life is what is important. It is to this that God has called him. A priest will be judged not as a priest but as a certain man who was a priest. A physician will be judged as a certain man who was a doctor. A mill-worker, by the same token, will be judged as a certain man who was a mill-worker. In every case, it is the whole life which matters, not this or that part of it.

Our state and its duties—this is the only setting within which vocation can be fully understood. The *vocation wherewith ye are called*, in St. Paul's phrase, is not that of teacher or soldier or doctor or priest. Our calling is to manhood, nothing less; to be the men and women God intends us to be. Each of us in his own state, each with his particular endowment and temperament, each with his particular choices to make. Our vocation is to be what our Lord would be if He were we.

THE CHRISTIAN PRINCIPLES OF VOCATION

When we think about these three uses of the word "vocation," and consider them against the background of the deep Christian meaning of the word, certain clear principles begin to emerge. We list five "rules" as practical guides to Christian living in these vocational matters.

First is the *rule of wholeness*. God calls us to follow Him and, as with the disciples, the call is peremptory. Our Lord said to St. Peter and St. Andrew, *Follow me. . . . immediately they left their nets and followed Him* (St. Matthew 4:19-20). What did they take with them? Only what they could carry, doubtless; for there was no way for them to live two lives; and to choose one meant leaving the furniture of the other behind. To say that they "sacrificed" their nets for the sake of obedience would be a trivial and debasing use of a great word. The point was that these two men suddenly belonged to Christ, wholly and without reservation; and from that moment nothing mattered except that they be free to follow where He led. This is the rule of wholeness.

This rule is quite applicable in our daily lives, even though the circumstances of our calling are quite different from theirs. It is not possible, nor are we asked, to leave our livelihood, our family obligations, or our community responsibilities in a physical following of Him. There are many times when we are tempted to do so (and there are some whose duties are such that they should). But for most, the following—the wholeness of our obedience—must be done within the complex of our duties, not by abandoning them. It is as mother or brother, as teacher or salesman, as citizen, as Churchman, that we follow. And the rule of wholeness, applied in those circumstances of our "state of life," involves us profoundly in the practical judgments of which all moral life is made. (I use the phrase "practical judgments"—my first impulse was to say "compromises," for that is what those judgments are; but it has a misleading connotation.)

Whatever we call them, however, the paradox is that if we are to follow Christ completely and wholly, we may have to offer far less than what our idealism might lead us to want to offer. One is moved perhaps to offer his life to be a missionary teacher, yet perhaps for twenty years he is not free to make that offer because of his family obligations. Therefore, his following of Christ, at least for the time being, may be no more than to teach a Sunday school class or lead a scout troop.

Or again, one is moved *to give my goods to feed the poor,* yet the livelihood of his employees depends on his maintaining, at least for the time being, the establishment he has. Therefore, his following of Christ, at least for a while, may be no more than a trebled tithe or a gift of time. Or one feels called to a greater service through his church, yet his is a divided family, with the wife (or husband) of another faith or of none; and if he should follow his call to personal religious practice to the full, he might thereby cause hurt or pain to another. In all such cases, for the time being (and God is the creator of all time), we take what seems to be half a loaf.

It probably only seems to be that. Usually we need to look more closely at what we can do, not at what we cannot. The frustrated missionary, who has to stay home at his job, learns to look again at that job and find how great his vocation in it may be. God is a partner in all these things; and it may well be that He has other plans and other uses for us than those that attract us so much.

Yet these compromise choices continue to disappoint and anger us, for our sense of vocation is sometimes a very imperious master, and we want to do what we want to do. Still, it is by just such choices that a free and whole person maintains wholeness and integrity in his obedience. If such a life of seemingly imperfect choices disappoints us and makes us rebellious against our human situation, it is well for us to remember the saying about saving and losing our lives (St. Mark 8:35). Who is he that *saves his life* only to lose it? It is (among others) the one who insists that he must be free of all duties except that of finding his own soul. Who is *he that shall lose his life for my sake*, who finds it again? It is (among others) the man who, soberly and thoughtfully, responds to the call as best he can, being what he is, and willing to give up the satisfaction of his own soul for the sake of humble and patient obedience within his duties. He is the man who *enters into life maimed* (St. Mark 9:43), who is willing to forego the full accomplishment of his own dream for the sake of the wholeness and integrity of his obedience to duty.

Wholeness it is, "not only with our lips, but in our lives," which is primarily at stake in our obedience. For it is a man's whole life that God is calling, not just his job or his prayers or his money. And to make that full offering is generally far less dramatic than to give Him an easy and vivid portion of our whole self.

Clearly, such a rule would be dangerously liable to deceit were it not for a second one—*the rule of present obedience.* We start to follow Him from where we are, not from where we hope to be or wish we were. One of the most perilous sophistications in Christian living is the impulse to say, "Well, if only I were somebody else, then I could follow." The "if onlys" are innumerable. If only we lived at another time, or had another job, or belonged to another church, or had married another wife, or were born in another family, or had a different set of problems. We are all well acquainted with this legion of "if onlys."

But there is an urgency about Christian vocation. The call is here and now, and obedience starts precisely where we are at this moment. It is *this* person, in *this* job, living in *this* century with *these* gifts and *these* handicaps, whom God is calling. And the humility of true discipleship is born precisely in that acceptance of present self. If the job is a bad one, then it must be changed. If the times are evil, then they must be made to yield good fruit. If my self is wrong, then I must be put right. But the obedience must begin without delay. When that rule is applied, we are saved from the dangers of the wrong kind of compromise, for it breeds a healthy resentment against anything that is not right and yet which must be taken as the only possible starting place.

A third rule, perhaps the most obvious of them all, is the *rule of faith,* not in terms of credulity but in terms of commitment. (Think back to our early discussion of faith and freedom, and apply those considerations here.) To take up our cross and follow Him requires that we shall go with Him wherever He leads. This may sound remote from what we were saying earlier about vocation and jobs; actually it is highly relevant. For, if we start where we are, it is inevitable that it must be through what we are that we will follow to where He is leading us.

To use myself for an example, He is calling me to be a true bishop and a faithful husband and a thoughtful citizen, because I have no other starting place except that of bishop, husband and citizen. It is in that context and no other that my faith in Him must operate. If I am to commit myself wholly to my vocation, then I must not be surprised if my obedience leads me into some pretty strange country. To be a true bishop may require of me the abandonment of a lot of familiar customs, attributes, traditions, habits inherited or acquired, and the exploration of new relationships, without precedent (for me, at least), and new and untested by the standards of our inherited pattern of the Episcopate.

If I am not willing to put my hand to the plow and not turn back, then I am not ready to follow His call to the Kingdom. Therefore, the rule of faith—of willing and absolute self-commitment to Him—is an essential ingredient in true vocation. My vocation is to be my true self, in the circumstances of my life. To achieve that self will require of me the freedom to put myself and my concerns, as far as I can, into the hands of God, who alone knows what the final truth about me is and can make that truth possible. This is the rule of faith.

The fourth rule is the *rule of relationship*. *All vocation is inescapably social*. We are members one of another; and our vocations necessarily involve others and are involved in others. Nobody chooses in a vacuum. Parents, friends, counsellors, even hostile critics, all have a hand in our choice of work or marriage or community or whatever else may be our vocational decision. Society puts its mark on all these choices, through school, government, church. Even marriage, that most intimately personal of all phases of our vocation, is hedged around by society with all sorts of regulation and control.

Such concern is inescapable because every man's choices ultimately involve everybody else. While we may dislike it, even resent it, we learn to accept it. Therefore, we are not surprised when we look at the Church and see in it this principle of the social character of vocation raised to the summit of reality in the "called society." *I beseech you* cried St. Paul, *that ye walk worthy of the vocation wherewith ye are called*. He said this to the Church in Ephesus, not simply to individual hearers. For all our separate vocations —jobs, homes, marriages, professions, hobbies—all are part of the life of the Body. Each is incomplete apart from the whole; each finds its fulfillment only in the deep companionship of the Body of Christ. It is here, in His Body, that the contradictions, frustrations, imperfections, limitations of all our separate vocations are resolved in the fullness of Christ. When men and women learn how we can bring our separatenesses to Christ in His Church, and there add them together to make an infinitely greater unity and comradeship in worship and service, we have come a long way toward understanding the mystery of vocation.

Last is the *rule of greatness*. *Vocation is as long and wide as life itself, indeed greater than this life*. Even the most satisfying work in the world will not contain or satisfy the whole of a man. There is more to us than any job can fully use, even the best; and most jobs actually use very little of us. And how tragic it is when men or women try to fit the whole of themselves into a job, having no interests outside of their daily work, being nothing except what the job can use—people with undeveloped selves, who work as hard as they can until they retire, then wander comfortless. in a world where suddenly they seem to have no status or usefulness, until death mercifully releases them from boredom.

We rightly are concerned with such people. We discuss the importance of hobbies, of education for retirement, of this and that which will expand their interests and give them a self outside of their jobs. These are good concerns, and the Christian should share them to the full, because the generous and mature development of a whole human nature is part of the Christian's business. But, by themselves, as ends in themselves, these devices may be as boring and frustrating as what they are intended to solve. A life lived for play alone is as empty as one lived for work alone.

The redemption of life—the redemption of play as well as work, of the home and the church and the club and the garden and the automobile as well as the office—is bound up with our full awakening to our vocation. When we learn to see that *our life is our vocation* and that all things in life are part of our vocation, then simplicity and satisfaction are possible. All our choices—work, play, marriage, politics, reading, speaking—all are part of our long conversation with God, which is our real life. He has made us for Himself; it is our calling to come to know Him, to love Him, and to serve Him. If "most men lead lives of quiet desperation," as Thoreau said, it is because we have not yet found the simplicity of a life single and whole, in which all that we do is in answer to what God has already said and done. Take the word *vocation* then, as a key to serenity. He has called us to His joyful knowledge and service. We are free, if we will, to answer. In that obedience we will find the full flowering of our selves, which is also our freedom and our peace.

PROBLEMS RELATING TO VOCATION

We have already mentioned incidentally some of the common problems that men and women face in the matter of their vocations. It might, however, be helpful to devote the closing pages of this section to some general aspects of these vocational problems and to Christian thought about them.

Generally speaking, we have three kinds of problems in finding and following our vocation. The first is that of the *missed* vocation.

The second is that of the *unworthy* vocation. The third is that of the *incomplete* vocation.

The *missed* vocation is distressingly common; and it is common, usually, for perfectly evident and familiar reasons. Many men and women have almost no freedom, no choice, in the selection of their jobs, particularly of their first job. It is pleasant to think of young men and women, on graduating from school or college, examining, with serene gaze, the whole field of employment before they make their vocational choice. Some young men and women are that lucky; but not all, perhaps not even the majority. For most go to their first employment without having had real alternative. The urgency of economic need, the pressure of family loyalties, the accidents of geography or acquaintance, and, most significantly, our own imperfect knowledge of ourselves—all these conspire to make our vocational choice about as unfree as any choice could be. The wonder is, really, that so many of us are quite happy in our jobs and make a good life for ourselves. Yet we are and we do, despite the rather haphazard and accidental way in which we came to them.

There are always some who discover, perhaps after many years, that they have really "missed" their vocation altogether—that they are hopeless misfits in what they are now doing, and, even more important, they have real gifts for another, a wholly different, vocation. What does a person do in this case?

The answer would surely be that he change his job *if he can—and if he should.* In making such a decision, he must be guided by many factors. His age, the obligations he has for his family, what real possibilities there are for his making a successful change—these are the chief "iffy" factors which come immediately to mind. But behind them are other and subtler factors. One is certainly the question of the accuracy of his judgment that he is a misfit. It may be that he is; it may also be that he is simply bored because he has not invested himself seriously in his present job, or because he is immature and irresponsible in his whole attitude to life, being unwilling to commit himself to life's stern realities. In this area we certainly owe it to ourselves and to God to get the best and most objective advice we can.

Another factor—an even more important one—is the degree to which his longing for another job is born in a romantic illusion about the nature of that other job. Many a man has looked with envy away from the drudgery of his office at the supposed freedom and creativity of a clergyman's life, for instance, until he found out that there is about as much drudgery in one job as in another, and that the secret of happy work does not lie in an absence of drudgery but in the degree to which the drudgery can be interpreted and accepted as part of a wider and more creative and more satisfying pattern. All good work is hard and routine and sometimes dull; there is no escape from this. But the dullness and drudgery of a job are swept away by the creative interest and purpose of the worker, if he is really interested in the job and the job is worth doing.

Many people come to think they are misfits because they cannot feel that their work is of any real importance or usefulness. It is unhappily true that they may be right. But it is more often true that they have simply not used enough imagination really to understand the place that they and their job have in the general scheme of human need and service. When they apply that much imagination and are helped in it, their boredom often disappears.

But suppose that all these factors have been weighed, and it is still pretty clear that Mr. X is a misfit, and really ought to be doing something else. The answer, then, would certainly be affirmative. If God's call is clear and persistent, and if there is no commanding reason except the purely personal ones of timidity or financial welfare, we ought to be encouraged to accept such clear guidance. A loss in salary (unless it be such as to lay an unfair penalty on one's family) is an unworthy reason for hesitation; and so is the natural timidity at leaving a known and familiar routine to start again in an unfamiliar one. After all, God will not call us to destruction.

Neither will He make up our minds for us. What He does is give us evidence, as clear as this human life permits, of what we are really and what we are equipped for; it is our part to trust the evidence, and trust Him, and make the change, no matter how our self-esteem may suffer. We are concerned, and rightly, lest we ask, in such cases, more of a sacrifice from our families than we ought; this is a godly concern. Yet families will often say to us, "We would far rather have you doing a good job and doing it well and happily, even if we lose some of our luxuries, than have you go on divided and unsatisfied." And to accept this kind of understanding and generosity is no imposition of unfairness. It may even be a profoundly good and humble acceptance of a common love more precious than any salary or income could be.

What about the jobs that are wrong in themselves—the "unworthy" vocations which are not really vocations at all? The answer here must be clear and short. Where a man or woman is trapped into a job which simply cannot, by any stretch of charity, be fitted into a Christian way of life, there is only one possible answer—*get out of it as quickly as you can.*

This is pretty heroic counsel, we might think. But what other answer is possible for the Christian? It is simply unthinkable that a man or woman should lend even a minute of his time to a work which does harm to his fellow-men; it would be the supreme wrong and weakness in us, and a blasphemy to suppose that God would ever call us to such a wrong use of our freedom. If the job cannot be changed, so that it be worthy, then let it be spurned. God is in command; He will not leave us defenseless.

The test of "worthiness" should be, primarily, a religious test. What society thinks of a particular job, as expressed in terms of reward or of dignity and acceptedness, need not be a particularly important clue to the essential worthiness of the job. Poetry generally does not pay the poet very well, for example; the role of the teacher is not usually very glamorous in the eyes of his or her contemporaries. But these tests are not necessarily important ones. The important test is simply *whether or not a particular job can be fittingly offered to God.* No matter how humble it may be, or ill-regarded and ill-rewarded, if you can soberly and devoutly offer your handiwork to God, week after week, as being a job worth doing and worth doing well, for Him, you have the surest test of its worthiness. Contrariwise, no matter how glittering our work may be, if our conscience protests against linking that work in our offering to God, then we have no right doing it.

The "incomplete vocation" is another problem. By this phrase is meant the almost universal experience that our work, and the way of life it imposes on us, is not entirely and fully what we are really created for. This is not a case of missing our vocation; we are doing a job we are fitted for, but the job does not exhaust our gifts; instead, it limits us, it requires that we leave undone much that is of primary importance to us, and it diverts our energies and time from much that we could do well and greatly prefer to do.

THE ESSENCE OF CHRISTIAN VOCATION

In this area we need to remember especially the great Christian lesson about our state of life and its duties. God looks at the whole of us, not just our jobs, and not at each part of us separately. His question is, "What kind of person are you, given your job and circumstances, your temperament, your family, your community?" In fact, the essence of Christian teaching about vocation is summed up here; the heart of vocation is not the job but the man or woman doing the job, and the way in which our work serves us as a means for praising and loving God and our neighbor.

No job, not even the most perfectly adapted one, will use more than a fraction of our selves. No life, no matter how rich in opportunity, can offer us more than a tiny fragment of all the possibilities there could be for us. The important thing here is not to hanker after what is not possible for us, but to seize and use what comes to hand to use. Christ is our great example in these matters. While others talked and disputed about who was to do what, He acted. While others dreamed and longed for better tools and better times, He acted. His action, limited and circumscribed as it was by time and all the other bondages of this world, is what saves us. God can use our acts, unimportant and incomplete though they be, where our restless dreaming and empty discontent will be no more than a hindrance.

Our imperfect acts, done as well as we can do them and offered to God with a humble and trusting love—this is the heart of our vocation. Through them God gets His work done. Through them He wins us to Himself, for the greater work we will sometime do in His presence and company.

CHAPTER ELEVEN

Death

THOUGHTS relating to death belong in a book on Christian living just as prayers relating to death are a natural and good part of our life of prayer. Our evening Family Prayer includes a beautiful petition, ". . . grant us grace always to live in such a state that we may never be afraid to die; so that, living and dying, we may be thine . . ." (P.B., p. 591) Living and dying belong together, to the Christian as to all men; as we think about life, so are we likely to think about death (and vice versa); even more, our life must inescapably be thought of as a preparation for death and what lies beyond it.

Hardly anything else in life so fascinates and disturbs mankind as the enigma of death, a fact so mysterious and so final as to seem, in some ways, the most important of all earthly facts. This is not particularly a Christian preoccupation. All mankind is at one here. Plato spoke for thoughtful people of every generation and belief when he said, "They who rightly practice philosophy study nothing else than dying and death." That is to say, we study humanity and its hopes, and then we confront the inescapable fact of death and mortality; and in the face of that fact we deliberately choose what values there are, if there are any, which can survive the gamble and test of death. Death, in this sense, is the ultimate and determining fact of human life. It is the horizon which is the present limit of our sight; and all human activities and values have got somehow to take death into consideration and come to terms with it. This is what Plato calls "the study of dying and death."

Thus it is both a mystery and a challenge to humanity. We do not know, and in this life we shall never know, what lies beyond that mysterious threshold. Nor is there any possible compromise with it. Death comes into life with its peremptory and arbitrary summons; man cannot reason with it or temporize with it. We have teased ourselves from the beginning of time with dreams of what it might be like if we could buy or barter a little time from death, but the dream is so sweet only because we know the reality is so irrevocable and merciless.

There is also a kind of ambiguity about death in humanity's eyes. Mysterious and peremptory as it is, it is also natural. In nature the cycle of life seems almost to depend on death; the tides of the seasons are tides of birth and death; the life of the forest or the life of the sea as we know them would be quite impossible without death. In those terms, death has almost a kind of rightness about it.

It is chiefly with human death that we quarrel. No matter how philosophical we may be about the naturalness of death, it is still an indignity that violates our deepest sense of the fitness of things when it brings human life to an abrupt and pitiless end. Physical death, we reflect, may be right enough in its own order, in the forest, in the sea. But in human life and consciousness there are values at stake—love, creativity, virtue—which show death in a truer light, as somehow wrong and destructive. Even when death comes with as much justification as it ever does, after long illness, perhaps, or to a lonely older person, we still feel that mortality itself is an indignity. The wonder and beauty of human personality deserves something better of existence than that it should age and wither and die.

I suppose that on this ground alone a doctrine of immortality seemed inevitable and right to humanity. Certainly there have been few people or cultures who have not come to such a belief; and there are arguments aplenty, which are as convincing as any such arguments can be, for a belief in the immortality of the soul. It should perhaps be noted parenthetically that the Christian doctrine is a good deal more than simply a belief in some kind of immortality. Christians would not necessarily argue with a doctrine of immortality; but the heart of the Christian doctrine of future life is not immortality but what is expressed in the Creed and ultimately in the New Testament, as "the resurrection of the body." To this we shall return in a moment.

Let it also be noticed here that there is a curious disparity between our human preoccupation with death, so absorbing and widespread, and the scanty, bare bones of official Christian doctrine on the subject. It is almost as if God were saying to us that we should not dwell overmuch on the details of what lies beyond death; our attention ought to be focused on this life as a preparation for death, and our confidence repose in Him that what comes after will be ordered aright. Certainly the Christian tradition has tended to discourage undue speculation and experimentation. It is not necessarily wrong for our imagination to play with the possibilities of life after death. Yet still there is a deep reluctance in Christian thought to make more than the simplest and briefest of statements about that life.

CHRISTIAN DOCTRINE OF LIFE AFTER DEATH

It is not the work of this volume to discuss Christian doctrine in itself except insofar as that doctrine bears on the problems of Christian living. Those who are interested in our official Christian teaching about life after death should read the relevant section in *The Faith of the Church,* a companion volume in THE CHURCH'S TEACHING.

There are, however, six elements in Christian doctrine which have a direct bearing on Christian living, and it is to the point to say something about each of those.

First, *in Christian teaching there is a clear assertion of finality about this life.* This life is not one of a series of existences for us; it is unique; it is the one period of probation that man has to prepare himself for judgment. Doctrines of reincarnation are common enough; but there is no Christian doctrine of reincarnation and, in the nature of things, there could never be. For one thing, any doctrine of reincarnation is almost inescapably associated with a belief that this life is essentially evil, something ultimately to be escaped, but in the meantime to be endured. Christians have, and can have, no such feeling about this life, for life is a gift of God and an act of love.

Nor is there any important biblical evidence to support a doctrine of reincarnation. Quite the contrary; biblical thought everywhere leads to a sense of the unique and unrepeatable character of this life, and there is no indication that there will be successive probations for us. Perhaps the clearest teaching from our Lord on this is the parable of Lazarus and the Rich Man (St. Luke 16:19-31), a most solemn and awesome picture of the seriousness of this life and its choices.

The second element in Christian teaching stresses *the certainty of judgment*. Like all our beliefs about life after death, our teaching about judgment must of necessity be highly symbolic. This is true of all such teaching and, doubtless, explains in part the Church's reticence, along with that of the Bible, in not speaking overmuch of such things. It is simply impossible to speak, except in the barest symbol, of conditions in another life, in terms which are understandable in this life. Therefore, the circumstances of judgment—times and places—are all to be taken in pictorial terms.

Two times, or moments, or phases, of judgment seem to be taught by the New Testament. One is an immediate judgment, a "particular" judgment, according to which at death each individual comes to the end of his probationary period. At death the data of judgment, so to speak, are completed; there will be no further change in the individual's fundamental disposition; he has finished his probation.

There is no suggestion in Christian teaching that this is God's final judgment on us. That final judgment is to come in the general judgment at the end of the world. Christians have always thought and wondered about the intervening time; and certainly Christian faith has held that there is every possibility of a cleansing, purifying period of development to follow the particular judgment.

The second and final judgment comes at the end of all things, when, as St. Paul told the Athenians, *God has fixed a day on which he will judge the world in righteousness by a man whom he has appointed, and of this he has given assurance to all men by raising him from the dead* (Acts 17:31). That will be the time when all things are completed, and *All things shall be subdued unto God.*

How appallingly difficult it is for us to avoid the imagery of time and space—to speak of an "earlier" judgment and a "later" judgment, when we know we are speaking not of time at all but of eternity. It is supremely important here to remember that we are straining at the outer limits of language and are perforce speaking of things of which we can have no clear knowledge at all.

Yet, despite that, the element of judgment, the certainty of human accountability before Christ for what we have done in this world, is a cardinal point of Christian teaching. The essential meaning of the "particular" judgment is that death ends a certain phase of probation for us, as individuals. The "general" judgment means that there will be a final end and a final accounting, when Christ "shall come again, with glory, to judge both the quick and the dead."

The third element in Christian teaching is that uniquely Christian assertion of *"the resurrection of the body."* This phrase has never been taken in serious Christian thought, and never should be taken, as an assertion of the physical reconstitution of a dead body, with the reassembling of its members and the reclothing of them in the original flesh. Such literalism has no place in Christian thought and never did. Christian thought on this matter largely began with St. Paul, in the magnificent passage in I Corinthians 15, which is one of the great lessons in our Burial Office. In that towering chapter, St. Paul works out the implications of all this, and proclaims quite simply and clearly that the stuff of the resurrected body will be totally different from the stuff out of which that body was made in this world: *it is sown a physical body, it is raised a spiritual body.*

What Christians believe is something quite different from any magical, physical reconstitution of flesh and blood. In essence, the Christian faith is that *the whole personality continues.* We have no experience of disembodied spirits in human affairs; every human person is a soul so intimately involved with a particular body that it is quite impossible to think of that soul and body separately. In a familiar contemporary term, man is a psychosomatic unity, which means simply what our faith and experience alike teach us, that the body is the essential vehicle of the soul.

This sense of the identity of body and soul carries over into our belief about life after death; and in this respect there are very important differences between Christian thinking and the general run of mankind's thoughts about immortality. To the Christian, what lies before us after death is not the existence of a disembodied spirit and certainly not the disappearance of individual personality by virtue of its being merged into some vague spiritual whole. I quote here a long, but important, paragraph by Dr. Ramsey, the present Archbishop of York:

While traditional Christianity insists upon distinguishing the revealed doctrine of Resurrection from a philosophical belief in the immortality of the soul, it regards the latter not as untrue and irrelevant so much as incomplete, distressingly dull and missing the gift of the Gospel. There are grounds, both philosophical and psychological and religious, for believing that the soul survives death; though the life of a soul without the body is a conception which is difficult to imagine. It is *incomplete;* because the self is far more than the soul, and the self without bodily expression can hardly be the complete self. It is *dull;* because it implies the prolongation of man's finite existence for everlasting years. In contrast both with the incompleteness and the dullness of the immortality of the soul, Christianity teaches a future state (not as of right but as of God's gift) wherein the soul is not unclothed, but clothed upon by a bodily expression, and wherein the finite human life is raised so as to share, without losing its finiteness, in the infinite life of Christ Himself.[1]

Our teaching about the resurrection of the body is simply another way of underlining our profound and fundamental faith in the significance of individual personality. As individual persons, souls inhabiting and influencing our particular bodies and being influenced by these same bodies, we live through our life of probation; we come to judgment; and, by God's grace, we have the opportunity of continuing that life with Him, in our particular bodies (except that the stuff of which those bodies are made will be something that can exist in eternity instead of the fragile, earth-bound flesh we know here.)

This conception of the community of individuals, known and loved in their bodies, is the basis for all our deepest thought about the ways of God with us, in death as in life. *Behold, the dwelling of God is with men. He will dwell with them, and they shall be his people, and God himself will be with them.* (Rev. 21:3) If, in the body, I have sinned, then I shall be judged in the body. If, in the body, I have been able to grow in freedom and in grace, then it is in the body that I shall come to the fulfillment of those gifts in eternal life with God.

The fourth element in Christian teaching is that *our ultimate blessedness lies in a life with God,* unimaginable in its joy and radiance, yet still the final glory that waits for us at the end of the earthly road. So too, whatever notion of ultimate punishment we may have, the one sure thing in it is that it will be an unspeakable loneliness and separation from God and from our fellowmen, a

---

[1] Arthur Michael Ramsey, *The Resurrection of Christ* (London: Centenary Press, 1945), pp. 101-2. Used by permission of the publisher.

loneliness chosen by ourselves. To man's insistent question, "Where is heaven?" the best answer the Church has ever given is, "Heaven is wherever God is, and where we, by His grace, some day may be."

A supremely important condition of this life with God is that it is a supremely social one. It is quite characteristic that in the Apocalypse, where the pictorial imagination of Christian thought rises to its height, the abode of the blessed is a city, a community, engaged in the highest and fullest and most satisfying of all social activities—the worship of Almighty God. I think that every biblical image, without exception, of the ultimate blessedness of the redeemed, is corporate and social. And granted that the conditions are unimaginable, it is of very great significance that this is so, in distinction to so much non-Christian though which suggests, at least, an intolerable aloneness and monotony, if not a complete disappearance of separate selves in an eternal silence and sleep.

So, too, the most vivid images of hell in Christian thought are often images of a total lack of community, of solitude, and lonely self-engrossment. The images of penal fire are attempts simply to imagine the worst thing that we can imagine, in physical terms; but the idea of a silent and solitary imprisonment with one's self for eternity is surely the most terrible thought any man ever had.

The fifth element is *Christianity's unconquerable certainty of God's will that all mankind shall finally come to be with Him in glory.* This is so basic with us, because of our certainty of the goodness and love of God and of His omnipotence, that it is almost inconceivable to the Christian that anyone should ever be finally lost. We admit the possibility of that final refusal, for it would be hard to imagine any perfect justice in God which did not include at least the possibility of a final condemnation of evil, and it would be hard also to imagine a real freedom in man which, at least theoretically, did not include the possibility of a final refusal of God's love, on our part. Yet we are understandably reluctant to imagine that God could ever ultimately be defeated by anybody, or that His love could ever fail in the end to win all men to Him.

This conviction must then wrestle with two practical questions. The first is, "What about people like most of us, who at our death are now by no means ready to live with God, yet whose natures have been formed during the period of probation, by His grace, so that ultimately we could be ready?" We can conceive of few more frightening thoughts than that, at death, any possibility of growth or purification would be closed to us. We would hope that, by the time of our death, we had some real freedom and a soul to be saved; yet we can understand that there might still stretch before us at death a long time of learning how to live under new conditions in the presence of God. Probably most Christians share some such feeling about themselves; and it is for this reason that belief in a place or period of purification, a belief in purgatory, became almost universal among Christian people.

Our Church rejects what the Articles of Religion call "the Romish Doctrine" of purgatory, specifically the doctrine that living men and women can by their prayers and good works, influence God to shorten the purifying period either for themselves or for others. But a belief in purgatory, as such, has been widely held by Christians, is quite permissible for Episcopalians, and indeed is included in our prayers as when, for example, in the Prayer for the Whole State of Christ's Church (in the Holy Communion), we pray that God will grant the dead "continual growth in His love and service" or, in the Burial Office, we pray for the departed that "increasing in knowledge and love of Thee, he may go from strength to strength." It would not be true to say that a doctrine of purgatory is specifically stated in our Anglican formularies, but it is perfectly true that such a belief is permissible and congruous with all else that we believe about God and His ways with us, and that it is expressed in our prayers.

The second question which must be faced, if we are to hold to our conviction about God's all-conquering love, is the question about those whose lives were untouched by the Gospel at all. What about the non-Christians, especially those who lived before Christ? What about the unbaptized babies? What about those to whom the Gospel has never been preached?

Part of the Church's answer to this question is found in the teaching of Christ's "descent into the place of departed spirits," the doctrine found in the New Testament in I Peter 3:19 and stated in the Creeds, wherein the Church affirms her belief that God saw to it that the pre-Christians heard the Gospel as well as Christ's contemporaries. Then, too, medieval theology tried to answer part of this question in the curious doctrine of "limbo"—the *limbus patrum,* where the Old Testament saints awaited the coming of

Christ, and the *limbus infantium,* where unbaptized babies were thought to enjoy a natural blessedness and joy.

The descent into Hades is biblical and credal doctrine. The idea of the limbus is no more than a sanctified guess and a permissible opinion. But both doctrines bear witness to an indomitable certainty in Christian hearts of the unconquerable, victorious love of God, who will not, if He can help it, suffer anyone to be lost. He will find ways to reach every created soul and offer to that soul the choice and chance of eternal life. Subject only to our own freedom—a freedom so real as even to make possible a final rejection of God—God means to win us all to Himself. He is on our side in this mortal adventure of ours, which, after all, began in an act of His love in our creation; He is on our side through death and even to eternity. This is the heart of the Christian answer to these perennial questions.

Finally and most important, the center of Christian belief about life after death is *our faith in the resurrection of Christ.* We believe in the resurrection of the body because of the resurrection of His body. He "who for us men and for our salvation came down from heaven and was made man," carries us and our state with Himself into glory. To quote St. Paul again, *Now is Christ risen from the dead, and become the firstfruits of them that slept. For since by man came death, by man came also the resurrection of the dead. For as in Adam all die, even so in Christ shall all be made alive.* (I Cor. 15:20-22)

In one sense or at one level, death is natural and inescapable, and so Christians understand it with all other folk reflecting on nature. In another and deeper sense, death becomes a punishment for our sins; the fear of it, the aweful solemnity of it, the pain of it, the arbitrary power it has over all human hopes and joys and achievements—all this is the mark of our punishment. We might have died anyway, but God could have ordered our death differently had it not been for the Fall. We sinned; and the manner of our dying bears the marks of that—*by man came death.* So then it must necessarily be that only through death can we be saved. Another Adam must come inside our manhood and go through our life and our death, this time obediently and victoriously, and so open the way for us.

> From death to life eternal,
> From earth unto the sky,
> Our Christ hath brought us over
> With hymns of victory.

So one of our loved Easter hymns puts this whole matter. It is through Him and in Him that our resurrection comes; it is as a band of pilgrims following Him that we find our way to eternal life.

But our eternal life, our sharing in His resurrection, does not wait until our death. This is the summit of Christian faith: that our life with God begins long before our death. As St. John says, *We know that we have passed out of death into life, because we love the brethren* (I John 3:14); and again, *This is the testimony, that God gave us eternal life, and this life is in His Son* (I John 5:11). Eternal life is to be with God; and the foretaste of that life is given to us in this world, long before death. This fact puzzles us, when we see it in the lives of men and women we know. We hardly know how to describe it; we fumble with words like "spiritual," "good," "holy," to catch the quality of people who seem already to be infinitely closer to God than we; they seem, in a phrase of one of the great mystics, "to see through a veil opaque to us."

The mistake we make is not in finding this quality in the great Christians—it is there, clearly enough, and they do seem, in some real sense, to have already passed through the gate of death and to have come to the other side. Our mistake is in supposing that this gift of eternal life is for the few and the exceptional. Christ did not die for the exceptional ones; He died for us all; and the gift is for us all, and it is no further away than our will to receive it.

How to receive it? *If we love one another, God abides in us and his love is perfected in us.* (I John 4:12) Such is St. John's answer: that the gift of eternal life does not depend on our accomplishments but on our willingness to accept the love of God and to show that love in our daily living. That love will drive out of our hearts every lesser thing. Even the fear of death cannot remain where there is love, for *perfect love casteth out fear.*

Eternal life begins here and now, in our willingness to accept the saving love of God in Christ. When we have entered into that eternal life, through our baptism and our sincere Christian living, death is no more than a change, a molting, a bursting of the cocoon of this world, to release us to enter into the fuller life where "we are delivered from the burden of the flesh and are in joy and felicity."

"LIVING WITH DEATH, DAILY"

This section, so far, has dealt only with matters of belief, with the six principal elements in Christian teaching about death. But the implications of this belief for our Christian living are clear enough, and can be spelled out briefly, under three main heads.

First, *coming to terms with death: it is an essential part of Christian living to learn to live daily with death, without fear, and with the gravity and soberness which becomes Christians.* We suggested at the beginning of this section that living and dying belong together in our thoughts and prayers, just as they do in the minds of thoughtful non-Christians. The difference between the Christian and the non-Christian in this is the profound difference which our faith in Christ and in that eternal life which is God's gift through Christ has made. All wise men should be philosophical and thoughtful about death; Christians may have, as well, great hope and infinitely more joyful expectancy, if they will only remember and accept what their faith teaches them.

We are living in a time when the fear of death seems to be more widespread and acute than it has ever been. There are doubtless many reasons for this. A widespread clouding and dimming of vivid belief in immortality, a growing emphasis on human right to comfort and happiness in this world, a heightened sensitivity to suffering are certainly three such factors. Perhaps the chief factor is the vast, almost unbelievable, sharpening of medical and surgical skills, and the immense attention we now pay to matters of health and sickness, in contrast to the sometimes almost fatalistic acceptance of such mortal ills in past time.

Certainly no one is going to quarrel with this generous and tireless fight for health and life. It has brought hope and happiness to countless millions who, even a generation ago, would have faced short and painful lives and faced them without hope of relief or release. Man is at his best when he is pitted against nature; and the torrent of ingenuity and devotion that has gone into our fight against disease may well rank as one of the supreme moments of man at his best.

But such devotion and concentration is not without its price. And the price, inevitably, has been a tendency to think of death as the greatest of all evils, and of physical existence as the most important of all values. We are reminded at every turn of life-preserving medicines, surgical procedures, appliances, ointments, capsules, wonder-drugs, foods, until it is no wonder that we come to accept it as a matter of course that the indefinite prolongation of human existence is the most important of all ends, and that consequently death is an utterly abhorrent enemy, to be feared and avoided as the worst of all enemies, and to be disguised and hidden in a blanket of silence and circumlocution. This, perhaps more than any other, has been the factor responsible for the horror with which our generation has faced death.

Customs and conventions have followed this, naturally. "Corpse" or "body" are words now thought to be slightly obscene in well-ordered, secular undertaking establishments; and the dead body is now referred to, often enough, as "he" or "she"—an obscenity almost without parallel in Christian minds, when one stops to think about it. Grief at our loss, which is natural enough, has been allowed to infect our feelings about the dead, until we seem almost to be mourning for them rather than for ourselves. Children's prayers (or adult prayers, for that matter), are rewritten to eliminate any mention of death. The "if I should die before I wake" of the familiar child's bedtime prayer has long since disappeared from many homes on the ground that a child would be hurt by being reminded of the inescapable end of his life; and this, despite the fact that he does think about death with great perturbation and needs the reminder that it is both inevitable and, in God's good hands, somehow right and true.

To live with death, daily and without terror or morbid fascination—this is the Christian gift of healthy-mindedness. The thought of our own certain death and of our need to be prepared for it; our steady remembrance, in prayer and thought, of the dead whom we have "loved long since, and lost awhile"; our relaxed and mature balance in understanding of what lies beyond death; and our help to others in interpreting the great certainties of our faith— these are instances of what we mean by "living with death, daily."

Both the pathological fear of death and the equally pathological attraction death holds for many people are beyond the scope of this book to discuss. They should be recognized for what they are—illnesses—and dealt with by physicians who are skilled in such things. Because death and life are so intimately tied together in our deepest thoughts and because our attitudes toward one are likely to be the same as our attitudes toward the other, a retreat from life or a deep need for the assertion of life and self is reflected profoundly in our death-fear or death-wish. These are not matters for amateurs.

But the provision of a healthy emotional and moral climate for people is decidedly a matter for general concern among church people. And since attitude towards life and attitude towards death are so intimately related, the whole of our Christian living is involved. To put this into its simplest terms, the fact of God is the first and most important of all facts. If He creates and reigns and judges, then existence is totally different in every respect from what it would be if there were no God. The life of church people or of a Christian congregation should be a clear and compelling witness to this.

For Christians, life is not a horrible accident, but rather the gift of God. Our individual personality is not a matter of chance; God has called us *by name;* He knows and loves us as we are; and no created person need feel the slightest fear or shame at being himself. Death is the gate to a fuller life, when the time comes for it. And over all, God reigns in constant knowledge of us and our affairs and in unalterable love and mercy. This is the climate of healthy-mindedness, within which death finds its normal and natural place because our existence, our life, has likewise found its place.

When we so live toward one another and when our community life is organized around these central facts, then it is easier for men and women to grow in maturity and to think with peaceful mind about death as about everything else. Thus, the whole of our Christian living cannot help but be involved.

Thus there is a responsibility for us to live with death, daily. In practice this doubtless means many changes in our current conventions and superstitions. In our prayers it means that every day we should remind ourselves that death may come suddenly and without warning, and that we should be prepared for it ourselves, and in our relations to others, so that there be no heartbreaking regret afterward. The reconciliation of differences and grievances while there is time, the avoidance of procrastination, the thoughtful self-examination at night or morning—these and the like need to be practiced in the steady remembrance of death.

In our affairs a similar thoughtfulness is needed. Many a man has created far more pain and injustice by his will, or lack of it, than he ever could have in his life; it is no wonder that one of the few specific directions in the Prayer Book for Christian living refers to this. (See the second rubric on page 320, as well as the third and fourth on page 313.) Every man ought to order his business affairs, insurance, check-book, and papers with consideration for those who, at a moment's notice, may have to act in his stead. So also is it an act of consideration to make provision for one's funeral plans and wishes—many a clergyman has, in his files, memoranda on such matters against the day when they will be needed.

Our attitudes toward death are, perhaps, most severely tested and developed in the way we ourselves meet the death of others dear to us, or try to interpret the Christian faith to those who mourn. We need here especially to guard ourselves against the infections of the world. To the serene and tranquil faith of Christians, death is not the unspeakable worst of all things; to that faith, it is a fact of nature which God Himself has undergone and transfigured. Christians are rightly made uncomfortable by the devious ways men find to disguise death or pretend that it does not exist. A dead body is a dead body; the *person* has been released from that burden into an infinitely closer life with God; and therefore there cannot help but be joy mixed with the solemnity. But that joy depends on our keeping the respect we owe to the physical body he once inhabited quite distinct from the affection and thanksgiving we feel for the person himself.

Grief is natural; grief is also, inevitably, self-centered—we are sorry for ourselves at the loss of a loved one. But the sharpness of our self-pity and the threat to us which someone's death may hold depend in the main on the security of our own inner life. To the Christian, this security is assured because of the fact of God. Therefore our comfort and consolation to the grief-stricken lies largely in our assurance that they, the living, as well as the dead, have a constant place in the thought and love of God.

Second, *dealing with the fact of death when it comes: it is part of Christian living to understand the customs and requirements of the Church and the reasons for them.* Perhaps there is no area where the infection of the world is more apparent than here, in the misunderstanding and sentimentalizing of the Burial Office, and indeed of our funeral customs in general.

The earliest Christian burial custom was the Holy Communion, celebrated at the funeral and on the anniversaries of what the Church beautifully called our "birthdays into eternity." By approximately A.D. 350, other devotions—psalms, scripture lessons, hymns—had come into use. By the Reformation, the length of these rites had become wearisome, and their character increasingly penitential with more and more concentration on the awfulness of death and judgment, and with less and less of the joy and peace of the primitive rites. The Reformers both simplified the services and restored the earlier note of triumph. Specifically, the prayers and devotions were concentrated into a single service of the general form and mood of the familiar Morning and Evening Prayer, to be used with the Holy Communion where desired.

The Burial Office is thus, inescapably, the corporate act of the Christian community; it is the congregational form of prayer appropriate to the death of a member of the flock. It is intended to be fully corporate in its recital, with the congregation joining in the psalms, responses, and Lord's Prayer precisely as they do at Morning Prayer. It is not a private service for the bereaved, nor a monologue for the clergyman.

Due provision is made (see the rubric on page 337) for occasions where the use of the Burial Office would be inappropriate. There are many such occasions when the Church is asked to provide a suitable public funeral for people whose lives and beliefs were such that it would be improper or absurd to use the Burial Office as it is; and there is no earthly reason why the Church should not minister to those people and their families as the Christian community would want to. The Burial Office itself is a service of the congregation, not of the clergyman alone, and it presupposes the participation that is characteristic of a common act of the household.

The parish church is the proper place for the Burial Office; we do not normally go to a private home or some rented quarters to celebrate the Holy Communion or Morning Prayer on a Sunday, and no more should we do so when we are burying the bodies of our dear ones. *There is no excuse for treating a faithful Churchman as if he were a second-class citizen simply because he is dead; he has the same full right to the Church that he had when alive.*

Because it is a congregational service, the clergyman is in full charge, as he would be of any other church service, and he should be the first one consulted about such arrangements. Where it is physically possible, the use of the choir is just as appropriate as it would be on a Sunday morning.

It is wrong to make a funeral the occasion of financial display, especially where means are limited. Embalming and the use of a coffin is now usually required by state or local law and accepted by most people as a matter of practical convenience. But the costs for these should be kept at a minimum. The intent of burial is to restore the dust of our bodies to the dust from which they came. This is right and good; and it is ridiculous in Christian eyes to make a fetish of the preservation of the body, through eleborate embalming or the use of coffins supposedly impervious to the elements.

It is wrong also to expend great sums on elaborate floral displays. Flowers in themselves are lovely, and as gifts to the living they are gracious and kindly. There are few performances sillier than the loading of a coffin or the cramming of a church with "arrangements" that serve no purpose except to advertise the wealth or formal concern of the donor. Many if not most of our churches now rightly forbid such displays in the church, and urge that the money involved be spent either in a more meaningful memorial or in helping even to pay for the funeral. Many churches now provide a funeral pall, a cloth to cover the coffin while it is in view, to remind us of how the love of God covers us all alike, rich and poor, good and bad, and to help demonstrate the equality of all mankind in death.

Because cremation was the custom of their pagan neighbors, the early Christians adopted the custom of burial—inhumation—instead; and this tradition has continued until recent years. The Roman Church still enforces it; our Church does not, and there is no reason why anyone who so chooses should not prescribe cremation instead of burial. No doctrinal point is involved; it is purely a matter of custom and tradition.

In many cases, particularly where the final illness has been of an unusual character, physicians are grateful for the opportunity of an autopsy. Certainly no Christian would have any hesitation about this, nor about the possibility of the use of eyes, skin, or any other part of his bodily equipment which could conceivably be of value to anybody else. It is not permitted to us to be superstitious about our bodies. When we die, our earthly tenement has served its purpose; it deserves no more than respectful disposal, in whatever simple way is possible; and if it can incidentally serve medical knowledge or the need of others, we are more than glad for that added possibility.

To sum up, our attitude toward our funeral customs should express our profoundest beliefs about life and death and reflect our Christian practices. This life is our period of probation, and from it we go to judgment, in our bodies. Therefore death is an occasion of sober thoughtfulness, when the transitory flesh has served its purpose and the person is released into another body, fit for eternity. For him—for the departed—this is a kind of "birthday"; therefore there is not only sorrow at our separation from him for the time being, but also joy at what gleams before him. There is also a profound and moving sense of comradeship; nobody has ever shared in a requiem Eucharist without knowing the deep companionship with the dead which that Communion expresses.

In all this, the Christian community is playing its rightful part. The service itself is an expression of our oneness and our corporate life, as of those who have already known and shared the eternal life which God has given and will give. And we shall continue to share that life; our prayers for the dead are as right and natural and Christian as any prayers we say, for we believe in the community of the redeemed, the Communion of Saints, in which death plays no greater part than do the steps we take between nave and chancel in our parish church. This is all part of our Christian living.

Third, *facing the hard problems: all these certainties of Christian faith need special application to the "hard cases."* Chief among these are the tragic cases of death by accident or warfare, which affect the young man or woman whose life is just beginning. It is easy to be philosophical and say that it matters little whether death comes at 19 or 90. In fact, it matters a great deal and we know it; when death arbitrarily cuts off the promise of new life and forbids the flowering of possibilities, it is wrong; and we know it is wrong.

We often make the mistake of forgetting that God knows it is wrong too; that the only reason it is wrong to us is that it is wrong in His eyes. We need to remember that He is on our side in this. He is not neutral, much less our enemy, decreeing cruel and evil death in some caprice of His will. God hates wrong and evil as we do, but infinitely more so; and He has showed us how to meet it, and turn it into victory. The greatest wrong in the whole world was the Crucifixion, the bitter death of "the young Prince of Glory," when God experienced to the full the tragic evil of life, but bore it in such a way that it became a door of hope for us.

This is not to suggest any easy solution, or any solution at all for that matter, to the persistent problem of evil. Christianity has no panacea in this respect. Evil is evil; and all we know at the start is that there is no use disguising evil or pretending it does not exist. Our only hope is to face it honestly, and remember that God is infinitely more concerned with it than we are.

Nor is this to suggest that we should be passive about it. The fact of accidental death on the highway, for example, is a matter of profound moral concern to Christians, quite apart from the statistics or the stupidity of it. Life—anybody's life—is a supreme concern to us. So to drive our own cars that we do not only protect ourselves but also do everything in our power to protect others, even from their own foolishness, is a Christian responsibility. For life is sacred to us, and there are few graver duties than the protection of it.

But in all this it is needful to remember that death does not have the last word. If there were nothing more than this life, then it would be an unbearable tragedy even to live at all. Accidental death, in the hands of God, however, has a meaning and possibility which man cannot fathom, yet which is as sure as anything in the world. *To win us to Him* is God's supreme purpose; and even an untimely death can be an instrument of that purpose.

Another problem area for us is the matter of the taking of life, either by the state, as in capital punishment, or in euthanasia, or suicide. Capital punishment, like death through warfare, has consistently been held to be permissible for civil government, where the cause was grave and the purpose clear. Probably most Christian opinion would still support that view. But it is an area of vital moral concern, and an increasing weight of Christian thought questions it, not so much in terms of the right of the state to exact it as in terms of the purpose it serves and the possibility of injustice. This question is, and ought to be, an acute one for Christian consciences.

A different question is posed by euthanasia—mercy-killing. This is a heartbreaking dilemma for physicians as well as for the men and women who must bear senseless pain and suffering or who must watch others bear it. There are few physicians who have not known the bitter temptation to ease the passing of a patient and spare him the final agonies of hopeless sickness, or to destroy life in a child presumably hopelessly handicapped at birth. This problem becomes more acute, too, with the development of techniques and medicines by which life can be prolonged almost indefinitely—"life," at least, in terms of biological functioning.

Most physicians seem to feel that they have no option in this matter—that their responsibility is to maintain life at all costs, not to destroy it. It is hard to see any other attitude possible for a physician; and most thoughtful moralists would agree with them. Indeed, it has been precisely this resolute refusal to accept death as a solution to anything which has done so much to strengthen and develop our means of healing. If a child, no matter how handicapped, must live, then we must work all the harder to find a way around his handicap. If old people, no matter how ill, must live, then we are spurred on to find ways to defeat their illness or to ease its burden.

If we ever failed to hold to the supreme sacredness of life, we would be lost. It is this sense of life as inviolable, as an end in itself, which, more than anything else, has brought us to our deeper knowledge of mercy and understanding; and this sense is an inheritance few people would feel free to tamper with or give away.

Yet the almost unbearable moral problem that is posed by hopeless suffering is sharp and crucial, as is also the problem posed by suicide. The basic Christian teaching is that this life is our probation, our preparation for judgment; and therefore we have, under no circumstances, the right to take that life into our own hands. In earlier times, the Church forbade us to give Christian burial to suicides on the ground that the fact of their suicide was *prima facie* proof that they had died in disobedience to God. More recently, our attitude has modified somewhat; and this not because we feel any less strongly about the sin of self-destruction but because we have come to feel that most decisions to commit suicide are made by individuals of unsound mind and irresponsible judgment, and that it is unfair to judge suicide as a deliberate, free act.

This may be true; and it probably is true in the great majority of such cases. Yet it is needful for Christians still to say that it is basically and fundamentally wrong for people to think of taking their own lives. Life is a gift of God; He has His purposes; and He has all eternity to work those purposes out. Man has no right to arrogate to himself the prerogatives of God; all life is sacred to us, even our own; and death is no escape from anything, least of all one's self. Thus there is a firm and undeviating "No" in Christian thought at this point. There is always an alternative to suicide; and if men and women so tempted will put themselves into the hands of God and into the company of other Christian people, they will find that alternative. In life and in death, God is the first and most important fact. He reigns, and all creation is safe in His hands. This is the supreme certainty in all Christian living and dying.

The answers to these problems are not perfect answers. The deliberate sacrifice of one's life as a supreme offering of love—such as when Titus Oates walked out of the tent into the swirling Antartic blizzard in the hope of saving Capt. Scott's expedition, or when a heroic man places his life-preserver around the body of another and so condemns himself to death—this is an act which defies any easy solution. Suicide it doubtless is, in technical terms. Yet, just as clearly, such an act is good and right and heroic in our eyes. Is it thereby justified? The quick answer, of course, would be that the *motive* in such an act is unselfish; it is done for others and not for one's own ease or welfare; and therefore it escapes the condemnation of suicide.

So God doubtless understands. But these exceptional cases only test more sharply the Church's teaching about the supreme and frightening certainty of the sacredness of all life, *including our own.*

So also are we aware that there is no easy solution to the problem posed by hopeless suffering. The time may come when biological existence can be prolonged almost at will. At what point should the physician feel that he may rightly "let go," and let the inevitable happen? Is the death of a sick, tortured old man so terrible that it must be postponed at all costs? Is the final passing of an aged woman's unconscious body the worst of all possible ends? At what point does our medical or surgical interference with nature become unwarranted and wrong?

To say that nature should not be interfered with but should take its normal course is no answer—the art of all healing is interference with nature, in one sense; and if any surgery or medication is justified, then what will be the standard by which we shall decide what is unjustified?

These questions are agonizingly sharp and contemporary ones. They are on the frontier of Christian conscience. To say that there are now no settled Christian answers is not to say that the questions ought not to be asked. They must be asked and answered, if there is to be any realistic Christian moral leadership at all. But the answers, when they are made, will doubtless reiterate the timeless Christian affirmations about life and death—that all life is sacred, including our own; and that God reigns, and all creation is safe in His hands.

PART THREE

Church, Community, and Nation

CHAPTER TWELVE

The Nature of the Church

THIS PART of *Christian Living* moves on from the personal and individual areas of home and job to the wider concerns of Church and community. Some may wonder why as many as three chapters are devoted to Church matters; certainly most of our Christian living is done outside the church building and apart from churchly duties as such.

The answer to that question is a double one. First, we ought to say that part of our world's problem is the artificial distinction we make between "Church" and "world"—as if Church were simply the building and the services and the little organizations of men and women. In Christ's eyes, Church and world ultimately are meant to be one thing. The Church is meant to invade the world, change it, convert it and restore it to God. Therefore it is dangerous to draw any clear and final line between the two. Nobody really knows where his Church life stops and his life in the world begins. It is better to vote as a Churchman and pray as a businessman than to "put on a Sunday suit."

Secondly, the brief time we spend in the congregation at worship may actually be far more important and basic than the long hours we spend in our jobs, simply because what goes on in church is really the heart and foundation of what goes on in our life in the world.

For both these reasons, it seems right to spend these three chapters on the Church and our part in its life; and we begin with a chapter on what the Church is like.

WHAT IS THE CHURCH?

There was a young businessman in a group I confirmed a few years ago. I do not know what motives may have impelled him to receive instruction and join the group. Doubtless he had children in the Sunday School—perhaps his wife was an active Churchwoman. At any rate he had been impelled to align himself with our little local congregation.

In preaching to the class, I used the text from Ephesians (2:19) in which St. Paul speaks of us as *fellow-citizens with the saints, and the household of God*. Developing the text, I spoke about the great company of people who, like the class before me, had similarly made their confession of faith and received the gifts of the Spirit. I spoke about the saints themselves, and the great men and women of all ages, who were our companions in the Church. I dwelt at some length on the great and rich inheritance of every Churchman, pointing out what it meant to be a member of the Catholic Church of Jesus Christ, one through the ages. I tried also to point out something of the responsibilities which followed from that wonderful heritage, and of the great trust that had been given to us in our membership in the household of God.

After the service, during the coffee hour, the young man came up to me, evidently somewhat troubled and amazed by what he had heard, and said, "Bishop, I never knew how big a deal this Church was!" Nor had he! I suppose he had had no further thought than that by being confirmed he became an Episcopalian and a member of his local congregation. Confirmation had doubtless seemed to him nothing more than the somewhat picturesque ceremony by which a man could join his strength to that of the local group of people who stood for something in which he had confidence, and which he felt deserved and needed his strength. Nothing had been further from his thoughts than that he had thrown in his lot with so exalted a company as I had described it. It had never occurred to him that St. Paul, St. John or St. Francis was a fellow Churchman, nor had he considered that what they had given to the common treasury of manhood was also an obligation on him.

I think the revelation must have been both disconcerting and frightening, for it expanded the horizons of the Church almost unbearably wide. This was far more than he had bargained for. To be a member of the little Episcopal Church in his home town was one thing. To become a member of this infinitely great body, this *household of God*, involved him in relationships and duties inconceivably greater than he had anticipated.

The revelation must also have been puzzling to him. As I dwelt on the greatness of the ancient and universal Church of Christ, he must have been looking around him at the little local congregation and wondering where all this greatness was. As far as he could see, the Church consisted of a few people, like himself, banded together because they believed in Christian ideals and felt that an association in support of those ideals was a good thing for the community to have. Where was this household of God of which St. Paul had written? Where were the fellow-citizens with the saints? Clearly they were not here; this visible Church, of which he had just become a part, bore very little resemblance to what St. Paul had described.

It is a familiar problem. You and I read in the Office of Instruction that "the Church is the Body of which Jesus Christ is the Head and all baptized people are the members." This is a statement which we are prepared to accept, at least in theory. But in practice the Church does not look like that nor act like that. In practice, the Church we know seems to have no such dimensions as those described in the New Testament or the Prayer Book; and in our day and age we are far too impressed with the present necessities and limitations of the local congregation to have any vivid idea of the Church as "the body of Christ," except perhaps in some vague, mystical sense.

We are, therefore, not surprised that all through Christian history, and particularly at the Reformation when men and women were impressed with the weaknesses and failures of the Church, Christians have been tempted to divide the Church into the "visible" and the "invisible." Such a division seems inescapable, when one first begins to think deeply about the Church. This earthly reality, composed of very imperfect Christians gathered in their local congregations, immersed in the world and marked by all the compromises and failures of humanity, bears little resemblance to the ideal Church of the saints and of the sanctifying power of the Holy Ghost. It is no wonder that we are tempted to speculate about a double Church, one in history and another quite outside of history, connected only by a mysterious bond, mystical or perhaps even purely imaginary.

But the New Testament knows nothing of any such double Church. The New Testament knows only one Church, the Church of the fellow-citizens with the saints. The biblical doctrine of the Church is that of the one and single body of Christ. True, that body is a very mixed one, as is suggested in the parable of the Wheat and the Tares (St. Matthew 13:24-30); and none of the New Testament writers were under any illusions about the shortcomings and failures and even the outright wickedness of many who were in the Church. But, as the parable of the Wheat and the Tares teaches, the task of dividing and purifying the Church is God's task and not a duty for theologians and reformers.

The Church in the New Testament is a clear case of all or nothing. Either you cast your lot with Christ, willing to accept the dimensions and standards of life as He had taught it and lived it, or else you were not in the Church at all. There was no other alternative. There was no practice Church for beginners; there was no diluted Church for sinful men; there was no way of postponing entrance into the great Church.

Similarly, historic Christianity knows only one Church. The great Church of the saints and of the holiness and power of God Himself is none other than the little local church composed of imperfect and half-converted disciples like ourselves. There is no easy way in Christian doctrine to escape from the greatness of our vocation as Churchmen. Attractive though it might seem to leave the great things of Christianity to the saints and content ourselves with the tiny, man-sized necessities of the local congregation, that pathway is closed to us. If we are going to be Churchmen at all, we have got to accept the fact that the saints are in the pews with us, and that our Lord is the real pastor of our congregation.

It is perfectly clear that most of us do not always live up to our vocation as Churchmen. It is perfectly clear that the little visible congregation to which we belong often does not act as if it were the Church of the New Testament. But there is no way of escaping from that difficulty by pretending that we have our choice as to which Church we are going to belong to—the great one or the little one. There is no possibility of watering-down the standards or teachings of the great Church until they are more comfortable for us, or conform a little better to the standards of the world. For there is only one Church; and with us as with the people of the New Testament it is a case of all or nothing.

This fact, of the unity of the Church, is both uncomfortable and also wonderfully strengthening. Examine the discomforts of it first. The chief of them is the stubborn fact that the teaching of the Church must, of necessity, always seem to be authoritative, uncompromising, and aristocratic. It must be so because it must be nothing else than the teaching of Christ, exemplified in the best and truest and fullest of the lives and teachings of His disciples. The great guaranty of this is the solemn promise which lies at the heart of the ordination of men to the ministry of the Church, when they declare their faith that "the Holy Scriptures contain all Doctrine required as necessary for eternal salvation through faith in Jesus Christ," and their determination "to teach nothing, as necessary to eternal salvation, but that which you shall be persuaded may be concluded and proved by the Scripture." The Church of Christ, whose doctrine is Christ's own teaching, recorded and reflected upon in the Holy Scriptures, is the only Church there is. Necessarily, therefore, its teaching must be authoritative and uncompromising.

A sharp instance of this is the Church's teaching about marriage. It is not really the "Church's teaching"—it is really Christ's teaching, as bold and stern as anything in the Gospel. In bearing our witness about marriage before the world, we must of necessity start with what Christ gave us. When we live, as we do, in a world whose practice is sometimes completely at variance with Christ's teachings, the Churchman is in an uncomfortable position. His instincts move him to the utmost of sympathy and conformity with the world. His best friends—sometimes he himself—are involved in marital situations which do not seem to fit into the Christian categories. He must live, do business with, and share a community with people who have not been able, or who have not chosen, to abide by Christ's teachings. It is small wonder that the impulse to modify or dilute the Christian attitudes towards marriage and divorce is very great.

But the Churchman is tethered pretty closely in such matters as these. Strongly as he may be moved to conform to the world's theory and practice, he is also a man under authority, commanded by the uncompromising witness of Christ. This does not keep him from merciful understanding and from courageous attempts to do what he can to rebuild shattered lives, and to bring forgiveness to bear on the marital tangles in which his neighbors are involved. But

Christ is his Master and he must bear his steadfast and honest witness to what his Master said.

The Churchman often finds himself in an awkward and sometimes tense relationship with his fellow citizens on other issues. Why does the Church not tolerate gambling as a means of increasing its revenue? Why must a Christian consider and discipline his influence and example on others when it comes to drinking? Why may not church people simply adopt and follow the general community patterns in race relationships? These are examples of the discomforts that arise from our vocation to be fellow-citizens with the saints.

On the positive side, the Churchman discovers that, despite these tensions and indeed in some measure because of them, there is an immense strength for him in faithful Church allegiance. If what is expected of him is exacting, then too what is given to him is very great. If he may not comfortably slump into a kind of satisfied worldliness, he also knows that God is calling him to a level of life far beyond anything he might dare imagine. And he knows that God will make that level of life possible for him, just as He has for myriad others.

To know the truth about life, and to be able to build one's life on that truth with courage and serenity, is a far greater satisfaction than any more comfortable half-truth could be. Indeed our deepest need and our greatest privilege is to find that rock of truth. The household of God offers just such a granite foundation to those who will accept it.

The granite, obviously, is not any human goodness or human opinion. It is the rock of Christ, first of all—the revelation of God's nature and will in His Son, and in the Gospel. The Holy Scriptures, and the continuing life of the people of God about which they were written, are our supreme guide. Flowing out from them are the creeds, the Sacraments, the ministry, the continuing tradition of moral and intellectual standards and values which compose the secure foundation on which Christian living is built.

But God does not offer this security without its price, the price of obedience to a teaching always uncompromising, sometimes austere and even frightening when compared with the easier life of compromise. This price is one of the discomforts of the Christian doctrine of the Church.

Another discomfort is the one entailed by the fact that the Church is not a group of completely developed, mature and redeemed people, but a cross-section of humanity who are in the Church not because they have "arrived," but because they have the courage to hope that someday they will.

The spirit of the "sect" is familiar to most of us. It is a quite different spirit from that of the Church. The spirit of the sect is that of an exclusive group who have qualified, who have "arrived" so to speak, and have earned the right, in their own eyes, of claiming the privileges of the Church for themselves.[1]

No true Churchman feels that he has any right to claim anything from Christ. The most that he will say about himself is that he is caught and bound by the hope that, in God's good time, he will be allowed to come to that maturity in redemption which God wills for him to have. In the meantime he is like one of our radio commentators, who, when asked if he were a "practicing Christian," answered, "I do not know that; I know only that I am *an attempting Christian.*"

Precisely because the Church has not arrived, but is on the way, it is an uncomfortable body. The accomplishment of Christian hopes and objectives in the world seems to require men and women of prodigious and super-human moral insight and courage. But there are not many people like that. Most of the people we see around us in the Church are like ourselves: not very impressive morally, and lacking many of the qualities which the Christian life seems to require. It is easy to imagine what an ideal Church could be and do in the world. But the fact is that we have got to live and work with very imperfect Christians, no others than ourselves and those who are in the pews with us on Sunday morning.

Because this is so, we have also to learn patience with ourselves in the measure of our accomplishments in the Church. It is humiliating to be so, and to wrestle with the imperfections of the Church. We are often betrayed into the attitude of the individualist, who insists that he will not be held back by the impurity

---

[1] The word "sect" is not used here as descriptive of any particular religious body, as if some were "churches" and some were "sects." The sect-spirit infects every religious body just as it does every individual. The difference between religious bodies in this respect is rather the degree to which they claim it as an ideal to be sought. Others would feel it was untrue to the basic ideal of the Church.

of the Church and will instead strike out on his own, and leave the Church behind.

At times like these, it is good for us to imagine what the impatience of Christ must have been, and how profoundly tempted He was to cut loose from the sluggish body of mankind. In fact, this temptation to escape from the slow process of the corporate life of the Church is precisely what is reflected in the test He describes to us in St. Matthew 4:5-7, when the tempter urges Him to jump from the pinnacle of the Temple and thus prove His claim, without the necessity of being involved in the slow and painful conversion of mankind.

To this temptation He has a quick answer—*Thou shalt not make trial of the Lord thy God.* It is enough for Him to know the task which God has set Him to do. He will accept the task and fulfill it without availing Himself of the attractive shortcuts which the power of evil suggests to Him. This decision should be the subject of meditation for every Churchman.

The idealist, who is trying to live and bear his witness in a very imperfect world, is in very great discomfort. In fairness, it ought to be added that there are very few Churchmen who are not idealists in one way or another. Our idealisms do not coincide, and therefore the inescapable collisions in parish life arise. Idealism is not something to be particularly proud of; it is part of the common endowment of mankind. The art of constructive Christian living is not simply a matter of being idealistic; it is a matter of the dogged pursuit of the possible, and of willingness to see that half a loaf is better than no bread at all.

The third discomfort of the Churchman is in some ways related to the second. It is the discomfort arising from the very limitations of human life itself. We thought about these limitations in Part I, and of how hard it is to accept the fact that it is only in this world and in this time that we can act. The Church we know seems ineffectual in the face of the massive and inscrutable problems which confront mankind. If the world were only the size of Galilee! Personal example and influence could then count for something, and it would be easy to be a Christian and a Churchman and feel that one's life were well spent. How futile it seems, in the face of the complicated world of the twentieth century, to go on bearing our pitiful little witness. Perhaps in heaven, the invisible Church, our witness can stand for something and will be evaluated aright. But of all possible worlds, our world seems to be about the poorest one in which to try to be a Christian with any sense of effectiveness.

It is not surprising that many of our contemporaries are drawn away from any wish to be involved in the visible Church. Many of them seem even to abdicate their part in life altogether, feeling that it is perfectly idle and hopeless to try to come to grips with the world we live in. To such people the idea of an invisible Church is an extremely attractive one. In God's good time He will make that Church visible—either in this world or the next. In the meantime the course of prudence is to withdraw from the hopelessly corrupted and ineffectual congregations of this world, and to find solace in mystical realities of one kind or another.

These are the common discomforts which our contemporaries feel with the historic Church. Doubtless we could list more of them. But it would be needless to do so, for they all arise from the same fundamental reluctance of mankind to accept the idea of a revealed, historic religion. From the very outset men have found it hard to believe that God could or would reveal Himself within the limitations of time and space. *Is not this the carpenter, the son of Mary?* is the incredulous question (St. Mark 6:3) from those who were with Jesus in His earthly ministry. And the same question has its echoes all through the ages.

It is the central question for Christianity. If it is not possible or right for God to accept the limitations of time and space and to reveal Himself in our history, then Christianity is impossible, and the Gospel is a wild speculation. But Christians do not read it so. To us, the fact of the Incarnation is the central fact of all. It is the fact with which we begin—that God did, at a certain time and place, enter directly and personally into our life. In the Creed and in Holy Scripture we are prepared even to set down the place and time of that intervention, in Him who was "born of the Virgin Mary: suffered under Pontius Pilate."

This faith in the Incarnation—this certainty that God did fully and willingly choose to become man—is the central pillar of Christian faith and Christian living. More than that, it is the principle which illuminates all that we feel and believe about the Church. To the difficulties which men find with the historic Church, we answer that they are no different from the difficulties which men have always felt about the Incarnation. The life of the Church is, like the Incarnation, a deliberate act of God in history, an act in which God freely chooses to accept the limitations of time and space, to use them, and in using them, to redeem and sanctify the world of time and space.

There are obvious limitations to this claim about the historic Church. Certainly, as far as man's part in it is concerned, we should not want to claim for the Church the sinlessness or the authority that we ascribe to our Lord. We are far too aware of the imperfections and failures of the historic Church to make any such claim. Men make mistakes, and men are sinful; and, as far as God is dependent upon men in the life of the Church, then His redeeming and sanctifying work can be corrupted and even nullified.

Christians do not claim that the holiness and goodness of God automatically are given to every member and agency of the Church. The Christian claim is that, at the heart of the Church, God is at work, in all His purity and goodness, revealing, redeeming, strengthening, sanctifying. More than that, all this cleansing and healing grace is there for man to use, if he will. Our Lord did not cease His work after His Ascension. He continues His work, through His historic Body of which all baptized people are members, and of which He is the life. This "Body," (in St. Paul's great word), is the community of men and women filled and invigorated by the Holy Spirit, through whom that Spirit reaches out into the world to penetrate and guide. It is the Spirit Who matters, not the people; it is He Who is good and pure. Like the Incarnate Lord, God the Holy Spirit moves and works among sinful men, Himself unblemished by our failure and sin, yet identifying Himself at every point with us, and fighting by our side for the winning of the world. This spirit-filled community, so like the Son of God on earth as far as God's action is concerned, is the Church.

THE INCARNATION AND THE CHURCH

Let us look, once again at the Incarnation, as a guide to our understanding of the Church. Specifically, let us examine four principal factors in that doctrine.

The first is *God's willingness to accept the limitations of time and space.* This is perhaps the crux of mankind's difficulty with

178 ·

the doctrine of the Incarnation. We are so well acquainted with the limitations of time and space—with our ignorance and our powerlessness—that we find it almost impossible to conceive how the great and infinite God could consent to come inside these limitations. We can imagine Him in terms of His absolute qualities—at least we try to imagine what He is like in Himself—but we find heartbreaking difficulties in conceiving how perfect knowledge could, in St. Paul's phrase, *empty itself*, and live out its perfections amid all the shadows of human ignorance. Thus, for so many it is far easier to believe in an impersonal God, a great Force or Spirit, than it is to conceive of a God who is in any real sense a person capable of personal relationships. Because personal relationships and personal qualities, as we understand them, imply also the limitations of personality, we are led to this cheerless conception that an impersonal God is somehow superior to a personal one. It is not the task of this book to examine the Christian doctrine of God. Yet we must say at least this, that the prime consequence for Christian living, of the doctrine of the Incarnation, is precisely that God *did* become a particular personality among many, and that in so doing He raised human personality to the highest and most central place in the created universe.

Second, *God not only accepted these limitations, in becoming man for us, but He used exactly these limitations as the means of His revelation.* To take the clearest example of all, when the Christian talks about freedom, he is not thinking of an abstraction or an ideal. The Christian knows something infinitely more satisfactory than a theoretical freedom. He has seen freedom in action; he knows what freedom means in terms of forgiveness, of strength shared, of love acted out in life. And the miracle of this freedom lies entirely in the fact that the stuff of which it is made is not some wispy, theoretical element, but is the vivid, real, limited world of time and space. The love of God is not revealed in abstractions. It is revealed in the way in which Jesus of Nazareth met and dealt with the particular people who surrounded Him. He had no merely theoretical choices to make; He had a completely particular and immediate and cruel choice of life or death, which was not presented to Him for discussion or reflection, but for decision and action. The wonder of the Gospels is precisely that the people in them are men and not gods, and are real and not dreams. It is among these real people, like ourselves, that God fully reveals His nature and His love.

The third factor is that *God not only accepts and uses the limitations of creation, but in that acceptance and use He redeems us and the world.* Our true nature could never have been revealed in any other flesh than ours. The real depth and significance of our choices could never have been shown us in any other framework except that of those very choices themselves. The significance of the temptations of Christ, and His victory through them, lies entirely in this fact. Those temptations are real ones, of the same substance as ours; and that they are deliberately chosen and used by God in order that we might be redeemed from inside our creation rather than by some unapproachable example outside it. When God meant to show us what it is to be human, He asked no other medium than the very life of man, with all its limitations. He lived it; and He fulfilled it; He redeemed it.

Finally—and this is the heart of Christian living—*God keeps on entering, using, redeeming, and sanctifying His creation from inside.* What was done once for all in the incarnate Lord has yet to be done over and over again in every created soul. Christ not only does something for us; He means to do something *to* us, and within us; *He means to reproduce Himself in everyone.* Nor does He wait until we have reached some unimaginable perfection before He comes to make us new. He takes us as we are, just as He once took all mankind as it is. And, as far as we will permit Him, He makes us over from within, redeems us, and begins the long process of making us His.

These four things are what we chiefly learn from our faith in the Incarnation. To what end did God become man? That He might, by accepting and using our limitations, redeem and fulfill them, and make them the means of His continuing perfecting of us.

And it is in the light of these things that we must examine and understand the Church, for this is exactly what God is doing in the Church as He did in our Lord. If we are troubled that the Church does not look more like the perfect reality which the New Testament describes as the Body and Bride of Christ, then we need to take another look at our humanity as a whole. It does not look very much like the ideal manhood of which we dream. Its possibilities are thwarted and blunted, and it is barred from that ideal reality by countless corruptions and distortions. Yet we have also seen our manhood glorified by the indwelling of God Himself. And the manhood of God is continuous with our manhood, whence comes the dignity and gravity of the Christian's knowledge of himself. So is it with the Church. And when we remember that Christ stands at the heart of this same Church, that it is *us* whom He has called and appointed, that it is through *our* hands and voices that He acts, then our understanding of the Church is truly and deeply changed.

So will we gain both humility and realism from our reflection about the Incarnation. Our Lord was not sent to men good enough to deserve Him. He was sent to those who were lost without Him. So does He come now. There is no man good enough to belong to the Church. There is no man good enough to receive the sacraments. It is precisely because we are not good enough, that the Church is necessary to us.

We might well ask whether the "good people" are commonly found in the Church at all. When one reflects on the excuses which are given by those who choose to stand outside the Church, it is hard to escape the feeling that they are not in the Church because they are too good for it. "I won't go to Church because it is full of hypocrites; I don't need all the externals of worship; I find my God out in the woods and under the sun." When people say those things, they are really saying, "I am too good for the likes of you. I'm not a hypocrite; I don't need all this childish paraphernalia; I can be an angel straightway and be my own church."

Be that as it may, the Church is a central and inescapable part of Christian living. To the man or woman who means to take his discipleship seriously, the historic Church is a fact to be reckoned with. He will have his difficulties in coming to terms with it. He will find its imperfections, or the imperfections of its members; sometimes he will feel that his churchmanship is futile and unreal; he will look at himself and his brothers, and wonder where the household of God is hiding.

But if he will only not stop with that reflection, but go on to remember how Christ walked the ways of earth with us, then he

· 181

may look with new eyes on his comrades in the Church, and rejoice that Christ is willing to use such as we are, to hear and receive His holy word, and to act it out in the world.

Most important of all, we must remember that the Church is not a museum. The work which Christ began in His Incarnation is continuing every day of our lives. There is the Holy Spirit as well as the Son at work. And that Spirit is steadily encountering us and leading us in the fellowship of the Church.

Here and now we are helped by God the Holy Spirit to find and see for ourselves the new self which Christ gave us. Here and now, among our fellow-Churchmen, we discover the present reality and power of God. *Lo, I am with you always,* Christ said; *the Holy Spirit, whom the Father will send in my name, he will teach you all things, and bring to your remembrance all that I have said to you.* (St. Matt. 28:20; St. John 14:26).

CHAPTER THIRTEEN

Ecumenical Churchmanship

IN THE LAST chapter we were talking primarily about the Church in its local and personal aspects. This second chapter deals with the Church in its most extensive aspect, as seen in the multitude of separate denominations, sects, confessions, churches, or whatever else may be the title of the separated bodies of Christian people which surround us. Some of those bodies are of very recent origin. Some of them date back almost to the beginning of Christianity itself. But no matter what their origin, they are most confusing to the non-Christian, and almost equally so to the loyal member of any one of them.

The United States has the widest variety of competing groups. Perhaps, therefore, the American Christian is particularly confused in understanding this divided Christianity, and experiences difficulty in coming to terms with it. But the divisions are world wide, and so is the confusion. Therefore it is not surprising that there is a world-wide concern among Christian people to grapple with these divisions and, if possible, to achieve some kind of corporate solution to them.

Actually, much of the strongest and clearest leadership in ecumenical affairs has come from the "younger churches"—those Christian bodies established by missionaries in the Orient and in other sections of the world where Christians are in the minority. We shall come back to this later on, for it is a fact which has an important bearing on our American life.

It may be helpful to analyze a little more closely the confusion which people feel in the face of the divisions within Christianity. That confusion lies, first of all, *in the variety and number of the bodies which represent Christianity.* The counts differ; but at the very least there are almost three hundred such sects or denominations of

Christians in the United States. Most of them are very small and transitory in nature, in many cases being simply local congregations of people attracted by a particular leader over the space of a few years. But even after allowing for these, there still remain many large and relatively permanent divisions, of which at least ten are of major significance.

To the man or woman seeking a Christian affiliation, this question of competing groups presents a real problem. In most cases, he probably solves it by allying himself with whatever Church is most convenient to him physically, or most congenial to his temperament. But this solution is unsatisfactory to many men and women, and probably ultimately unsatisfactory to almost all, for it overlooks a second and more important factor about these divisions.

That second factor is *the variety of the claims which they make for themselves,* and the consequent attitudes which they take towards each other. If it were only a case of selecting one denomination among many, as one might select one brand of automobile or paper towel, the choice would be a fairly simple matter. But the competitive religious market is quite different from the one in retail sales. No automobile manufacturer claims that his is the only real automobile on the market, and no manufacturer of paper towels maintains that his are the only ones which will do the job. "Live and let live" is a maxim of competitive enterprise in the world; but it is by *no means* applicable in the religious sphere.

Not all Christian bodies make exclusive claims. Some would go very far in the other direction, and claim for themselves only that they were a reputable body of Christian people, who do as good a job as anyone else at their discipleship, and who have some qualities and characteristics, even secondary ones, which are true and have a certain merit of their own. Yet, because of the nature of religious convictions, it is difficult if not impossible to hold that there is no essential difference between the claims of one presentation of the Christian faith and another.

Even the most convinced individualist, who professes no creed whatever and has no doctrine of the Church, is still likely to be convinced that his particular creed-less and doctrine-less Church is the true interpretation of the Church, and therefore has a claim on his allegiance, and on the allegiance of other thoughtful people, stronger than any other. Clearly, some such convictions are unreasonable and are held because of some emotional or psychological need for them. We call such claims bigotry or fanaticism. But this is very far from saying that the ideal religion ought to be free from convictions altogether.

The claims appear to be inescapable. Certainly the ecumenical movement has taken them seriously, and has never tried to attack the problems of division by maintaining that the rival claims either did not or ought not to exist. They do exist, and in the nature of religion they must exist; and they present a very confusing challenge to the person exploring Christianity from outside.

They present an equal challenge, perhaps even a sharper one, to the man or woman inside the Christian faith. A "non-denominational Christianity" simply does not exist, nor does an "individual" Christianity. To be a working Christian necessarily implies membership in an organized body of Christians, a church. And to belong to a church necessarily implies belonging to some one of the bodies which make their separate claims on our allegiance. Whether, for example, you chose to be an Episcopalian, or were born into it, does not make very much difference in this. In either case, your own loyalties are involved; "our Church," with its own particular doctrines and traditions, has a profoundly deep emotional hold on you.

We have always to reckon with this third factor, *of our own particular and personal loyalty to our Church*. It is perhaps needless to point out how this personal element complicates and confounds the confusion. It is no wonder that we are so likely to crawl into our own ecclesiastical shells and try to forget the existence of the other Christian bodies. It we cannot forget them, then we may simply work out, in the top of our minds somewhere, an easy explanation for them: "German people are excusably Lutherans," "the Irish are of necessity Roman Catholic," "it is proper for Negroes to be Baptists," or some other simple explanation of religious differences.

These superstitions are not very deep or very important; and of course they do not stand up under examination. They are simply an attempt to shrug off the troubled confusion of our consciences. We would like not to have to come to terms with these divisions; we wish they did not exist. We are happy where we are, and are convinced that our own allegiance is the right one. Therefore we are eager for any easy and attractive theory which will let us go on in our own congenial discipleship, without hurting the feelings of people who hold different convictions from our own or without violating any deep convictions we hold ourselves.

Clearly, there are exceptions to this attitude; and the exceptions are coming more and more to be the rule among thoughtful church-people. We have come to see that the divisions of Christendom cannot be accepted as is the accustomed competition between manu-facturers of different brands, nor can they be waved away with some convenient and painless theory. Few things have been more marked in recent religious history than the concern of the ordinary churchman to know more about his own church, its doctrines and claims, and the doctrines and claims of others.

Side by side with this deepening of thoughtful church member-ship has come the *Ecumenical Movement*. Which one of these developments gave birth to the other is probably a question without an answer. It is certain that they have developed side by side, and that we are living through a time when the relationships between separated Christian bodies are being examined as never before in human history.

Archbishop William Temple, the loved and respected Archbishop of Canterbury during the last war, said of the ecumenical movement that it is "the great new fact of our time." In describing it that way, he was calling attention to precisely this recent concern for inter-church relationships, and also to the means that the churches had found to attack their separations and, if God wills, to end them.

THE EPISCOPAL CHURCH AND THE ECUMENICAL MOVEMENT

In the remainder of this chapter we shall ask five questions about the ecumenical movement: What is it? what is our Church's participation in it? what is its goal? what is its motive power? what are our responsibilities as Churchmen?

First, *what is it?* Basically, the ecumenical movement is a com-mon awareness, alive in all Christian bodies, of a troubled con-science at our divisions and a determination to study them and, by living and working together, to give expression to our hope that they may be ended. The movement is far more than a spirit, however; for the spirit is expressed in some major inter-church activities. Chief among them is the World Council of Churches, an organization of churches which include substantially all of the historic Christian bodies with the exception of the Roman Catholic Church and the more extreme, fundamentalist sects. The general basis of membership in the world Council of Churches is that any organized and recognized Christian body, which holds the historic Christian faith in the deity of Jesus Christ, is welcome.

The World Council of Churches is itself the product and fulfillment of several earlier movements. Perhaps the earliest was the impulse toward cooperation in foreign missions, which found expression in the nineteenth century in such bodies as the International Missionary Council. An antecedent of a different kind is found in the Faith and Order Movement, a movement for the common study of the doctrinal differences between churches, initiated early in the twentieth century, largely under the leadership of Bishop Brent. Still another antecedent was the Life and Work Movement, a development somewhat parallel to Faith and Order, which concentrated chiefly in the area of common Christian witness and cooperation in the social and political arena. The notable world conferences in Stockholm, in 1925, and Oxford, in 1937, were both fruits of this movement. There were similar inter-church movements of lesser scope, all of which played their part in accustoming the churches to think and work and talk together.

In effect, the World Council of Churches is a fulfillment and amalgamation of all of these separate concerns and activities into one world-wide organization. The World Council of Churches actually came into existence in Amsterdam at the first great assembly there in 1948. It has had one world assembly since, in Evanston in 1954. In between its assemblies, the work of its several departments goes on steadily.

The old Faith and Order Movement, for example, continues as a division of the Department of Studies. Theologians from all of the member churches meet together for common study and for occasional conferences, one of which was held in Lund, Sweden, in 1952. Another large Faith and Order Conference was held at Oberlin, Ohio, in 1957, under the presidency of Bishop Dun of the Diocese of Washington. At present, the Faith and Order

Movement is working on the general theme of "the nature of the unity we seek"—an experiment in common thinking about what a united Christian Church might be like.

Faith and Order is but one of several major segments of inter-church work. Parallel studies are going forward in the field of inter-church cooperation in such areas as refugee settlement, evangelism, the work of laymen and women in the Church, and social and international affairs. The World Council of Churches is not a super-church nor a competing denomination. It is an organization of existing churches, designed to hold our separate bodies together in common study and work—and in common meetings with one another, to provide an arena in which, we pray, God the Holy Spirit may lead us to find a way through our differences and divisions to a deeper unity.

As far as we in the United States are concerned, the second major expression of the ecumenical movement is the "National Council of the Churches of Christ" (not to be confused with the National Council of the Episcopal Church, which is our own chief administrative body). Within the United States, The National Council is generally, the counterpart of the World Council. Many of the fields of work and interest of world Christianity are also of concern to American churches; and the divisions and departments of the National Council are organized and function in similar manner to those of the World Council. Our own Church is a full and active member of the National Council, just as we and all our sister Anglican Churches around the world are members of the World Council of Churches.

Second, *what is our participation in the ecumenical movement?* The fact that our Church is a full member of these central ecumenical bodies, as cited above, is not necessarily significant in itself. The significance lies in the degree and amount of participation we take, expressed both in terms of financial support and especially in terms of the personal leadership provided by the clergy and laity of our Church. Bishop Sherrill, our Presiding Bishop, has been president of the National Council of the Churches of Christ, and is currently one of the six presidents of the World Council of Churches. It is impossible to list names; there are hundreds of our clergy and laity who are active in various areas of the National and World Councils, and a number who are members of the working staff of those bodies. At the official meetings of these organizations, our Church is always represented by a full delegation of clergymen, and laity. Also, in our own organization we have a Commission on Ecumenical Relations especially appointed to insure the full representation and participation of our Church in these activities.

We can say that the participation of the Episcopal Church in the ecumenical movement both at the world and national levels is wholehearted, and adequate to our minimum responsibilities. Our participation in local and regional councils of churches, ministerial associations and the like, is probably far less complete, and varies a good deal from area to area. The danger here is primarily that of giving lip service to local inter-church cooperation. In nearly every case, we have an officially cooperative attitude; but the degree of participation varies widely, and often reflects purely local and personal situations.

Third, *what is the goal of the ecumenical movement?* No one answer to this question is likely to be very satisfactory. The aims of the World Council of Churches might be expressed in this way: "It is an organization of the churches for fraternal study and action, that provides a meeting of the churches in the hope that, with better understanding, they may come eventually to full unity with one another." This definition is the author's, and not an official statement of policy. Yet it reflects the various official statements made from time to time, all of which testify to what is true for most if not all Christians, that the ultimate end of the ecumenical movement is unity, and not cooperation alone. The Episcopal Church clearly accepts this principle. Our Joint Commission on Approaches to Unity is an important agency of the Church, and is specifically established to explore ways towards unity with other religious bodies.

Different individuals and churches within the ecumenical movement would have widely different answers to the question we ask. Some might feel that cooperation alone was a sufficient end; that it is hopeless to work toward a unity which only God can give in His own time and way; and that we should content ourselves with finding the areas within which we can cooperate without danger of a collision of convictions. At the other end of the spectrum, there would be those who would feel prepared to regard the World

· 189

Council of Churches as a Church itself, as the ultimate super-Church, within which all of our differences will be lost or merged. Between those two extremes, there would be almost as many ways of answering the question as there are individuals.

Yet running through all of them there would be a common conviction that, until our divisions are ended and there is one earthly body of Christians, the ecumenical task would not be done. Thus it would be true to say that, in the minds of all who share in it, the ultimate goal of the ecumenical movement is the unity of Christians.

Some might phrase this as "the reunion of Christianity." Others might prefer to use some phrase suggestive of the fact that Christianity never yet has been wholly unified, and a true unity lies still to be imagined in the future. There would also be different emphases placed on the meaning of the words reunion and unity. Some would feel that a close cooperation in all esssential matters would be equivalent to unity. Others would press for a mutual recognition, by churches of one another, as true and complete churches. Still others would see a united Christianity in terms of free and complete intercommunion between all Christian bodies. Again, some would not be satisfied with anything less than a full organic unification into one organization, with a unified life and administration. The study and exploration of the varying concepts of Christian unity is the task in which the Faith and Order group are now engaged. It is a difficult task in its details. Yet it would be true to say that there is very deep agreement that, whatever form our ultimate unity may take, it must be a true unity in which diversities may exist, but division and cleavage will not.

Fourth, *what are the dynamics of the ecumenical movement—* whence comes its motive power? All that this section has said so far is by way of description. With this fourth question we come to the motivation which bears directly on our central theme of Christian living. It might be phrased thus: "why should a Churchman concern himself with ecumenical affairs?"

Fundamentally, the answer lies in what we said in the last chapter about the nature of the Church itself. There is only one Church. It is the great Church of Jesus Christ, and the apostles and the saints. It is the household of God, the Body of Christ. In the less lyrical language of the Offices of Instruction, "the Church is the

Body of which Jesus Christ is the head, and all baptized people are the members." In the creeds the Church is described as "one, holy, catholic and apostolic."

These are the stubborn realities which make us uncomfortable when we try to reconcile them with the day-by-day realities of our own congregations. These are also the same stubborn facts which make us uncomfortable in our divisions and separations from one another. How can there be any reality to these separated churches, when there really is only one Church? By what right do Christian people persist in their differences from one another, when there is only *one Lord, one faith, one baptism, one God and Father of all?*

The reflection of most thoughtful people is likely to start with just such questions as those. But there is a danger that the reflection may not start at all. It is the danger of a complacent acceptance of things as they are. Therefore, we need to examine ourselves first as to our complacency before we begin the reflective examination of our divisions and how we shall interpret them.

The only way a man or woman can accept, without a troubled conscience, the disunity of the Christian Church is by keeping his conception of the Church trivial and unimportant. In any major community, a man has his choice of at least three service clubs. He understands that they are all well-intentioned and useful, differing only in the composition of their membership. He makes his choice between them, either on the basis of invitation or because of some associations which draw him to one or another. This kind of competition is an accepted and normal part of American social life.

If a church is nothing more than the religious or theological equivalent of a service club, then his choice of his church allegiance need be no deeper or more costly than his selection of Rotary or Kiwanis or Lions or whatever his fancy may choose. If a church is no more than that—if all there is to a church is the little local group of congenial fellow-citizens working for the supposed good of the community—then he may freely take his pick.

This relaxed and genial acceptance of competing merchandise is especially characteristic of the Church in the United States. It is for this reason that attention was called earlier to the fact that much of the powerful and concentrated leadership in the ecumenical movement has come from the younger churches. The Christians in India, for instance numbering only a tiny fraction of a hugely non-Christian population, have no such trivial conception of the Church as do some of us. Therefore, it is not surprising that there is among them an insistent concern for ecumenical Christianity which is often lacking among us. Many of them realize, as we should, that because there is only one Lord and one baptism, the appearance of division and the calm acceptance of it is a profoundly shocking thing.

We Americans are so accustomed to our divisions that we are often quite unreflective about them, and are sometimes even tempted to defend them. More than once it has been pointed out that there must be a church for the country-club people and a church for the working men and a church for the foreigner and a church for the minority groups of one kind or another; and that this kind of sociological division is good and necessary. More than that, it will be argued that even within a single social group, it is still good to have competitive denominations—that it sharpens the wits of clergy and laity when they are pitted against ingenious and persistent competition.

As far as our divisions are historical facts, it is idle to quarrel with them. As far as they reflect a real diversity in modes of worship and manners of organization, diversities may even be nourishing and fruitful. The ideal of Christian unity is not an ideal of a uniform Christianity; men have never been alike nor will they ever be. A real part of the hope of the ecumenical movement is the hope of mutual enrichment through our diversities and because of them. There is this much truth, then, to the vulgar defense of a divided Christianity.

What this defense does not realize, however, is the transcendent meaning and solemnity of what lies at the heart of the Church, nor the true significance of the factors which divide Christians from one another. We are not talking about community objectives or retail trade or the passing political scene when we meet together in common worship. We are talking about God Almighty, the Creator and Father of all mankind. We are talking about sin and salvation and man's universal need to be set free. We are talking about the love of Christ and the unique and majestic symbol of the cross.

What we do in church is the holiest and the most universal of all human activities. Therefore, it is utterly grave and serious when men are separated one from another in these deepest of all experiences and truths.

More than that, it is precisely the depth of the issues involved which makes the division so complicated. Christians are not divided, at any deep level, by trivial matters of organization or tradition. They are severed by convictions that stem from the most profound issues, and partake of something of that same dimension. A sacramental church is not divided from a non-sacramental church simply because their rituals differ. The sundering is as deep as life, for there is no meeting place between a sacramental and a non-sacramental conception of the universe. Similarly, a church whose faith is built on the historic creeds finds far more at stake in its relationship with a non-credal church than merely the liturgical question of whether or not the creed is recited. One church interprets history one way and the other in quite a different way. And it is foolish to disguise the depths of these issues; nor does the ecumenical movement intend to do so.

At this deepest point of separation is precisely the point where the deepest motivation is found. When we have reached the point of understanding how profound the subject matter of our Christian religion is, and how serious the real divisions are, then we have taken the first step toward healing them. The Episcopalian looks anew at his ministry—he hears or reads the words used at ordination—and realizes, perhaps for the first time, that his clergy are not ordained as ministers of the Episcopal Church. They are ordained as "priests in the Church of God." He looks anew at the sacraments as they are spelled out in the Prayer Book, and realizes that nowhere are they referred to as *Episcopalian* sacraments. They are *universal* sacraments, for there is only one Lord, and therefore He has only one way of acting. We take a closer look at Holy Baptism, and realize the peculiar and tragic anomaly that it is only here at the beginning of life, that all mankind stands together; for there is almost no reputable church which does not accept the validity of this basic sacrament, no matter where or by whom administered, as long as it is baptism with water in the name of the Triune God.

In short, a member of our Church comes to the realization that everything of any importance in his religion is really not Episcopalian at all, but part of the single and universal Church of Christ.

The title page of the Prayer Book is worthy of some reflection in this connection, where it speaks of "the Sacraments and Other Rites and Ceremonies of the Church"—meaning the one, great Church of Christ—and then indicates that the Episcopal Church has only a "use" of them. Therefore, the ministry and sacraments of the Episcopal Church, like the Bible and creeds, are instruments and organs of the one, holy, catholic and apostolic Church. It is curious to note that even the Episcopal Church herself has only a shadowy kind of existence as far as her own Prayer Book is concerned—it is a peculiarly difficult problem to determine just what reality the Episcopal Church has in our own eyes. Holy Baptism does not make us Episcopalians, nor does confirmation. The Episcopal Church has no ministry of her own, nor any sacraments nor creeds. The Bible is not hers. The only identification an Episcopalian has is that he attends that Church and contributes to it. No other identity can be found anywhere.

This is a curious fact and also a somewhat moving one. When we discover, perhaps for the first time, that when we have thought we were talking about the Episcopal Church, we were talking about the one great Church, we realize, with something of dismay and penitence, the tragic falsity of divisions in that Church. Then it is, perhaps for the first time, that we are driven to a sober and thoughtful appraisal of all that the ecumenical movement means.

Episcopalians do not have any one single answer to this problem of disunity. Not many of us would be likely to adopt either of the possible totalitarian answers: either to say that the way to end disunity is for all Christians to become Episcopalians, or the alternative, that we all cease to be Episcopalians and simultaneously become something else. Our first response to this new sense of the deep, given unity of the Church should be a fresh appraisal of our own Church and her teachings and practices. Nothing could be more healthy than this, as long as it does not end simply in a renewed smugness and complacency. If the Episcopal Church and the Anglican Communion have been entrusted by God with certain profound insights into the truth about Christianity, those insights are a trust and not a gift; and their ultimate destiny is not to enrich us alone, but to enrich humanity. Thus, the more we know about our Church's doctrine and nature the better, as long as our love for her and her ways does not become idolatry.

If it is not to be idolatry—if our own treasures are to be taken as a measure of God's trust in us—then the only alternative is for us *to work unceasingly to find the ways in which we can add our inheritance to the undoubted treasures of others,* to bring about in the end a Christianity which is deeper and richer for all. This is the ultimate motive power of ecumenical action.

In all our great Anglican meetings, such as the Lambeth Conferences or the Anglican Congress, this has been the thought uppermost in our minds. I am sure also that it is the thought which dominates all the individuals who participate in ecumenical affairs. But we shall never get the job done until every clergyman and layman feels the same earnestness and the same sense of stewardship. Mankind is one in the love of God, as well as in birth and death; and until this unity is reflected in the unity of the Body of Christ, true and deep Christian living will be heartbreakingly difficult.

Finally, *what are our ecumenical responsibilities as Churchmen?* It has already been suggested that our first responsibility is the deepening and development of our sense of the obligation of the ecumenical task. If we as individuals are not disturbed in our consciences by our divisions, then we should begin to worry about the depth and thoughtfulness of our religious life as a whole.

But when this hurdle is cleared, we may expect to find no easy solution. If there were any easy solutions to be found, then the problems would not be very serious ones. The fact is, however, that there are some extremely thorny ones, chiefly revolving around four main points, and especially around two of those four. Many years ago, our bishops meeting in Chicago, and then later at Lambeth, set forth what were felt to be the four essential elements which must be found in any reunited Christian Church. One is the Holy Scriptures, and a second the practice of at least the two "necessary" sacraments, Holy Baptism and the Holy Communion. While there are sharp differences between churches in their interpretation of the Bible and of the sacraments, it is still in these two areas that the greatest measure of common agreement is found.

The other two elements set forth by our bishops were the historic creeds and the historic Episcopate. It is on these two points that the churches are most widely separated. To many Christian churches, the use of the historic creeds as definitions of Christian doctrine is no longer practiced, and our insistence on them creates real difficulties. Similarly, there is very great reluctance on the part of many non-episcopal churches to accept our teaching about the central place of the historic Episcopate, that conception of the bishop as the chief pastor of the diocese, by whose hands alone Holy Orders are conferred.

To have thoughtful knowledge of these issues and their importance, and to be able to interpret them to our neighbors of other traditions, would be the first obligation on the Churchman. It would be good also to know and make known what things we do not regard as essential. It is sometimes quite surprising, to us as well as our neighbors, to realize how little stress we lay on what seems to others sometimes to be our primary characteristics—our ordered liturgy, our vestments, our parochial or diocesan organization. They are not so important to us as they seem. But there are deep matters which are of great importance to us; and it is part of the life of the Churchman to know them and to be able to interpret them.

We are infinitely more concerned, for example, with continuing a deep sacramental life in the Church than we are with the outward forms the sacraments may take. Again, what is at stake in our attitude toward the historic creeds is not a mere interest in their frequent repetition, but a profound concern that the living, working faith of Christians of every age shall be securely rooted in the historic revelation with which Christianity began.

Second, it is an obligation of the Churchman to know his neighbors and to share as much common life with them as it is possible for him to do conscientiously. This means more attention to local councils of churches and ministerial associations than we sometimes give. It means, perhaps, even the visiting of one congregation by another. It means sharing in common tasks except where real convictions deny this. It means the establishment of a common front in our communities wherever that common front can be powerfully and realistically established. Only by knowing one another and by sharing together the things we hold in common, can we begin to make a realistic assault on the complacent acceptance of division which faces our church life almost everywhere.

Finally, it is an obligation for the Churchman to be steadfast in his prayers that God's will may be done and that there may be one flock under the one Shepherd. Not only at the special times of prayer during the year, but in our daily prayers, we need to hold constantly before ourselves and before God the shame we feel at our division and the hope we hold that it may soon be done away with. Thought, action, and prayer are surely the commanding obligations of a Churchman in facing the ecumenical Church.

Let the familiar prayer for unity in our Prayer Book be the closing reflection of this chapter.

O God, the Father of our Lord Jesus Christ, our only Saviour, the Prince of Peace; Give us grace seriously to lay to heart the great dangers we are in by our unhappy divisions. Take away all hatred and prejudice, and whatsoever else may hinder us from godly union and concord: that as there is but one Body and one Spirit, and one hope of our calling, one Lord, one Faith, one Baptism, one God and Father of us all, so we may be all of one heart and of one soul, united in one holy bond of truth and peace, of faith and charity, and may with one mind and one mouth glorify thee; through Jesus Christ our Lord. Amen.

CHAPTER FOURTEEN

The Churchman in Church

THIS CHAPTER, dealing with the Churchman's duties, should begin with the definition of those duties contained in the Offices of Instruction in the Prayer Book. "My bounden duty is to follow Christ, to worship God every Sunday in his Church; and to work and pray and give for the spread of his kingdom." (page 291)

This is a brief statement—far too brief—and it is also somewhat childlike in its extreme simplicity, as are indeed both the Offices of Instruction as a whole, because they were written, in part, with confirmation classes for children in mind. But there is another and deeper reason for this simplicity, namely that any prescription of duty needs to be as simply and unmistakably said as possible. A generalized duty, or a duty expressed in general terms, sometimes creates more problems of conscience than it solves. Man wants no rhapsodies about his duty; if he believes in duty in any area, he wants to know what it is in the clearest terms.

Our first questions are probably questions as to the use of the word "duty" about God and Church at all. To many the word seems to be out-of-place here. We have clear duties toward our neighbor, say, or toward our country, or toward our family. If we accept the notion of duty at all, it is certainly in those areas that we will be quickest to accept it and to welcome all the help that simplicity can give.

But we are likely to question the use of the word in connection with such exalted and transcendent realities as God or the Church. How do we know what duty we have toward God? Who defines it? Does not God wish the free and glad response of a heart deeply moved, rather than the rather pedestrian and unemotional performance of certain obligatory acts? Should we not approach God when we are moved to do so, rather than when someone tells us to do so?

These questions become even sharper when we remember that the Prayer Book also tells us that it is our duty to believe in God and to love Him. This is a separate question, dealt with elsewhere; but the hesitation about the word duty in both contexts is the same, and must be recognized at least before we go any further.

THE NATURE OF DUTY

Our answer to these questions might well begin by looking more closely at the word. Duty implies reality. That is to say, a duty is created by the state of affairs which exists. A requirement imposed arbitrarily by a superior authority may not necessarily be a duty. Although we may obey such a demand because it may be better to obey than to resist, the obedience will not imply any agreement that it is right to obey.

Duty is not merely obedience. *It is obedience willingly and gladly given because the facts make such action the right one.* We understand the facts at least sufficiently to perceive that there is a duty arising out of them and that it is right for us to obey. Military duty, for example, ought not be, and usually is not, simply blind obedience to one's superior. We may not understand the reasons for an order; but we know enough about the facts and circumstances— we know enough about reality—to know that we owe obedience to those who are above us in the chain of command and who know more than we do about the circumstances. We are prepared to submit our wills to the general good, as we understand it, because we have already felt that the general good requires a military body and all that goes with it.

Duty is obedience willingly and gladly given because the facts make such action the right one. Nowhere is this more clearly seen than in our religious duties. It is not simply blind obedience that is required when we are told that it is our duty to believe in God. To believe in God is clearly far more than simply to accept intellectually the fact that He exists or to admit His power. To believe in Him, like believing in anybody we know and love, is an act of the will, for it requires not mere credulity, but a certain degree of deep moral commitment. I believe in the honesty of my friend or the virtue of my wife or husband; and in saying this, I am also involving myself with them and on their behalf—"going their bond" so to speak. So is it with God. So should my duty also require my faithfulness and loyalty, even where it is not "deserved." But with God, this possibility does not exist. To "believe" in Him is in large measure something that I do with my will; and this is a duty born out of the fact that God exists. The reality of His existence creates the duty to commit myself to Him.

As with these greatest matters, so is it also with such day-by-day concerns as our duties as Churchmen. If they are true duties, they are created and ratified by relationships that exist. If they are true duties, they reflect honestly the way God has made us and our society, and what He expects of us, in our society. Therefore, the answer to the question "Why have I these duties to perform?" must lie in the very nature of the Church itself and of humanity.

If the Church were nothing more than a voluntary association of men and women, banded together for the accomplishment of a worthwhile purpose, we might still have a duty to it; but the dimensions of that duty and its authority over us would be very much less than what the Prayer Book assumes. The Prayer Book does not believe that the Church is simply a voluntary association of men and women. The Prayer Book assumes what the New Testament teaches: that the Church is a creation of God, His household, called into existence by His love and power, to which men and women are both called and appointed at the initiative of God. According to the Church's teaching, the Church of God is not limited to those now alive in this world, but it transcends this world and bridges the gap between time and eternity. In the Church we rub elbows with those who have gone before us, with the saints of long ago as well as of today, indeed with the angels and archangels as well.

The Church is humanity in process of being redeemed by God, at His will and choice, and through His grace, and the Church is also humanity responding to His action. Of course, it is likewise—at least in its present phase—an association of living human beings. In this respect it is simply a chunk of humanity, a cross-section of the creation. But its true limits and nature go far beyond this present society, so that it is a supernatural body, whose common life is not that of human beings alone but primarily that of God.

These are the assumptions upon which the Church is built, for they are the assumptions of the Bible. When we interpret these assumptions in terms of duty, then the authority and scope of that duty begin to loom pretty large. Suppose, though, that we still resist the conception of duty, as many do, and seek for another defense against it. We should probably find that second line of defense in the question as to the way in which such duties are established. We might accept all that the New Testament teaches us about the Church and still raise the question as to where we find the voice of the Church which defines these duties. By what authority, or through what officer or organization, does the Church establish these duties?

The basic answer of the Prayer Book is that Holy Scripture is the ultimate authority for any duty. No clergyman or group can require of the Churchman anything which cannot certainly pass the test of Holy Scripture.[1] If any of the duties laid down in the Prayer Book or anywhere else were in conflict with that basic principle, the duties would have no moral authority for us. But where the teaching of the Church, as established by her legitimate officers or organs, can be established in Holy Scripture or is clearly based upon what Holy Scripture teaches, then we rightly feel that it has commanding authority over us.

The legitimate sources of authority in our Church are, in general, our legislatures—our conventions. It is perfectly conceivable that a particular convention might be grievously wrong, might mislead and misdirect us. But if anyone were to go so far as to reject entirely the right of this representative body of the clergy and laity of the Church to define our duties, then it would be open to question whether he truly intended to be a member of the Church at all. The lesser question would be swallowed up in the greater; and in this chapter we are concerned with this lesser question, not the greater one whether we mean to be Churchmen.

The Prayer Book has authority for us because it is the product of the considered judgment and will of the Church, acting through her legitimate authorities. It is consonant with all else that we know of historic Christianity: it is a legitimate phase in the continuous Christian tradition, and it fulfills, and is in harmony with,

---

[1] "Proved" is the Elizabethan word used in the Prayer Book, as in the priest's vow on page 542, in the Ordination Service. Its sense is "test," as in "the exception proves the rule."

the teachings of Holy Scripture. Therefore, the Prayer Book is an authoritative voice of the Church for us; and its statement of our duties has the right to claim our obedience.

THE CHURCHMAN'S DUTIES

All we have said so far is really introductory to the duties themselves, and it would be well to refer again to the statement of them in the Office of Instruction. (This is not the only statement in the Prayer Book about our duties; there are others throughout the Book, in the rubrics and in the introductory material; they are, however, generally summed up in the statement we are examining.) The first phrase, "to follow Christ," is, of course, the general, all-inclusive requirement of Christian life and is hardly to be described as a "Church duty." Two groups of duties then follow this general phrase: first, "to worship God every Sunday in his Church"; second, "to work and pray and give for the spread of his kingdom."

The first group of duties, implied in the injunction to worship, are these three: *worship, discipline,* and our *responsibility* to the *community,* specifically the worshipping community. Let us look briefly at each of them.

1. Worship: This duty to God is one which is taught by God Himself, in many places in Holy Scripture, and supremely by our Lord Himself, as, when in the wilderness, our Lord confronts the tempter with the solemn reminder, *Thou shalt worship the Lord thy God, and him only shalt thou serve.*

But here as everywhere, Holy Scripture simply ratifies what the thoughtful Christian already knows. When we lift our eyes from ourselves and from our imperfect lives, our impurity, and our long weary history of compromise, and look at the awful purity of God and the almost unbelievable depth of His love, amazed and humble adoration is the only possible response that human beings can make. Nobody needs to tell us of our duty to worship, as long as we are mindful of the One whom we worship. What actually happens to us, when we grow cold and careless in our worship, is that we forget that it is really worship of God, and see only the routine ceremonial and ritual embodiments of that worship, as they are contained in our Prayer Book or in our forms of service.

I do not mean to suggest that Episcopalians are any different from the rest of humanity in this. No doubt, most of us are prone to forget the reality of God and become all too engrossed in the details of our own activity. This universal danger is, however, enhanced in proportion as our worship is rich and beautiful. It is distressingly easy for us, who have all the wonderful heritage of the Prayer Book and of the ordered worship of the Anglican tradition, to become almost idolatrous of that heritage and tradition.

"Idolatry" is a strong word, perhaps too strong; yet every Episcopalian knows the danger in which he stands, the danger of losing, in the dignity and beauty of our forms of worship, a sharp and objective awareness of the reality of God. Insensibly we are led to feel that our form of worship is the "right" form. If we are not thoughtful and watchful, we come almost to the point of feeling that God is the prisoner of the liturgy rather than the supreme Creator and Actor in it, and that there is no other authentic way of dealing with Him save in the ancient and lovely language of our services. Clearly, nobody really thinks this. Yet we often act, in our devotional lives, as if this were so; and the beauty of our worship tends to become an end in itself, full of grace and adorned with every human art, yet troublingly empty of any clear sense of the frightening and commanding presence of God.

It should be said again that this is a universal danger and not one to which the Anglican alone is prone. Yet this does not excuse us from taking the greatest care that our reverence be both thoughtful and real. Our preparation for worship should be as reflective as we can make it, so that we approach worship, prepared and expectant to find that we are coming into the presence of the supreme and holy mystery of God. This preparation of our hearts and thoughts is not simply a matter of devotional habit; it should rather be a deep attempt to make real to ourselves the fact of God, His creating and redeeming and sanctifying Being. Because duty is the reflection of reality, worship is the only possible response for us to the reality of God. Because that reality is the central one of our existence, then we need not be surprised to find that worship is one of the supreme duties of mankind.

2. *Discipline:* The Office of Instruction states next the requirement that the duty of worship shall be performed *every Sunday*. This, of course, reflects the biblical teaching about the Sabbath, a teaching as deeply embedded in the religion of Israel as any, and one, beyond doubt, faithfully kept by our Lord.

The primitive Christian was, necessarily, in something of a quandary about the Sabbath rules. In many cases, he had been brought up as a good and faithful member of the community of Israel. But even when he had come to his Christian faith from outside the biblical religion altogether, the question of the Christian day of worship had still to be faced on its own merits. The governing consideration for the Christian, in his discipline, was that the first day of the week, the day of the Resurrection, must be for him the supreme memorial of God's revelation. Whether or not the Sabbath, the seventh day of the week, was to be observed was a matter of detail; and in fact, it quickly disappeared from the Christian calendar. But the first day of the week was immediately appropriated for the weekly commemoration of the Resurrection, and became therefore the equivalent, in Christian terms, of the Sabbath.

Indeed, it became more than the Sabbath, for it included all that the Old Testament had enjoined, and then added to it the particularly Christian elements of thanksgiving and praise for the gift of the risen Christ. Thus, Sunday became, from the beginning, the supreme day of worship for the little Christian community.

It is important to remember the unique Christian character of the first day of the week. Sunday is not the Sabbath (although much of the Sabbath tradition attached itself to Sunday),[2] it is more than the Sabbath. It is a day of rejoicing; therefore, it is never a fast, and is omitted, for example, from the Lenten fast, for it would be inappropriate to celebrate a great feast by the sober disciplines of fasting. (This fact sometimes concerns our friends outside the Church, who may feel that it is somehow unworthy to relax our Lenten rules on Sunday. But whatever may be said about our motives, the reason for that relaxation is deep and true; and if we live up to the reason, we need not worry about our motives.)

The problem of Sunday duty is accented for many people in our secular culture by the fact that Sunday is also our weekly day of recreation and rest, one of the two days each week set aside for those good and necessary purposes. The problem here is, of course, the familiar one, that the man or woman who does take his duty as a Churchman seriously is often thrown into a painful dilemma. He

---

[2] Sunday was, of course, a normal working day for the early Christians, but it was prefaced by their worship.

must choose between Church on the one hand, and legitimate and often necessary personal and social duties on the other. "I would love to go to church more often," he says, "but unfortunately church always comes on Sunday, which is the only day off I have."

There is no easy solution to propose for this. In most cases the only solution for us is to try somehow to do both duties, even at some personal inconvenience. For the Churchman ought not to take this duty of worship lightly, nor easily dispense himself from the obligation to obey it. The duty is not simply one of a number of minor directions by the Prayer Book. The duty is, first of all, a reflection of the reality of God Himself and of the consequent duty of worship; and even more it is a reflection of *the need of mankind for a disciplined and ordered pattern of his time.*

This last is probably the most important factor of them all in this matter. Let us go back, for a moment, and remember what we said in the section on our personal religious life about the use of time in our self-discipline. Time is given to us to govern and control. There is not an unlimited quantity of time; we are allowed the use of only a certain number of days and weeks and years; and one of the major obligations of freedom is the right ordering of the use of that time. The man who lightly discards the duty of Sunday attendance, and instead indulges himself, because it is more pleasant to go off for a day's recreation or to sleep late one morning a week than it is to join with his neighbor in public worship, is not only being disobedient to a duty. He is really abdicating his freedom, in deliberately giving over his time to that which makes the most insistent and clamorous demand on it.

The question of the use of our time is the same as the question of any discipline at all; it is the question of who is to be the master, ourselves or the pressures outside of us. If a man chooses that his life shall be simply the result of all the forces that play on him—if he intends to take no initiative himself and simply do what happens to be easiest to do at the moment—that man has simply given up the responsibilities of human life altogether. God did not give us our freedom in order to have us turn it over, lock, stock and barrel, to the chance impulses and influences of the world. He means for us to learn how to use the world—time, and all that time contains—for right and true purposes. If we are not willing to discipline ourselves so as to become, in some degree at least, the masters of time, then we have really abandoned the fight to be mature and free human beings.

There is also the question of comparative values to be considered. Just how important is our duty of worship? Or, to put it in a truer perspective, just how important is the reality of God to us? The man or woman who feel that it is justifiable to spend forty hours a week or more in his job, and adequate additional time in his recreation, and yet begrudges one hour a week for corporate worship, has an eccentric standard of values, to say the least—if not a corrupted one. Weekly worship has behind it every conceivable biblical tradition. More than that, it has the weight and authority of all historic Christianity. It deserves, therefore, to be taken with very great seriousness and ranked among the most important duties which the Churchman acknowledges.[3]

3. Community Responsibility: Our duty is to worship God every Sunday and do it "in his Church." This is what we termed "our responsibility to our community." Although this seems to present fewer questions than does the duty of regular weekly worship, or of worship at all, yet it often arouses quite profound and troubling questions in people's minds. Why is there this requirement that our worship be corporate? Why is the Church involved in this? As we ask these questions, we think of the number of friends we have, whose belief in the existence of God may be quite clear and strong, yet who say to us, in effect, "I don't know why I have to join in common worship—I find God, when I am alone, in the trees or on the water, and I worship Him by myself."

Obviously the answer to this is not to say, "No, you don't." The experience of God which is granted to us, through nature particularly, when we are by ourselves is very profound and true. Music

---

[3] Many of the clergy and laity of our Church, and doubtless also of others, grow weary of hearing about the remarkable faithfulness of Roman Catholics in attending public worship, and about the way in which the law of that Church is obeyed. If it is true that Roman Catholics are among the most faithful of Christians in fulfilling the duty of worship, then let full credit be given them; but let it also be noted by Episcopalians that the law is the same for us as it is for them. The difference, if any, is in the degree of seriousness with which the law is received and taught, and the amount of self-discipline which individual Christians display. It is easy for Episcopalians to talk about the "fear" supposedly inculcated in Roman Catholics. The question for us is what have we that is better, to teach us to obey our duties faithfully and at real personal cost.

can be such a vehicle of a personal experience of God, as can any art. Reading will do it for those who read much. Even fishing or golf or a walk through the woods will do it, no matter how often those activities are abused by the careless. The answer of the Church to the man who prefers to be an individualist is not that his experience of God is unreal. It is rather that his experience of humanity is sub-Christian.

To the man or woman who does not believe in God, the Church, of course, is highly unreal and has no claim on his thought or allegiance. But to the believing man or woman, as most of us are, the Church is the expression, at the top, in the highest and fullest terms, of the unity of humanity as a whole; and to deny that unity is to deny our own nature. For we are born as members of the community of mankind, and we shall live, work, and die as such. And if that community is recognized as real in the less important things, then it must also be recognized as real in the most important things.

The man who chooses to be an individualist in his worship, although he is a good enough citizen every other way, is simply saying to himself, "I propose to secede from humanity, in anything that really matters." He is thereby doing violence to a basic truth about himself and the way God made him.

More than that, he is shutting himself off from all that the corporate experience of the race can give him. Nobody has very much knowledge of God by himself, nor a very wide experience of God. Each of us, no doubt, has a little. But the way we get our knowledge of God is precisely parallel to the way we get our knowledge of anything else—we draw from the resources of humanity as a whole, to supplement and complete what we ourselves, as individuals, may have found out on our own. To leave out this element of corporate worship is as unreal, in its way, as it would be to say that we will read only the books that we ourselves write.

All that we have said so far would be true, at least to some degree, of any group of human beings. There is an added dimension in the Church, however, that needs to be taken into consideration. The Church is not simply a human group. While it is that, it is also infinitely more than that. It is mankind in the process of being redeemed. The participle is important—it would be wrong to say that the Church is "redeemed humanity," if by the word "redeemed" we understood a finished job. The Church makes no claim to being a community of the saved. It makes every claim, however, to be the community of those being saved, and even more to be the community of the saving.

For the work of redemption goes on without haste and without rest; it goes on continuously, through those who are themselves both being saved and also a part of the saving process. No man is ever the end of the process of redemption in himself. God's work in salvation touches him and changes him; but in doing so, it inescapably makes use of him as the means of touching and helping to bring the saving health of God to others.

This truth hardly needs illustration, for the parallel truth is to be found everywhere in life. The alcoholic, to whom Alcoholics Anonymous has brought release and redemption, becomes, in that very act itself, a minister to those others with him in the group as well as to those outside the group. Many men and women in our society have learned that lesson, and indeed have learned the further lesson that the surest way to establish and fulfill one's own redemption is by giving oneself to the redemption of others.

People who have been through the rigors of a severe heart illness, or who have endured a time of sharp emotional crisis, once again find that their own feeling in large part depends on the way they minister to others who are, at least, potentially like them. So, too, many clergymen observe that men and women who come to them for counsel and are helped, at least momentarily, find the best healing for themselves by turning at once to help others.

These are all instances of the most profound of all Church principles, that the Church is a body of men and women, whom God is in the process of redeeming, and among whom that redemptive love expresses itself in their attitude to others. This is the reason why the Church is an essential part of the redemptive process. It is our duty to worship God and to worship Him with disciplined regularity, and, above all, to worship Him with common prayer and praise in the company of others who are with us in our situation.

If this element were lacking, the Church would be a travesty of its true self. It would be simply the club of those who, in great self-satisfaction, choose to pay their conventional respect to the Deity by periodically going through a corporate religious ceremony. Indeed people can be, and often are, that alone in church and that passive an audience. But such people never understand the genius of the common worship of the Church. People who are engaged in corporate worship are not an audience—they are a congregation. They are not passive and individual recipients of God's acts—they are ministers of God's love, one to another, and together as a group to those outside.

The very nature of common worship itself reveals this. There is nothing so uncomfortable as Prayer Book worship, particularly to those who are inexperienced in it. They long to be allowed to sit quietly by themselves, and be inspired or moved or taught by the professional ministers in the chancel. Alas, they are not suffered to sit in peace. No sooner have they come in than they are ushered to a pew. Someone promptly gives them a Prayer Book opened to the proper place. And while they are seeking to orient themselves, they suddenly discover that the people around them are standing and reciting the office together, or kneeling and joining in a common prayer, or singing in a corporate act of praise. This can be overpowering, making real demands on the patience and the imagination of the stranger, demands of which we Episcopalians are not often enough conscious.

But the significance of all this must not be missed. It is the genius of common prayer that it drives us out of ourselves and our separateness into a joint activity, by which we learn, little by little, the fact that there are no passive passengers in the Church of Christ, but that all are ministers and share the common and single work of Christ.

Our liturgical symbolism is but the surface of this profound fact, of course. It is not by common prayer alone, however, that men and women are saved from their loneliness and brought into the life of the household of God. Indeed, the whole life of the parish and congregation must reflect this single and common ministry. More than that, the ministry must go beyond the walls of the church into the community in which we are set, as yeast into dough. But the act of common worship is the lens through which we see all these other things. For that reason, our duty to worship God in His Church is a commanding one.

Nor is this the only reason. There are many other factors, of authority in teaching and worship, of regularity and authenticity in discipline, and of simple obedience, which are also involved. But each of them, in its own way, reflects the underlying truth, that in our redemption we are members one of another.

The other half of our duty towards God as Churchmen revolves around three simple words: *work, pray,* and *give.* Each of these is for a purpose, for the spread of the kingdom of God; each of them also reflects a certain aspect of human life; and we ought to think about them for a little while separately, and about the great purpose they serve.

4. Work: The injunction to work for the spread of the kingdom summarizes all that we have been saying about our dual role as the redeemed and the redeeming. But it carries us a little further than those thoughts did, for work connotes not simply those within the congregation but, even more, those entirely outside. To work for the spread of the kingdom, above all things, means that we shall bear our steadfast witness to Christ and His teaching and life.

Inescapably, for almost all of us, the greatest opportunity we have for that witness is in our daily work. That is not the only opportunity, however; there is almost nothing that we do, the whole week long, which does not provide an opportunity for witness. But simply because we spend most of our time at our daily work, it is in our jobs—our office, our classroom, our home, among our friends—that the persistent opportunities come for us to do our work for the kingdom.

That work may mean, and always should mean, direct personal witness to individuals. We should worry about ourselves if each one of us did not have at least one person for whom we were doing everything we could to win him to Christ. In our prayers, certainly, there will be more than simply one remembered; but for our own soul's sake, we are never safe unless there be at least one person, still unable or unwilling to follow our Lord, to whom we are steadily and consistently doing our best to bring the Gospel of Christ.

If we do this, then we are not likely to forget the less direct and more diffused witness which is also the responsibility of Christians. Every day we have countless opportunities to make it clear that our Christian belief is important to us, and that it makes an important difference in the manner of our life. Even the very way in which we do our daily work may be such an opportunity. The job itself will be no different from that which our unbelieving neighbor does. Yet there will be opportunities, both in word and deed, to make it clear that to us the job is not simply a job but also, and above all, a way of working out our faith in God and our ministry to our brother man. As we have suggested before, if a job is not fit to be a ministry of Christ, if it is not fit to be offered to Him, then it is not fit for a man to do. But if it is a true and useful work, then it can be a means of grace, a way through which we recognize and strengthen the brotherhood of man, and so let our light shine before men.

Our homes are likewise sacramental means of witnessing. One of the most depressing questions to ask oneself is this: In what way does my own home differ from that of a thoughtless and unbelieving stranger? A home, after all, is a church of sorts; and it is a sorry thing to find lacking from our homes any silent evidence of the fact that we believe, and mean business by our belief, in the Gospel of Christ.

So, too, is our conversation a continuing opportunity to witness for or against Him. Even courtesy itself is but an outgrowth of faith; and in an age grown increasingly careless of the gentle and the courteous, the impact in manners alone of thoughtful and understanding Christian faith is very great.

Parish guilds and activities afford still further opportunities for work "for the spread of his kingdom." Even though we may take it for granted that all the members of our church group are converted Christians, the life and work of the kingdom is still going on. We all live, spiritually, on the strength that is given one to another. Our conversion, so we pray, is a process that steadily continues and deepens from day to day. So also is our practise in the Christian life. Parish groups are laboratories and classrooms; they are cells in which the life of the whole body is born and nourished; they are a missionary frontier for those who are already missionaries.

And such groups should be not simply for the converted, but also, and perhaps most of all, for those who are just on the fringes of the Church. A men's club or a woman's guild that exists only for the companionship of the faithful members of the parish is missing its best vocation. These are the places where the stranger and the novice should come, to see what the Church looks like in action and to learn from the faithful what the Christian life is like.

5. *Pray:* The second great word is "pray." Once again, it is needful for us to look outside the conventional and the accepted

modes of prayer. We may take it for granted that the prayers of the congregation in church will include our petition that the kingdom of God will come on earth as it has already come in heaven. We may take it for granted that we shall pray for all sorts and conditions of men.

The question here is not simply one of whether or not we join deeply with the congregation in those prayers. The question here is more one of the degree to which, *in our own daily prayers,* we bear the redemptive work of Christ in our hearts and minds. No matter what else we can do to bring a friend or neighbor to conversion, at least we can pray for him, and we should.

More than that, we should remember that the life of the Church is itself a web of intercession. The work of our parish priest, which we often respect and admire very profoundly, is not really his work, so much as the work of God through him, supported, strengthened, and made enduring by the steadfast prayers of the congregation. Some congregations are fortunate enough to have an organized group of church men and women who periodically join in corporate intercession and prayer for the work of the clergy and of the parish. Such congregations are blessed. But there should be no congregation in the Church where at least the prayers of its individual parishoners, are not regularly and faithfully offered for the mission of the Church, both in one's own community and to the uttermost parts of the earth.

6. Give: Then, lastly, we are admonished to give for the spread of the kingdom. This duty involves the whole question of stewardship, of which we have already thought at some length; and it may be needless here to do more than mention it. Yet with all our wealth and generosity toward the Church, it is an astonishing truth that, outside of our own parish churches and their needs, we give a meager pittance to the central task of the Church. We are lucky if, in any year, we give a fifth as much to the work of the Church as a whole as what we give for the support of our own congregation. Surely, there is something grotesque about this. The question seems almost inescapable as to whether we measure the relative importance of these things in terms of our giving.

This disparity is made all the sharper when we grumble with one another, as we commonly do, that "the Church is doing so little" in this or that or the other area. We marvel at the sections of our own country which are in such great need of the ministry of the Church and receive so little. We travel to Africa or the Orient, and come home troubled and curious about the pathetic, tiny dimensions of the Christian enterprise in countries which cry out for the witness our Church can bear. We look at our depressed urban areas, which breed social problems of heartbreaking dimensions, and again we ask, "What is the Church doing?" We are aware of all that the ingenious mind of man is doing in laboratory and factory and, again, our consciences are troubled by the fact that the Church does not seem to be keeping pace with the great technical and scientific developments of our time.

These, and countless questions like them, are a measure of our sincere concern for the Gospel. What is grotesque about them is that we who ask the question are often the ones who give the least of ourselves toward providing an answer. There is always at least one reason why the Church is not doing a better missionary task, the reason that it cannot afford the men and materials it needs. Ask any bishop why there are weak spots in his diocese, a condition of which he is often the most conscious. Again, one answer is perfectly clear—he does not have the money to employ the clergymen and laymen to do the job. Ask why there are not more books or radio programs or study courses or social institutions to help meet the appalling ignorance and apathy of our society—ask why the Church so often seems poor and ineffectual against the massive misery of mankind—ask why communism makes such enormous inroads in great areas of the world, and the only possible answer to communism, which is Christianity, seems to hold such a flickering light—ask those questions, and then reflect on the answer which is common to all of them, the fact that these things happen because we do not give enough for the spread of the kingdom.

These are sober truths that conscientious Christians need to remember and think about carefully. Part of our bounden duty is that we shall give. And it is not out of kindness, or out of the goodness of our hearts, but simply out of the fact that God has created us, our duty to give arises. If we do not question the fact that God created us, and that He is redeeming and sanctifying us, then we have no right to question the duty of right stewardship, of stewardship worthy of the children of God.

It is perfectly true to say that money alone is not the whole answer to the world's need. The world's need cannot be met by money; it cannot even be measured in terms of money. The world's need is, most of all, a need for a deeper and truer understanding of itself and of God's will. If the Church had all the money in creation, and did not have the Gospel, it would be as sounding brass and a tinkling cymbal.

But put the statement the other way—the Church has the Gospel. Then what? This is the setting within which we ought to look at our stewardship, not asking how much the world needs, or the Church needs, but asking what we must do because God has done so much.

And we need to ask that question and think not only about the far distant places and the great world-wide opportunities, but also about our own parish, the nearest missionary outpost we have. It is hard to draw the line. The Church in South Africa, the Church in China, the Church in the slums of an old city, the Church in the isolation of a rural village—this is the same Church, living the same life, hearing the same Gospel as our own Church. The "others" for whom we give turn out to be people just like ourselves.

Therefore, we need to remember always that every parish is a missionary outpost, and every dollar we give is a missionary dollar. This fact will not keep us from supporting our national Church's work, or our diocese. But it will help us to understand our own parish and its program and budget in a truer light.

To worship God every Sunday in His Church, and to work and pray and give for the spread of His kingdom—these are our clear and simple duties as Churchmen. They do not need much discussion, for they are quite unmistakable. They need devoted and thoughtful obedience. They need practice within the household of our own parish church. They need to be worked out with our comrades in the Church. They need to involve us in a living allegiance with our fellow-Christians and fellow-citizens, remembering the great and single Church of Jesus Christ to whom these duties are owed.

In other words, they are not a sermon; they are a plan for living, designed to help us become people of gravity and soberness, of thoughtful devotion and of deep charity, people who take their responsibilities seriously and who mean what they say about being members one of another in the Body of Christ. As such, these duties play their great role in the strengthening of our freedom.

CHAPTER FIFTEEN

The Churchman in Politics

THE LAST three chapters have dealt with a consideration of the duties inherent in Christian living in relation to the Church. Now we turn to the radically different field of the Churchman's role as citizen.

Politics is a highly debatable field, and some would claim that there are no specifically Christian duties involved. Many more would admit that while religious issues are involved in politics, the gulf between them is so great that there is no satisfactory meeting ground. All of us will concede that religion and politics are two sensitive and highly charged areas. We fear their potential as sources of friction, and in personal relations we learn to steer clear of these areas. Some men's clubs even make it a rule that neither of these subjects ever be made an official part of their business. Yet, in spite of our caution, religion and politics remain perennially interesting and attractive areas; and there are few discussion topics more attractive for congenial conversation. Also, there are no themes which draw more deeply of our thought and concern.

In our American tradition we have tried to guard against the explosive mixture of religion and politics, and have adopted the principle of "the absolute wall between church and state." But this is neither a perfect nor an absolute principle in that we do not mean to separate *religion* from the state. The concern is to prevent the incursion of *organized* religion—the Church—into the political area. Yet, we say that our government exists to protect our God-given rights. Therefore, religion, in its deepest and most universal aspects, is part of our political tradition.

Thus this "absolute wall" is not so easy to build and to maintain as we might think.

But we shall think more of this later on. The theme of this chapter is simply that of the political duties of Christian men and women, as citizens. At this level our feelings about the distinction between religion and politics would probably be mixed. To the question "How much should religion and politics be mixed up with each other," our first answer might be a quick "not at all." If we were pressed a little, we might concede that there is some connection between the two, yet we would be inclined to play it safe and say that the further apart they are the better for all concerned.

WHAT IS THE RELATION BETWEEN RELIGION AND POLITICS?

If we were to analyze our feelings still more closely, we would find elements of, at least, four points of view involved.

First would be our feeling that *religion is private and individual, and politics is public and social.* Religion is, after all, very largely an individual matter; it is concerned primarily with man as an individual; and in a free society a man's religious choice must be his alone. More than that, his religious association in the Church is again on an individual and voluntary basis; and the Church itself is a private association, permitted and, to some degree, protected by the state, but still eminently private and quite personal in its implications.

By contrast the world of politics is the world of the public and the social. Political action has to do with men in the mass, and with their common life in society. Therefore, we say, the two realms of religion and politics must be by their nature utterly separate.

It may well be doubted whether this distinction has very much validity. There are elements of truth in it, particularly as they relate to the relationship of the Church to the state. But even here there are sharp limitations. The Church is by no means a private institution in many states where the state legislatures must and do legislate for the Church. In our national life, our clergy are employees of the state when they are chaplains in military service. Indeed, it is open to question whether any association of people as numerous and as entrenched as the Church, whether it be religious or secular, could really be described as private.

A far deeper question arises as to the use of the word "individual" in relation to Christianity. It is clearly true that the individual—his duty, his nature, his destiny—is at the center of the Church's con-

216 ·

cern. But it is impossible to find an isolated individual. Wherever you find him, man is inescapably social, and inescapably involved in the lives of other people both dead and living. Society is not something which men construct because they want to live together. Society is the fundamental condition of man's existence—he is a product of it, a victim of it, a member of it, and, one also hopes, a ruler of it. The one thing he cannot be is a refugee from it. Therefore it is hard to justify any distinction between the world of religion and the world of politics on the basis of any supposed individualism in religion as against a supposed social quality in politics.

Most people recognize this, and say that what they really mean is that *the world of religion is a world of the voluntary and idealistic, whereas the world of politics is a world of coercion, of necessity, of law and power*. There is certainly deeper validity to this second distinction than to the previous one, for it is quite clear that the first concern of the Gospel is not with what men must be obliged to do by law, but with what men should be led to do in their freedom, by grace. There can be no possible confusion between these two approaches to the human problem. The state is an organization of power, primarily, and should be; the Church is an association of free individuals; and no confusion between the two can be tolerated.

Yet, again, it must be noted that this is no final distinction. Granted that the state has power over men and uses it. Whatever the state does, therefore, must be of the greatest concern to Christian judgment, because individual men and women are so completely at the mercy of the state and its power. Granted that the Church believes that its way is better than the way of coercion. Nevertheless the Church must always be aware of the circumstances within which men and women must live and work; and these circumstances are, in the last analysis, determined not by the voluntary ideals of Christianity but by the effective power of the state. Therefore, while the distinction between the two ways of dealing with life is a valid distinction, the distinction cannot be pressed to the point of any fundamental separation.

Pursued a little further, many people would say that *politics is by its nature liable to corruption and sinfulness, whereas Christianity by its nature deals with the ideals by which men are guided*. The world of power, they say, is inescapably a corrupting world;

and it is necessary that the Church be spared any involvement with power, in order that its own proper concerns may be kept pure and inviolate. This is a distinction which has gravely important elements in it. Power is an invitation to corruption, because man is man and not God; and the experience of twenty centuries of Christian history has been quite unmistakable in pointing out the inevitably corrupting influence of political power in the life of the Church.

Yet it would be a terrible thing to say, and quite unacceptable to most Christian men and women, that the Christian should not soil himself in the grubby world of politics. Indeed, our response would probably be the opposite—an assertion of the duty of the Christian individual to concern himself with political life. There is a noble tradition of just such service for which Churchmen may well be thankful. And when we rejoice in such dedicated Christian men and women, it will also help us to a little greater clarity in thinking out what we really feel about the relationship between religion and politics.

Ultimately we are quite likely to be forced back to a fourth consideration, one of an eminently practical nature. When we are moved to say that we do not want any confusion between religion and politics, we may really be saying that *we do not want our clergy telling us how we should vote, or attempting to organize us as a political force.* It is not likely that there will be any fundamental disagreement with this feeling, least of all among the clergy so much of whose time and effort is devoted to the establishment of unity and common life among people of diverse opinions. This is as it should be; and this book would find no fault with the principle which is involved.

We might well, however, indicate certain reservations, chiefly about the meaning of the word "church." In common use, when a person says, "I don't want the Church to get involved in politics," he is saying that he does not want the clergy to be involved; and he makes the unconscious identification of the clergy with the Church.[1] There is no merit or justification for this; the clergy are not the Church; they are an order within the Church, much less numerous

---

[1] Of course, it may be also that he does not approve of some resolution or action of a diocesan or General Convention. This is anyone's privilege; and conventions are not infallible. But the answer is surely not to say that conventions should be silent about Christian principles.

than the order of the laity, but with specialized duties which the laity do not have. But it is not one of the special duties of the clergy to speak for the Church in practical issues. The man who has the best right, usually, to speak for the Church on practical issues is the man who knows those practical issues personally, who is expert and experienced in them, and who can bring to bear all the resources of that experience, tempered with Christian faith and judgment.

The tragedy lies in the failure of most of the laity to understand that they are an order of the Church's ministry, and are competent to speak for the Church and fulfill their ministry by taking part in industrial, social and political life. Part of our job in Christian living is to re-establish this unity and wholeness to life, so that the laity will understand that their ministry is in every respect a ministry of the Church, even when it is concerned with quite non-religious things. When this lost unity is found again, then we may find with it a very much clearer understanding of the true relationship between the Church and politics.

However that may be, it is certainly clear that only an eccentric and unthinking minority want to see a restoration of the kind of clerical-political society which was characteristic of the later Middle Ages. That unhappy episode brought a corruption and rot to the life of the Church from which we are not even now free. It is not the Church's function to be a judge and divider over secular society; it is the Church's function to be a yeast within that body, and a light to shine clearly and brightly so that men may be guided to the truth and may see themselves aright.

Yet it is completely within this picture that the Christian man and woman should learn to think of his political life as part of his Christian duty, and that the clergy should teach and preach to us about those duties and the principles which should control us. God is as much concerned with how we vote as He is with how we pray. Christian living is expressed as vividly in the share we take in our political communities as it is in our life in our parish church. You cannot draw a line between the two, nor cut humanity up into chunks. Man is one; and all that he does must be kept within one single framework. And for the Christian that framework is the framework of the Gospel.

CHRISTIAN POLITICAL DUTIES

How, then, shall we describe the political duties of the Christian? First, *the paramount duty of the Christian citizen is to exercise his sovereignty—to vote.* Our government is built on certain fundamental assumptions, of which perhaps the clearest is that the power of the state is rightly only derived from the consent of the people who yield it to the state but retain the directive control of it. In its essence, this political doctrine is profoundly Christian. This is not to say that Christians were the first to imagine such a state, or that this is the only form of the state which can be called Christian. Rather it is to say that, of all our political experiments, this doctrine gives the clearest expression and the widest scope to the Christian ideal of free and responsible humanity.

It is also quite clear that God will expect an equivalent responsibility from the people who have the power and the control over it. To whom much is given, from him much is required. While the parable of the Talents, and of the stupid and fearful man who buried his talent only to lose it, is not a parable of politics, it could very well be a parable of the fate of power in a democracy when it is not responsibly used. Time and again, history has proved this point. With all its excellences, democracy can become a hopeless tyrant if the mastery over it is not retained by those who have the power, namely the voters.

Thus it is that the first political duty of the Christian is to vote, in primary elections as well as in the final balloting. Indeed, this duty is so clear that many moralists would say that a citizen who deliberately does not vote is thereby sinning.

The second duty is in some ways an extension of the first—it is the duty of the Churchman to take as active a part in political life as he can, with fairness to his other duties.

An example of such participation is the town meeting. In the simple democracy of early New England the town meeting was an inescapable opportunity for direct personal participation. It still is in some small towns, although the "representative meeting" more and more now takes the place of the old gathering of the community. Such direct participation is not possible in larger political areas, although there are still innumerable smaller units—districts, neighborhood communities, and the like—in which such personal participation remains. Where it does, Christian duty would certainly imply an obligation to take one's proper share in such meetings.

A more vexing area is that of participation in political parties. America has never made its mind up about political parties to the degree, for example, that England has. The political party in America is the preserve of the professional. It is touched in the popular mind with vague suspicions of compromise and corruption; and in general, many Americans like to think of themselves as independent voters. This would be true even though they had always voted for the candidates of one party; and they would still tend in the direction of independence, resenting any attempt to enforce party discipline.

This is a widely mooted question, and this book does not propose a single Christian answer. The extent of Christian duty in this direction may be no more than that we shall examine our political parties and the role they play in our government, and persistently ask ourselves whether or not our duty does not lead us into closer personal involvement with them. Granted that no party has a monopoly of truth or of Christian conviction, they are still the only organized and responsible organs of effective political opinion and action in a complex society like ours.

Because this is so, it is also true that the real power of the state often is actually wielded by organized political parties. Consequently the individual voter, be he ever so conscientious in voting, is in danger of abdicating part of his power if he does not exercise it in and through the actual instruments of power, namely the political parties. He need not necessarily feel that the party of his choice is the only party that has a claim on the Christian conscience. He need only remember the realities of political life—that parties, through their candidates and programs, direct and use much of the effective power in human society—to see that it may well be a Christian duty to take an active part in party life, and thereby to bear his Christian witness.

It is sometimes alleged that the professional dislikes the amateur in politics. It is not at all clear that this is so. Even if it were, a democracy has no professional rulers; and such an argument would simply underline the responsibility of the Christian amateur to let his voice be heard and his influence known. Non-partisan groups play a very important part in American political life, but they do not have the final say as to candidates or issues. Their study and thought must be translated into practical policies and action; and this last is the area where political parties and Christian conviction and witness meet.

Participation supremely means our willingness personally to undertake the responsibilities of public office. We Episcopalians are prone to be quite free in our criticism of both clergymen and politicians, and yet we expose ourselves to the charge that we help create the problem because we do not encourage our own sons to enter either profession. There is enough truth to this charge, particularly in politics, to make it hurt.[2] It is still the rare young man who seriously contemplates public office as his chosen career. It offers few financial inducements, it exposes a man to the vagaries of political fashion, it involves him in a personal conflict for his livelihood which is distasteful to most of us. All these difficulties must be admitted.

On the other side, it would be hard to imagine any vocation which was a more direct expression of Christian responsibility than that of political service and political life. Fathers and mothers would do well to contemplate these things when they counsel with their children about the future. The clergy would also do well to deal with political life as they do with the ministry, as a real and live option for the young men and women in their congregations.

The third political duty of a Christian churchman is *the duty of knowledge*—knowledge as full and as impartial as is possible to achieve. Thoughtful knowledge of candidates is the beginning of this. Here we are helped by the vast development of means of knowledge and communication.

But the far more difficult field of information about the issues involved in political action, and the possible effects of such action, is not so easily explored. Political decisions in the twentieth century are often of such complexity, and have such far-reaching consequences, that it is probably impossible for any person to have trustworthy knowledge of all that is involved or that will be affected. In some cases, as in legislation governing the development and use of nuclear energy, the requirement of secrecy prevents the free exchange of information needed. But in most cases, secrecy is not the

---

[2] Yet it is heartening to know that 12% of both houses of Congress, in 1953, were members of the Episcopal Church.

issue, but the complexity of our national life. Who can foretell or fully understand the effect on our national economy of a particular bill for price support for farm products? or, in legislation affecting particular groups, such as the Taft-Hartley law? The effects of these as they concern attitudes and relationships within national life are incalculable.

Thus, perfect knowledge is an impossible ideal; and all legislation must involve a considerable element of the conjectural and the unknown. This does not relieve the legislator or, ultimately, the voter of responsibility to know, nor does it relieve the responsible agencies of communication—newspapers, radio and television, and political leaders themselves—from a clear obligation toward the whole truth.

Fourth, *Christians have a duty to test all political action as moral action*. Twentieth century people have grown dangerously hazy about this. Even though there would be a decided revulsion among our own fellow citizens against any idea that the state was above the moral law, or that the state was an end in itself, still we are tempted to give way to a kind of unthinking pessimism about the possibility of applying moral judgments to the actions of the state, to political action. We have grown accustomed to a double standard in these matters, which is an extremely dangerous mood for a democratic republic.

The theology of political action is clear enough. All power comes from God and belongs to God. In this world, men are the trustees of the power of God, to use it aright and according to His will and for His glory. In this world, the end which all power exists to serve is the welfare of man in the natural community in which God has created and established us. The state—the political organization of men—exists to serve the natural community of men. In a democratic state like ours, it is very clearly established that the ultimate power, under God, lies in the people who are the rulers. The state is their servant and the instrument by which they propose to use their power to serve the needs of men and ultimately to glorify God.

This, or something like it, is the theological outline of the American Republic. In this outline, the moral responsibilities and the moral judgments on political action are very clear. A political decision—the act of a legislature—is subject to exactly the same judgment as a man's individual action.

All of us would agree that the decision of a legislature, facing a complex problem in national or state life, is bound to be much more difficult and far less clear than the choice any individual might make in facing his own problems. Further, a public and political decision, which must take into account the attitudes and backgrounds of many millions of people, will almost of necessity attempt far less than a particular individual might decide for himself. Politics is "the art of the possible"; and expediency must play a much larger part in group political decisions than it does in individual ones. Precisely for this reason, individual witness and decision play an exceedingly important part in a democracy. It is an incredibly dangerous situation when group standards, majority standards, are ever permitted to take the place of the higher, more exacting and more austere standards of the individual.

In this matter the voice of the American tradition has been very clear. We are quite willing to understand that the majority has the right to decide the practical issues of day-by-day living. We are not at all willing to understand that the majority is necessarily right. Indeed, we are quite prepared to find that the standard of the majority is far less than the standard we as individuals would feel right to set for ourselves. This is political expediency, and it is quite understandable and necessary. But it is only safe to have a doctrine of expediency as long as there is ample freedom for expression of principles and for individual witness to these principles.

The root issue is that the actions of the state—of society acting politically—shall always be understood as serving an end greater than themselves. Only in this way can the state be kept from becoming the god and tyrant which it has become for many millions of people in our world. The state quite clearly and rightly may do things that individuals cannot do; quite rightly it may reserve to itself whole spheres of action which cannot and ought not be left to individual initiative. But this is a wholly different thing than it would be to say that the state can violate moral laws which are binding on the individual. The standard of judgment, morally, must be the same for political action as for individual action.

Thus, the fifth political responsibility of Christian living is to *relate our political action to all the rest of our life,* under the single common framework of our religion. Here, perhaps, we suffer most from our timidity about relating our religion and our politics. It is in this area that we need far more interpenetration of our politics by our religion, and vice versa, than we now have.

It may well be that the pulpit is not usually the place for this; but this is so, not because there is any improper connection between religion and politics, but because the pulpit is not the place for the kind of frank give-and-take in discussion that such consideration requires. The pulpit is a place for proclamation; and on most political issues there is no such clear one-sidedness as to make it right for the preacher to proclaim a single Christian voice. There are exceptions to this, of course; and it is always appropriate and right for preachers to proclaim the Christian principles which must be involved in legislation.

What we are discussing here goes beyond a statement of principle. For legislation is not only an expression of principle, but chiefly an essay in the possible; it is eminently practical; therefore there are almost always two sides or more; therefore the need for searching examination and discussion in common, under the judgment of God, by all points of view.

An instance of this, for example, would be the so-called "right to work" laws which have been adopted in some states. Such laws seek to use the power of the state to regulate labor unions. Specifically they forbid the union shop, making it illegal for labor and management to agree that every employee in the labor force must join the union within a certain period following his employment.

Probably the bulk of Christian opinion would be against such laws, partly on the ground that their popular title is misleading, but mainly because they seem to weaken the bargaining position of labor without any compensatory gain, and thus introduce retrograde and disturbing elements in the American labor-management picture. But there is an honest division of opinion about such practical judgments as this; sincere and intelligent Christian opinion will be found on both sides of this issue; and it would be foolish and rash to feel that all Christian duty lay clearly on one side or the other.

Yet there is a clear Christian principle involved, namely the right of labor to organize and bargain collectively and the duty of society to protect that right. "We hold the right of employees to organize and to bargain collectively is necessary"—so said our bishops in

1934; and so also have said the responsible Christian authorities in every major communion, for seventy years and more.

The kind of decision that the "right to work" law represents is, of course, a practical and regulatory one; but it must fall within the general principle of labor's necessary right to collective bargaining, if it is to be acceptable to the Christian conscience. And precisely here, in such an area as this, is there need for the free interchange of thoughts and ideas by Christian men of differing opinions. This exchange must be made by Christians *with* Christians *as* Christians, because the right use of the power of the state to establish, to regulate, or to destroy is necessarily a matter of grave concern to Christian conscience. Our political action must be related to all the rest of our life, under the common framework of our religion—this is the guiding duty.

Another example of an area that needs deep common Christian study by men and women of all shades of opinion is that of taxation and tax laws. Our tax laws have grown so complicated, as a result of the growth of our economy and our political structure, that it is sometimes difficult to recall that a tax law is perhaps the supreme instance of a moral act on the part of the state. There are few clearer and more decisive instances of the state's power to destroy or to build up than these instances where it invokes its taxing power.

What should be the moral foundation of our taxes? What should be the right division of the taxing power as between national and local bodies? What standards should guide us in the percentage of our income or property which ought to be taken for the use of the state? What methods of taxation are legitimate to the Christian conscience?

In truth, our tax laws have run so fast and so far ahead of any concerted and sober Christian thought that it would be impossible to give clear answers to such questions as these. Yet, year after year, we pass tax laws which have almost literally the power of life or death over millions of citizens in their homes and in their industries, and it would be hard to conceive of an area more important for Christian conscience to study than this. It might be added that it would be hard to imagine a forum more appropriate for such a discussion than a group of the clergy and laity in a community.

The sixth of the areas of Christian political responsibility is that *of man's responsibility to man, for man.* This area may be illustrated by a quotation from William Temple, when he was Bishop of Manchester. Writing of God and the state, he said,

The individual is immortal and the state is not; that is the fundamental conviction which must always distinguish Christian politics from secular politics. As Plato saw, the doctrine of the immortality of the soul is of cardinal political importance; for if it is true, it is the state which is transient while the individual is permanent, and the state must serve the individual, only claiming from its citizens such service as it is in their own interest that they should render; while if that doctrine is false, the state is permanent and the individual transient, so that the individual's interest may reasonably be sacrificed to that of the state.[3]

It is, of course, on this point that the sharpest political divisions now arise. Temple did not exaggerate the absolute clarity of the two principles involved. The choice is ultimately just as clear as that —either man is immortal or the state is; and one or the other must be accepted as holding the supreme claim on our allegiance.

The only trouble with this confrontation is that it is so seldom clear. It is not the way of history usually to reveal such unmistakable conflicts of principle. The state just goes along from one act to another and from one policy to another; and citizens go along with it, accepting, obeying, grumbling, hoping; and progress towards tyranny can be just as imperceptible and unquestioned as anything in life.

Because this is so, there is always the most profound need for vigilance and thoughtfulness. It is perhaps here that the sensitive and awakened Christian conscience has its clearest obligation and greatest opportunity. To ask of this or that piece of legislation, or this or that political platform, whether it be grounded on the immortality of man sounds like a very non-political question; actually it is a profoundly political question that needs asking in a multitude of ways by a multitude of inquiring people. For there can be one master, and one only; and in the end either the state and political power will serve man under God, or else man will awaken to slavery and to the terrible judgment of God. The justification of democracy is that it is a way, and perhaps the best way man has yet

---

[3] William Temple, *Essays in Christian Politics* (London: Longman's Green & Co., 1927), p. 39. Used by permission of the publisher.

found, to avoid this tyranny and to establish the true service of man. But that justification needs constant renewal at the hands of thoughtful and concerned Christian citizenship.

It might be well to close this chapter with another quotation from Temple:

Democracy is akin to Christianity; but Christianity is a great deal more than democracy. It lifts it to its true origin which is faith, not primarily in man, but primarily in God, and in man because he was made to be a child of God and member of God's family. Nothing in democracy itself needs to be changed in the process of its spiritualization; but very much in most democrats must be changed. And only in the degree in which that change takes place, only in the degree in which democrats put duty before right and recognize that the rights of human personality are derived from its dependence on and relation to the Divine Personality, can democracy become the ideal form of society or be secured against the danger of degenerating into the worst.[4]

---

[4] *Ibid.*, p. 80.

CHAPTER SIXTEEN

The Churchman and Minorities

THE PROBLEM of race relationships is one of the most urgent and challenging problems our world faces. No matter where you go—in the Americas, Africa, Asia—the old, "safe," stratified racial structure is breaking down, or it has disappeared completely. We in the United States sometimes think that our problem of Negro integration is the most important; but that illusion quickly disappears when we come to know something of the problem Africa faces or to examine the tensions in East Asia. Everywhere in the world the subject-status of native peoples as well as the old patterns of discrimination are being rejected in the most prodigious social and political convulsion in human history.

Actually, we in America are only caught in the backwash of this world-wide conflict. Our problem is real enough, to be sure; yet real as it is, it cannot be understood by itself. Nor can our solution to it be evaluated or interpreted only in terms of its possible usefulness as a political compromise for the American scene. The problem is a world-wide one; and the American solution to it will echo around the world.

Indeed, in this crisis, both the sincerity and the effectiveness of our way of life is being tested. Subject peoples, coming for the first time into political independence, are aware that the western, Christian solution is not the only one that is offered them. They watch with cool and critical eye to see just how competent is our idealism and social machinery to cope with their problem and find a just and humane solution to it. It will do our western civilization and our Christian tradition no harm to be tested; but the test is not an easy one; and we will not pass it unless we take it with the utmost seriousness, understanding how radically important it is that we both see the problem honestly and sympathetically, and have the honest courage to meet it and solve it in its own terms. This is the challenge we face, and it is one about which this chapter must speak.

THE CHALLENGE OF MINORITIES

Americans have certain advantages in facing this challenge. Chief among these is that the story of America itself is largely a story of ethnic minorities, of the gradual integration of immigrant racial and religious groups into the nation. The experience of this kind of immigration is by no means uniquely American. There is hardly a nation that has not gone through such a process at some period in its history, and has not had to face and solve those very problems which America confronts.

An English lady once told me, in answer to a question, that she felt it was the French in her that made her so susceptible to the rigors of the English climate. Upon further questioning, however, it developed that the last French element to enter her family did so in the days of William the Conqueror, in 1066! Although we chuckled at this, we were reminded that for hundreds of years England confronted a problem of minorities and ethnic integration similar to our own contemporary problem.

On another occasion, the late Bishop of Ely told us about a village in his diocese, divided by a stream, with an age-old tradition of hostility between the two parts of the town. He was not surprised to discover that the reason for the hostility was that the stream had marked the utmost penetration of a wave of Viking migration and that the old majority had stayed on one side looking down their noses at the new minority across the brook.

No, America's experience is by no means unique. What is important is that we are in the middle of it, instead of looking back on it over the comfortable distance of several centuries. We still face urgent problems of integration, and we are facing them at a time when they are dominant problems in world history. Whether we like it or not, we are a laboratory upon which is focused the intent gaze of hundreds of millions of people.

What has been our experience thus far with this problem? First off, most of us would probably answer positively that our experience has been good. We do remember that all Americans have been immigrants and any difference in status on this score arises only from where we came and when we came. This fact is a good one from which to start our thinking. But whether we start there or not, we soon confront another fact—namely, that immigration has brought an exciting and nourishing enrichment into American life.

Let us see, for example, how American speech habits have been enriched and given variety by immigration. The man who grew up in New York speaks as he does because he and his forebears have heard from childhood the unique lilt of Irish speech as well as the unmistakable, expressive dynamics of Yiddish. Those in the Northwest are likely to absorb much of the plain directness of the speech of the Scandinavians who settled that section in large numbers. Food, architecture, social customs, political habits of mind, accents, gestures, legal traditions, party politics, jokes on television, styles in clothing—where in American life do we find one feature that does not lead us straight back to some mother country, whence came some of our fellow citizens?

It has not been a one-way street, of course. We say "we," as if there was a basic stock onto which all these fresh gifts were engrafted. And in a measure this is so; the old have always gained by the gifts of the new. But the trick of it is that the new gain also, in full proportion. America is not a series of grafts; America has been justly called a "melting pot," which is much closer to the truth. And even though this melting pot may be scorned and called "mongrelizing," most of us would shrug off the word and keep the reality.

This American character, like the English character in its time, or the French, Italian, Greek, Israelite, or Egyptian character in their time—this American character is a continually renewed thing, particularly in a vigorous period of transfusion and integration like our own, and it can stand on its own feet.

This renewal is not achieved, however, without effort and pain. In our own experience we can see at least five factors which have created this difficulty and pain. Although we all know these factors, it may be of help to our main task to list them.

THE SOURCES OF OUR DIFFICULTIES

First, *the perennial problem of the "ins" and the "outs."* Any immigration means that there are those who are there first, and there are those who are strangers. Most of us have had enough experience with this situation to recognize it—we have, in our time, moved into a new community, joined a new church, or found a new job, and learned, in that way, what it is to be an "out" confronting the "ins." Every minority that has ever entered American life has had that psychology to face and been marked by it. The Anglicans in colonial New York, the Presbyterians in tidewater Virginia, the Roman Catholics in Boston, the Germans in Pennsylvania, the Swedes in Wisconsin, the Mexicans in California, the French in Rhode Island, the Negroes in Detroit, the Poles in Western Massachusetts—there are not many Americans who have not had to learn what it is to stand on the outside and look in, and who have not been marked for generations by that experience. It would be quite impossible, for example, to understand the dynamics of twentieth-century Roman Catholicism without knowing the history of the immigrant Irish on the Atlantic seaboard a hundred years ago; and the future of the Puerto Ricans will doubtless be predictable on much the same terms.

Second, *the fear of strangers*—that dark, mysterious attitude which goes by the cultivated name of xenophobia. To be an "in" is to be in a comfortable situation; we know a good thing when we see it. But this strange, chilling fear is something else again; it seems to call up shadows long dead, and having forgotten what makes the shadow, we see only the darkness. I can remember to this day the shudder that swept through me when I first heard of the machine guns that were stored in the basement of the Roman Catholic church in our neighborhood. I do not know that I ever really believed in the guns themselves (even a boy of five has some perspective on such things); but the story might have been true, and the guns were only a symbol of the frightening *difference* that I felt in my bones.

Difference, this kind of difference far below the level of rational thought or argument, has played a recurring part in American life. Roman Catholics have known it. Jews have known it. Protestants have known it. White people have known it. Negroes have known it. Indians have known it. And while it is tempting to think that civilization grows away from such primitive feelings, nobody who examines closely the emotional texture of the word "communist" in our own time is going to be very optimistic in that respect. "Difference" is a perennial dragon that has got to be hauled out of its cave and killed in every generation.

Third, *our jobs are threatened.* America has never yet known a wave of immigration that did not present itself as an economic threat to a large segment of our population. Fear of this threat was certainly an important, if not the dominant, element in the attitude of West Coast people toward the Japanese, for example. An able, industrious folk, eager to work and accustomed to work harder than people here, so frightened men and women as to cause them to forget that men make jobs and that a society cannot have within it too much ambition and too much industry. Massachusetts people can remember the picture of Polish families, from babies to grandmothers, crawling down the rows, planting onion sets, and the Yankee farmer shaking his head and saying that it was hard to make a living any more because of "these foreigners."

The threat is real enough, and not simply to be waved away as intolerance. The Yankee farmer is speaking for a whole way of life when he comments bitterly on "foreigners" who let their womenfolk work in the fields; he is expressing the challenge which he feels they present to a certain standard of life—a challenge that may be quite real and quite important.

The point to be observed is that mere resentment and fear will not meet such a challenge successfully. What is needed is a positive, understanding attitude which interprets and communicates, rather than fear and suspicion which only exaggerate the threat and prevent the very assimilation that alone can eliminate it.

Fourth, *newcomers do not understand our values.* The people who are here first always have things their own way. They are secure in that they know what they want and know how to get it their way. The people who come disturb that; they want different things, and they have a different way of getting them. And because most human beings are people of little faith and really do not trust their lights except as a kind of symbol of their security, the old settlers feel threatened and try to fight off the new, fearing the conflict.

Fifth, *they go to different churches than we do.* This perhaps comes closest to being a peculiarly American factor. Our multiple religious divisions look like chaos sometimes to observers from outside. Actually they are not chaotic at all; there is a very reasonable order about them; they are predominantly based not on chance or on geography or on a difference in beliefs, but upon profound ethnic and cultural factors. There is a reason, in our country, why a family named O'Flaherty will probably go to the Roman Church, and a family named Olson will be Lutheran, and the Robinsons will be Congregationalists. It is not a very good reason, but it is a highly effective reason; and it has succeeded in producing the bewildering variety of religious groups we know.

People from the same country and the same background will tend to bunch up anyway; and they bunch up religiously as well. Sometimes their religious inheritance was important in that it involved convictions; sometimes it was no more than a matter of language or local geography. But whatever the reason, the result was, and still is, that the Church, which ought to have been the heart of the melting pot, more often than not only succeeded in making the process of integration more difficult.

Accusations have been rather freely made about the failure of churches in the South to give a lead in the task of racial integration between Negroes and whites. The accusations are by no means deserved; but even where there is truth to them, the truth is not that the Christians were so much *imperfect* Christians as that they were *segregated* Christians, imprisoned in their own inherited prejudices, so that they never had the experience of integration at all, to begin with. This will be so everywhere in American life just as long as there is an Irish church and an English church and a farmers' church and a laborers' church and a country-club church and a Bible church and a Negro church and a white church. To overcome this difficulty is a special task for Christians; nobody else can do this but we ourselves.

This list does not pretend to be exhaustive; it is simply an attempt to bring together the common, obvious reasons why assimilation and integration have been difficult, in spite of the wonderful wealth and vigor that comes when minorities cease to be minorities and become simply Americans, part of *us*.

HOW DO WE KEEP INTEGRATION FROM HAPPENING?

What are the means which we have commonly used to prevent integration and assimilation from happening? There seem to be four main ones; and again they ought to be listed, not because they are unfamiliar, but in order to take an honest look at ourselves and our practices.

First, *we segregate our homes and theirs*. This is probably the most common form of discrimination, so common and so nearly universal as hardly to be noticed. A segregated Negro community is pretty obvious, and we are fairly sensitive to it. But Negroes are by no means the only ones to find their freedom limited in selecting a home. Orientals find much the same problem; Jews are familiar with it. The Germans found it, on the whole, much easier to live together, when they came; and so did the Irish.

This is not to equate all such discrimination. There are clear degrees of it, and it would be foolish to say that all discrimination is equally bad. For the frightened strangers from Poland, Italy, or Puerto Rico, it was a real blessing for them to have a community that welcomed and understood them, when they first landed on this soil. Not many could have made it alone on the sparse and hostile reception they got from most of us. Thus it is, for instance, that so much segregation in housing is self-segregation. This kind of segregation does not excuse anything; it simply points up the problem; for when families huddle together for fear, it does not make too much difference what they are afraid of. They should not be afraid of anything.

But we have used segregation in housing as a defensive weapon. And we have suffered from it, as a majority always suffers when they segregate the minority and thereby prevent, or defeat, precisely the one process which will remove the problem—integration.

Second, *we discriminate unfairly in jobs*. Thanks to a changing climate in both labor and management, and thanks also to laws which have shown that we meant what we said about fair employment practices, the job picture is infinitely better now than it has ever been in American life. But it is by no means a satisfactory situation in any American community. Opportunities simply do not exist for many in minority groups. And the results are tragic. Whether you measure them in terms of unused manpower, in terms of enforced poverty, in terms of the "typing" of jobs and people, in terms of the bitterness of frustrated abilities, the cost of this type of segregation is incalculable. Everybody is impoverished by it, chiefly the majority groups who again, as in housing, have imprisoned themselves within their own prejudices.

Third, *we break up our society into fragments.* Laws can help to eliminate job discrimination and segregation in housing. But there is no conceivable law able to prevent the subtle and powerful discriminations within society itself. Men and women will rightly say that no law can dictate to them, who their friends are going to be or whom they will invite for dinner or a glass of beer in their homes. No possible law could do this, nor would we want one that could.

This is on us. In this area there is no substitute for the decisions that men and women must make on their own. And often, tragically enough, the decisions we make are short-range decisions: there is no reason why we have to consort socially with Jews; we do not want our daughters to marry Negroes; we do not trust the Irish Catholics. On the basis of decisions like these we, once again, lock ourselves up behind the walls of our fears and prejudices, and keep the rich, natural cross-fertilization from happening.

There are no absolutes in this, as far as I know. Intermarriage sometimes presents appalling problems, and it is idle to pretend that these do not exist. There is no point in letting a young Roman Catholic about to marry an Episcopalian girl think that everything is going to be rosy and that love will conquer all. Love will do nothing of the kind; there will be real and costly problems every step of the way! And problems far deeper are involved in inter-marriage between races.

Yet whatever progress mankind has made, in understanding and integration, has been made because men and women had the cour-age to take the long-range decisions rather than the short-range ones. For better or for worse, American society has got to be one. A house divided against itself cannot stand. It has been this cer-tainty which has guided men and women of courage to face the task of a divided society and to solve it in the only way in which it can possibly be solved. There is only one way to have a unified America, and that is to unify it.

Fourth, *we look at them but do not see them.* We look right through them. Here is both the most effective and cruelest tool we use. We do it—and this is the heart of the tragedy—without being aware of it much of the time. We do it in statements like these: some of our best friends are—; my old nurse was a —; my room-mate at college was one of —; I think the man who washes my car is a —.

Anyone who has talked much with Negroes about their problems knows how sharp this is. We can talk politely about discrimination in employment or about their housing difficulties; but we are not even close to the heart of the problem until somebody is honest enough to say that what really hurts is the way white people have of not really seeing or recognizing them as human beings. This is the ultimate offense that can be committed against human beings anywhere. We really ask very little from one another. We do not ask for another man's money, or his favor, or his affection. But we do ask him to admit our reality and to accept us as human beings like himself. We want the Golden Rule observed—not lip service to it, but the psychological and spiritual reality that underlies it. We want to be *real* to our neighbors. We want our hopes and needs to count in their minds along with their own hopes and needs.

Thus we can do nothing worse to others than to deal with them as if they were simply scenery on our stage. Thus, too, this subtle form of discrimination is both the most effective in accomplishing the immediate purpose, and the most costly in the price that we ultimately pay in resentment, bitterness, and in the implacable and undeviating purpose in the heart of the minority to get on top and stay there. There are few who would blame the minority for feeling that way; they have almost earned the right to resentment (if that right can ever be earned); but the answer is not to turn the minority into a majority—the answer is to do away with minorities altogether and let men and women stand on their own feet in each other's company, and deal with one another with dignity and charity.

These then, are the four principal instruments with which a defensive majority can prevent, or at least postpone, the coming of the rich unity of human society which God wills for us. As we said before, we do not list them with any thought either of a complete inventory or of suggesting things everybody does not know. They are listed, more than anything else, for the sake of our own self-examination and penitence.

The cost of this refusal to assimilate and to be assimilated is very great. It is a two-edged sword. Part of the cost is paid by the minority groups who suffer from the unfair discrimination; and part, a very great part, is paid by the majority in their deliberate self-impoverishment.

One of our bishops, who is at the center of the sharpest and most critical racial conflict of our time, the Bishop of Johannesburg, Ambrose Reeves, said this to the Anglican Congress:

Further, we are bound to draw attention to the fact that human beings suffer and are degraded because of the present conflicts and tensions between various human groups, and that happens not only to those groups which are frustrated and oppressed. *Such conflicts do terrible damage to the members of a dominant racial group, warping their humanity and making them the prey to all kinds of fears, some of which are the product of their prejudices, and others which are entirely groundless."* (Italics mine.)

It may be that the most searching self-examination, in the souls of the majority anywhere, ought to be an accounting of what our fears cost us and our children. Not only do we lose by our fears, in denying ourselves the rich human treasure which God has provided in the variety of the multiple races and cultures of mankind; we also create a bitter entail for our children and their children in a fragmented society, divided at its very heart.

WHAT DOES OUR CHURCH TEACH?

What is the plain teaching of the Bible and the Church about these things? Let me quote again an admirable summary by Bishop Reeves of what New Testament teaching is:

Certainly the Bible allows for people out of all races being members of the Church, but it knows nothing of any divisions in Church based upon race or color. Similarly, the Bible says nothing for or against the intermarriage of people of different ethnic groups. Its concern is with the building up of the body of Christ, composed of people drawn from all nations, peoples and tongues. Truly, Jesus was the Messiah of Israel and a member of that racial group who were God's chosen people. But the decisive thing about Jesus Christ was not that He was of the house of David, but that He was the Son of God, come into the world to be "a light to lighten the Gentiles" as well as "the glory of His people Israel." Through Christ Jesus sin is conquered and the wall of partition which separates man from God and from his fellows is broken down. Now a new race appears in the world. So St. Paul can write, "There is neither Jew nor Greek, there is neither bond nor free, there is neither male nor female; for ye are all one man in Christ Jesus."

Bishop Reeves goes on to add that

there can be no question that for centuries the Church included within its fellowship people of any color and race . . . for over sixteen centuries the Church never took race or color in account when considering qualifications for membership . . . because this problem is so great and so urgent we need to assert emphatically the plain teaching of the Bible that all men are created and sustained by God, for God has "made of one blood all nations of men." For that reason we cannot view racial differences as an instrument for keeping ethnic groups apart, but as a means by which the life of humanity may be enriched. . . . Whatever men may do to their fellows in pursuit of some racial ideology which distorts their judgment and obsesses their thoughts, we must proclaim insistently in the Church that the future does not lie in their hands or ours, but in the hands of Jesus Christ, Who is ever re-making men, replacing their fear by trust, and Who has the power to do away with injustice and oppression.[1]

We have quoted at length from Bishop Reeves, partly because he is living at the heart of a racial conflict of surpassing intensity in South Africa, and partly because he has put so succinctly and directly the clear elements of Christian teaching.

This teaching has been crystallized and underlined time and again by the Church in official statements. In 1948 the Lambeth Conference declared:

The Conference is convinced that discrimination between men on the grounds of race alone is inconsistent with the principles of Christ's religion. We urge that in every land men of every race should be encouraged to develop in accordance with their abilities; and that this involves fairness of opportunity in trades and professions, in facilities for travelling and in the provision of housing, in education at all stages, and in schemes of social welfare. Every Churchman should be assured of a cordial welcome in any church of our Communion, and no one should be ineligible for any position in the Church by reason of his race or colour. (*Resolution 43*)

In 1954, the Anglican Congress reaffirmed these principles in so many words:

We reaffirm the statement on race relations of the Lambeth Conference of 1948, and are penitent for our failure to put it into full effect. We urge

---

[1] All the quotations from Bishop Reeves are from his address, "The Church and the Family," in the *Anglican Congress, Report of Proceedings* (New York: The Seabury Press, 1954), pp. 112 ff.

members of the Church to continue to witness strongly and wisely against all forms of discrimination, to work in each land for justice in racial relations, and to teach the full implications of our faith with regard to race. Those living in multi-racial areas must put Christian principles into practice by improving social relations between people of different colour. In the work of the Church we should welcome people of any race at any service conducted by a priest or laymen of any ethnic origin, and bring them into the full fellowship of the congregation and its organizations.

The General Convention of 1955 again reaffirmed this teaching, and applied it directly to the American scene. One resolution adopted by the Convention expressed our deep thanksgiving for the fellowship of many races which we experienced in Hawaii, and went on to say "this experience has served to deepen our conviction and strengthen our resolution to witness as a Church in our lives and in our parishes both home and abroad to the oneness of man and to the breaking down of all racial barriers within the Christian fellowship."

A second resolution adopted by the General Convention expressed the intention of the Church to make our own the statement of the Anglican Congress already quoted, and also urged "all the clergy and people of this Church that they accept and support this ruling of the Supreme Court, and, that by opening channels of Christian conference and communication between the races concerned in each diocese, they anticipate constructively the local implementation of this ruling as the law of the land."

It is hard to see how any Christian body could do less than this, in the light of what our Lord has taught us and the Church has believed. The Church does not simply set out a hopelessly idealistic social doctrine, and then sit in judgment on mankind for failing to meet it. God does not ask the impossible and then condemn us because we cannot achieve it. God has taught us what the full truth about human relations is. If we choose to live by a half-truth, that is not because the full truth is impossible; it is because we are afraid, and needlessly afraid, of the full truth. And doubtless God's judgment on needless fear and faithless anxiety is very sharp.

THE AMERICAN SCENE

Finally, we must think these principles out in terms of our present, immensely painful, American situation. Our problem here at home is part of the very much wider problem of racial conflict the world around. Yet it has its own, particular American character. Color, as well as race and creed, are involved; and color is a differentiation between people that has a uniquely strong psychological effect.

The long years of slavery have played their part in our attitude toward Negroes, and they have suffered particularly from the "typing" which grew out of this—the "Uncle Tom" stereotype.

By sheer number (in many southern regions they are a majority of the citizens), the tensions are aggravated and the problem sharpened.

The fact that Negroes are often unable to compete successfully when they are suddenly turned out of their second-class situation and are plunged into competition with better-educated and better-nourished whites, is an added aggravation. The results of segregation and discrimination will last for a long time; they persist from generation to generation; and it is utterly unfair to expect untrained men and women, whose minds and bodies have been impoverished, to be able in the twinkling of an eye to come up to the standards of more privileged people.

Such factors as these, and others, play a peculiar part in the American scene and doubtless make our problem at least different, if not more difficult, than the problems mankind has faced at other times and in other places. It is for this reason that "gradualism" is a doctrine that appeals to almost everybody in the North as well as the South. The Supreme Court itself, in its basic ruling, took a "gradualist" position, in saying that the necessary changes in our system of public education should come with "deliberate speed."

Some of us may feel that this poetic phrase is out of place in a decision so far-reaching and basic as that decision; it is better to be clear, than to be literary, in a crucial judgment like this. Nevertheless, the Supreme Court recognized what nearly all of us do, that such an immense social change cannot happen overnight.

In a most thoughtful and moving statement to his diocesan Convention in 1956, Bishop Penick of North Carolina says as much:

To attempt a speedy answer, or even to expect it, seems to me unrealistic, for it ignores the experience of history, including an era of tragic fratricidal strife. It does not take into account a massive psychological adjustment, affecting basic attitudes and traditions centuries old, but, for good or for evil, do actually, at the present time, make up the pattern of modern society. This is a mountain of fact and circumstance that only faith in Christ can remove. And with all my heart I believe that this realistic mountain will be moved and cast into the sea. But the process, inevitably, must be slow.

Men and women of good will on both sides of the conflict recognize that the necessary changes in social habits and social institutions must come gradually. It will be, literally, generations before the social and psychological marks of the hundreds of years of this racial conflict will disappear from the American people.

This is well understood, and doubtless Negroes can be as patient as white people can, and as realistic. But changes in attitude can come a lot more quickly than changes in habit; and changes in belief and in intention can come even more quickly. *And these changes—the purposes, the intentions, the working commitments of people—are the heart of the problem.* I quote again from Bishop Penick's noble statement:

These are the things to my mind that indicate the direction in which a solution lies.

1. The Supreme Court of the United States is the highest tribunal of this nation. Its decisions are final.

2. It is my duty as a good citizen to obey the law of the land. This conforms to St. Paul's admonition: "Let every person be subject to the governing authorities."

3. I am under serious obligation to "think and do such things as are right," knowing that no permanent answer to life's questions can rest upon any other foundation than righteousness.

4. I accept the Christian doctrine of man, namely, that we are all created by God the Father, redeemed by Christ the Son, and sanctified by God the Holy Spirit. To distinguish and differentiate between men is right; to discriminate against them is wrong.

5. I believe that justice is not man-made, but comes from God; that it is a balanced thing, impartial, impersonal, giving preference or advantage to no man at the expense of any other. I believe that justice is invincible, incapable of being set aside by emotion or false reasoning, and eventually, in all cases, for all people, will prevail.

If we—in the South and in the North—mean this and intend to fulfill it as fast as we can, we will have broken the back of the problem. We will not have solved it; there will be years to come when the patience of men will be tried, and when we will be tempted to take counsel of our fears and move more slowly than we need to. But if Negroes feel that white men are fighting side by side with them against a common evil, and if white men feel that Negroes are sincerely anxious to contribute and are not merely seeking advantage, the task will finally be accomplished. For God reigns and His purposes are sure.

One of the greatest of Americans, at an earlier phase of this same conflict, had this to say about it:

Yet, if God wills that it continue until all the wealth piled by the bondsman's two hundred and fifty years of unrequited toil shall be sunk, and until every drop of blood drawn with the lash shall be paid by another drawn with the sword, as was said three thousand years ago, so still it must be said, "the judgments of the Lord are true and righteous altogether."

It has been nearly a hundred years since that was said, and the end is not yet. But the judgments of the Lord are still true, and our hopes are secure.

In all this, the essential ingredient will be a willingness to entrust ourselves to God. This is as true for the Negro taking his adventurous steps in a new kind of life as for the white man. The courage to endure suffering, even to offer that suffering in reparation for the long years of man's inhumanity to man, is the highest gift of faith as well as the clearest test of it. All of us need to remember that God is on our side if we are standing shoulder to shoulder in facing a common problem. It is part of Christian living, then, to thank God and take courage.

CHAPTER SEVENTEEN

The Churchman in His Community

THERE HAVE probably been few periods in our history when Americans have been so aware of "communities" and "community responsibilities" as we are now. We are not necessarily meeting those responsibilities any better than our fathers did, but we are certainly more conscious of them. Our lives, in most neighborhoods, are complicated by what seems to be a never-ending variety of community organizations; our loyalties are enlisted for a multitude of community purposes; there are moments when we wonder whether we still hold title to any time for ourselves and our families.

Doubtless, there are clear reasons for all this busyness about community affairs. One reason, certainly, is that our communities—our neighborhoods, towns, cities—are far less permanent than those of a century ago. We move around the country more and have fewer roots in the land and less time to grow into our place and duties in society, as those are traditionally understood. Therefore, we are likely to be far more conscious of those duties and of the relationships between people which they express.

A suburban community in mid-century America is filled with community activities on a scale almost unbelievable a few years ago. School districts and their duties, parent-teacher activities, neighborhood associations, tax study groups, church clubs—the number of them is great, and the proportion of time and energy they command is large. The most obvious reason for all this activity is that we are all newcomers, and the community itself often is new. None of us was here a few years ago, and many of us shall probably not stay very long. Therefore, there is an urgency about our participation in the community that a more static age did not know.

Another reason, perhaps even more important, is that our communities tend to be less and less complete in themselves. Our jobs are often carried on at a distance from our homes. Indeed, in suburban life, we live with a foot in two wholly separate communities, one the community of work, the other of play and sleep. But even if there is not geographical separation, there is likely to be spiritual and emotional separation (save perhaps in the small city or town where our work fellows are also neighborhood friends). More than that, the more complicated our economy grows, the less clear and direct is our sense of interdependence. The days when one member of the community fished and another farmed, one prayed and another hunted—or even more, when a whole group did these things together, as the proper season came—were days that nourished an easy and unmistakable sense of common life and dependence one on another. But such a sense of partnership in a common economic and social life is hard for a contemporary American community to have.

Perhaps the greatest block to our developing a community sense is that we do not share together the deepest experiences in life as earlier societies were privileged to do. I mean, of course, primarily that we do not worship together. We worship separately; and thereby deny ourselves the most fundamental bond of unity that life provides. Our worship suffers thereby, and our churches look more and more like clubs; and it is not surprising either that our clubs look more and more like churches.

But analysis is not our main interest in this book. It is enough to know that there are many good and sufficient reasons for our peculiar preoccupation with "community." We are filled with questions about its nature, its structure, its duties, and its privileges. How to see these and share fully in them, as Christians, is our major concern. Where does this concern find its answers?

THE NATURE OF COMMUNITY

To begin with, the Christian starts with one profoundly important, and quite unique, insight into the nature of a community. That insight is this: That a community is not created by geography, law, or economic interdependence, or by our human desire to have a community, or by anything else except *the aware-ness of duty owed by one man to another and by all to God.* This principle is unmistakably illustrated in the story of the Good Samaritan.

First, a lone man on the highway is beset by disaster. Then comes the dreary procession of conventional little men, each with a good reason for not perceiving the duty which clamors at his feet. It would be a mistake to suppose the Priest and the Levite to have been bad men. They are no worse than anyone else equally trapped in the moral blindness of unimaginative and conventional legalism. There was, doubtless, a good reason in their minds for the elaborate side steps they took, if no more than an understandable desire to avoid the nuisance of ritual impurity which they might contract should they even touch the shadow of one who looked dead and might even be dead. Their service in synagogue or temple was, after all, a greater good, one which might be imperilled, were they to be involved in the wretched affairs of this unknown. So they step elaborately, yet not without regret, to the other side, and so escape even the shadow of contamination, perhaps even reminding themselves that one cannot play with pitch without getting dirty.

Finally, one comes, with amazing freedom to see the real situation. He sees; he stops; and, even though by no stretch of the imagination could a Samaritan be held to have any responsibility whatever for a Jew, he perceives a duty and performs it. And, amazingly, in the very act, a community is born. There are no longer two unrelated individuals. There is a human society. And the root of transformation lies in what the Samaritan saw in the situation. He saw need, a capacity to respond to need, and consequent duty. The Master need hardly ask *Which now of these three, thinkest thou, was neighbor unto him that fell among the thieves?* The answer is perfectly obvious; what differentiated the "neighbor" from the casual passer-by is the former's awareness of duty.

We would do well, for a moment, to apply this parable to our own affairs. Some of us are likely to use the word "community" simply in the sense of locality. An adventurous investor buys a tract of land, subdivides it, lays out streets, provides some basic services, erects some houses, and then advertises the houses for sale, calling it "this desirable community" or "this modern community" or this something-or-other community. He names it so because the word "community" has most agreeable overtones for many people, and suggests, at least, what lies latent in any group of houses. But one may question how seriously he intends to use the word, for like the word "vocation" and some others of the great words of our tongue, "community" has lost its rich meaning in much common use. Or it may be that he uses it simply as an alternative to some balder phrase—"a community of homes" sounds a lot more attractive than "an aggregation of houses for sale."

If this realtor had stopped to think much about it, he probably would have remembered what most of us have learned, that *locality* does not necessarily mean *community*. Mr. Eliot, that distinguished Churchman-poet, puts the question into the mouth of the Stranger, who asks:

> What is the meaning of this city?
> Do you huddle close together because you love each other?
> What will you answer? "We all dwell together
> To make money from each other?" or "This is a Community"? [1]

The answer we make to this question cannot be one equating community with mere locality or propinquity. As the jungle implacably reclaims every foot of man's cleared ground unless he exercises perpetual vigilance to keep the land cleared, so a subtle force in life invades and captures every city of man except for the watch and ward of men of good will, who know that a city or a community does not just happen, but is created by the will of men resolute in desiring a true human community and in keeping it.

Some will say that this is certainly true about any purely geographic community, but that the human community, sharing propinquity, is not really comparable to a jungle clearing. The human values, exuded like the sweet sweat of bees, will continually regenerate the community and keep it true and fit for man.

But this is simply not so. There is no lesson of experience more pitilessly clear than this—that men, in their human association, get what they want. It is, no doubt, part of divine judgment that this should be true. We have got to choose what we want; and our choices are real ones, for we get what we choose. If men want an all-powerful state they can achieve it, with all its massed power,

---

[1] T. S. Eliot, *The Rock* (New York, Harcourt, Brace & Co., 1934), pp. 30-31. Used by permission of the publisher.

obedience, and conformity. We have seen just such desires and their tragic fulfillment; nobody, reading history or remembering the events of the last twenty years, will be under any illusion about this. What men want by way of their association is as important as their wanting the association.

A community requires a place, a locality, and it requires, of course, people. But it is always more than a place and more than the people.

It is a network of obligations shared, a web of responsibilities and freedoms accepted and sustained by the will of free men. A community requires place and people; but it has imperative need also for freedom within itself, for the privilege of offering itself, and for judgment over and beyond its own ends and needs. Freedom, Offering, Judgment—these are the absolute necessities of a true community.[2]

There was a local collection of people on the road from Jerusalem to Jericho—all the makings of a community. But the community did not appear until duty was seen and accepted. This is the first great Christian insight.

The second insight is that there is a fundamentally *given* quality about these duties. They arise, as we might say, out of the nature of men and our relationships to one another. Indeed, the duties and the relationships are hopelessly bound together; a duty is simply what a man "has to do" when he perceives a relationship. And man, in his creation, is a certain somebody in relationship to other somebodies. He is the son of one, the brother of another, the neighbor of yet another, the child of God (although this cannot be taken for granted). These and myriad more relationships are the conditions of our existence. We could no more exist without them than we could exist without oxygen. They are given factors. And with them come the corresponding duties.

The Declaration of Independence reflects a sense of this givenness in the tranquil assumption of the "self-evident" truths that "all men are created equal, that they are endowed by their creator with certain inalienable rights, that among these are life, liberty, and the pursuit of happiness." It goes on to place the function of government in a certain perspective relative to those given quanti-

[2] S. F. Bayne, Jr., *The Optional God*, (New York, Oxford University Press, 1953), p. 52. Used by permission of the publisher.

ties: "to secure these rights, governments are instituted among men, deriving their just powers from the consent of the governed."

This perspective and its Christian background we will examine more closely in the next section; it is mentioned now only to underline this massive and central dogma of our American tradition, that the foundations of political community are laid by God in our creation, not voted into existence by a human legislature. They are "given quantities," the conditions of our very existence. Such has been the American tradition, and such, of course, is the Christian faith from which the American tradition draws its fundamental beliefs.

It is at this point that much of the confusion about "community" arises. The Christian, to whom the fact of creation is a living truth, finds no difficulty in accepting these conditions and their duties as part of the scheme of a rational universe. But the atheist or the determined agnostic—particularly, perhaps, one with an over-developed veneration for experimental science—has real and deep difficulties about this. His dogmas seem to forbid him to believe in any such givenness about human life and its circumstances.

He is consequently driven either to discredit the duties of man to man, or, more commonly, to find the roots for them in either "an instinctive mode of human behavior" (which is really only a rose by another name), or else in constructions of purely human intelligence and government. The rights of man? To the Christian, they are nothing less than the gift of God and inescapable attributes of humanity. To the unbelieving man they present a real problem, for they seem to be the precarious favor of a constitution or a legislature with no more robust reality than any other political guarantee has; and they can be swept away with the same ease as that with which they were proclaimed.

Perhaps for this very reason the warmest supporters of human rights are quite often unbelieving men who fight all the harder for them, almost in proportion as they feel such rights to depend solely on human initiative. The danger of an accepted belief in God's gift of dignity and freedom to man is that we then take the gift for granted, forgetting that nations need to live up to what God has given lest they come under His judgment. It is to our shame that the Church is sometimes laggard in bearing witness to these things, and that God not uncommonly *shaves with a hired razor,* as Isaiah noted in the case of the Assyrians (7:20).

It is, however, with Christian witness that we are basically concerned here. When we come to examine the nature of living in a community, we must begin by finding the duties that are hidden in the community itself. Who are these people? What are their circumstances? In what relationship do they stand, to me, to one another, to God? These are the essential beginning questions, to which the answers are given in terms of the duties of the Christian as he works these duties out in service to his community.

Finally, the great gospel images of yeast, salt, and light emphasize the unique quality of the Christian's participation in his community. The Christian is not simply a critic or a spectator; he is not simply one who knows the truth about the community; he is one who, in St. John's phrase, *does the truth.* More than this, in doing the truth, the Christian always stands in a peculiar relationship to the community of which he is a part. They used to say about the Church, in the beginning years of its life, that it was "in the world, yet not of the world." This is a witness again to the peculiar relationship between the Christian and his community, a relationship suggested by the simple and vivid images our Lord uses.

Yeast is different from the dough in which it works; salt derives its virtue from the fact that it is different from the meat which it preserves; light invades darkness from outside, not sharing the nature of the darkness. What is suggested by these images except the fact that the Christian is "in the world, yet not of it"?

Clearly, this unique relationship should not mean that the Christian thereby abstains from full participation in his community. Indeed, his sense of duty ought to be all the clearer because of the deeper insights of Christian faith into the nature of a community. The images, however, suggest a certain quality about Christian participation which is worth examining more closely.

THE ATTRIBUTES OF A TRUE COMMUNITY

I suggested above that there are three essential attributes of a true community—Freedom, Offering, Judgment. Each of these words is a biblical word, and each is richly and deeply conditioned by the Christian revelation; and in each is hidden a special quality of Christian participation in community life.

A community without freedom in its very tissues is inconceivable to the Christian. A mob, an army, a herd—these are ways in which we describe different kinds of involuntary associations of people. We reserve the word "community" to describe a voluntary association of people, living together and sharing a common life and tradition. They choose to live thus in community, accepting both its limitations and privileges, for the sake of achieving something greater than what the sum of their individual freedom offers.

More than this, a wider and deeper freedom ought to be one of the products of a true community. We discipline our freedom, individually, even to the point of curbing it sharply, for the sake of producing a community life that will in the end enhance our individual freedoms. We willingly, for example, accept the restrictions of the law or the necessity of taxes, for we recognize that only by accepting these limitations can a true community exist. We do it gladly, for we understand that law and taxes are the necessary price we pay for passable roads and peaceful streets, for schools, for all of the common wealth of community life. Thus, as we understand it, a limitation of individual freedom results ultimately in a greater freedom for the community and for ourselves.

A community requires *Offering as well as Freedom—that is to say, the community must exist for something beyond itself, if it is to be a true community.* Nobody would deny that self-interest is a commanding factor in community life. We all want a higher level of life for ourselves, and we know that only by having well-organized and cooperative communities can we have what we want. But we also recognize that our self-interest inescapably requires that all of our activities and our goods shall serve some satisfying moral end.

The question "what is the point of it all?" lies at the heart of every community as well as every individual's life. If we say that all this prodigious economic and social and political activity is only to make life more pleasant for ourselves, we understand that we are only postponing the real question. What makes a thing pleasant to ourselves is that we feel it is inherently worthwhile. If we say that the end is not to be our own satisfaction, but that of our neighbor or our children, again we are simply postponing the real question.

Man's basic question is "To whom, and for what, may I offer what I am and what I do? Who is to judge it, receive it, evaluate it, fulfill it, perfect it?" A constituent element of a true community is the answer to such questions as these, an answer that says in effect "This community exists to offer itself and its goods to ———— for the following ends ————." The job of filling in the blanks is the most urgent and pressing question before the twentieth century.

Lastly, a community is *a place of Judgment—that is to say, the higher end which the community exists to serve is always, in part at least, a law by which the community is judged, and judges itself.* Again, what distinguishes a community from a herd or a mob is precisely this sense of judgment running through all that we do and all that we are. The laws of a community depend, in part, on force for their effect; but only in part. The major sanction for law arises from a basic conviction, shared widely enough by the community, that the law is right, and the command to obey it is justified. This is a form of judgment.

Even clearer are the appeals to the unwritten laws by which a community governs its life. Written law can cover only the minority of offenses, the obvious ones. Most of our life is governed by unwritten law, by the accepted standards of life and judgment that are shared by the members of the community from their youth upward. A true community, then, is always the servant of an ideal; it exists to offer itself for a greater end than its own life, and in so doing accepts standards for its own life which it does not itself create.

THE CHRISTIAN CONCEPT OF COMMUNITY IN ACTION

These three necessities of true community are familiar lessons to the Christian. They are lessons that are learned, in the first instance, from the Holy Communion itself. For twenty centuries, Christian men and women have joined in the truest of all communities—that of the Lord with His people at the altar. As we have joined in the liturgy, we have experienced all three of these central necessities. We have come *freely* to *offer* "ourselves, our souls and bodies," and to make that offering with Christ and through Him, an action which means accepting His *judgment* on us and on our fellowship. As the Church has rehearsed these three great axioms, Sunday by Sunday, we have come to see how the Holy Communion is the truest community of all. It is no wonder, therefore, that the Christian turns from the altar to the world, and is impelled to bring out into the world what he has learned at the altar.

This is far more than an attractive theory; it is a description of what happens when the Church and her people do their work well. Christians take their part in the activities of neighborhood or city just as other citizens do: we belong to the same organizations, we take our turn at responsible leadership, we try to carry our end of the load. All the while, however, as we do these common tasks, we have the privilege, at least, of importing into the common life of the community attitudes and values which are not necessarily native to the community at all, but which are really born in our experience of the spirit-filled community of the altar.

The clearest illustrations of this process are often quite simple and commonplace ones. For example, a parish study group decides to explore the public library and finds astonishing gaps in its collection; timidity and a lack of funds have combined, as so often they do, to limit the selection of books or even to eliminate certain kinds of books altogether. The group makes its feelings known and even ventures to offer help in the purchase of new books.

Or the "community-study" section of a parish council discovers that, for many factory girls in a downtown neighborhood, there is no place where they can eat their lunches brought from home except on the job in the plant itself. The parish hall is opened to them; and groups of parishioners greet them and make them welcome.

In another instance, when a Japanese family moves into a sensitive, white neighborhood, and meets the all-too-familiar difficulties—social boycott, threats, anonymous letters, and all the rest of the apparatus of cowardly resentment, Church people give the lead to organizing a neighborhood committee, where fears and ignorances are threshed out and reconciliation is made possible.

Of such things—small, personal, inconsequential—is the kingdom of God. For what is at work here but the yeast, the salt, the light, the memory of the altar? By these things are directions changed, and deeper thought and understanding created. Many times a community tolerates a social condition subversive of its own good simply because it is not aware of it, because it has lived with the situation so long that it has accepted it. What is needed is the pinch of imagination, of concern, which preserves the body of the community, and the sense of offering and judgment which bring into the community the qualities it desperately needs—sympathy, forgiveness, penitence, and brotherliness.

Most frequently, our participation is in positive ways. Often we find, or we can help to establish, agencies through which our community can look at itself as a whole and plan wisely to meet its needs—councils for social welfare, city planning commissions, councils of churches and the like. Church people ought to feel a deep responsibility for such agencies and the establishment of them, because through such broad thinking and planning, with all major interests represented, we can help ourselves avoid the danger of overlapping and conflicting groups—the sub-communities—into which our life is often divided. The Church ought to be, and often is, an excellent nursery for such broad and unified planning, for it is, by its very nature, a kind of super-community which holds together and integrates all the separate, smaller groups—social, business, educational, political—into which we are divided.

Sometimes our participation is by abstinence—by withholding ourselves from community activities and thus bearing the most effective witness we can to Christian convictions. A neighborhood club adopts a policy of exclusion of Jewish citizens, a policy that offends our sense of justice and deepest convictions about democracy. A protest—even withdrawal—seems the only positive step we can take, at least for the time being; and we reluctantly say this, only to find that actually a majority of our fellow-members feel exactly as we do, but lacked the courage or the constancy to say so.

A parents' group wishes to raise money for school equipment, and elects to do so through a community-wide gambling scheme. Objection is rightly made to this by Christian members, not from a mere prejudice against gambling alone, but from a conviction that the problems of the school are of far greater weight and dignity than such a proposal recognizes, and that the energy and leadership of the parents' association should be directed to the root of the problem. It turns out that a majority of the group have felt this all along, and needed only the stubborn witness of a few to find the courage to say so.

Small matters?—of course, they are small. A community and its life is made up of small matters, mostly; but small matters, which a cap-full of conviction and a sense of judgment can often bring to a good resolution. And where there is faithfulness in such small things, there is the likelihood of faithfulness in the greater things as well.

Yeast, salt, light, the altar—these are the Christian elements. Self-righteousness is not one of them. Christians are sometimes lumped as part of the "better element" in a community. Christians would be the first to say that, indeed, Christ and His Gospel are the "better element"; but their participation is certainly not on any basis of pride or condescension. The Christian has no feeling that he is necessarily a better person than his neighbor. *He serves a better master;* and he believes that if his neighbor did so too, the life of the community would thereby be enriched and deepened beyond measure. But yeast becomes part of the dough in which it works, and salt disappears into the food, and light spreads everywhere until the darkness is done away; just so does the Christian identify himself fully with his community, confident that the holiness and power of God will, in the end, win the victory.

One more comment ought, perhaps, be added—that the hall-mark of Christian participation in a community is not necessarily that of frenzied activity. We do our part; and it is a matter of our duty to God that we do our part. But it may well be that quiet moments of solitary prayer, or the regular intercession of a group of men and women whose only community participation can be a weekly hour in common prayer for their community, are the most valuable forms of witness and service we can give. An ounce of consecrated thought may be worth a pound of unconsidered activity. Just as the church building serves a community simply by being there as a reminder, a silent, voiceless admonition, so is the Christian's part in the community quite often that of a few thoughtful and reflective words rather than feverish multiplication of group activities. As always in life, it is quality rather than quantity which counts. The essential word, spoken at the right time by the thoughtful Christian, may be a far greater contribution to the welfare and happiness of a community than hours of busyness.

Therefore, community concerns and affairs ought to be much in our thoughts and prayers, in church and out of it. The preacher who does not continually have his own community in mind, and often in word, in his preaching and conversation, is not fulfilling his function. The women's guild or men's club which does not spend a high proportion of its time in reflection and study about its own community is again likely to be failing in its duty.

For the final truth about these matters is that they are matters for the community of Christians, not the individual alone. Community matters are church matters; there is no way to draw a line between them. The ultimate unit of the Church's life is the parish—a town, a community, a section of the countryside, with its multitudes of people and of interests. This is the parish, as our Church understands it—all these people, whether they are in our congregation or in some other or in none. "The Church," said Bishop F. R. Barry to a group of us once, "is the one institution in society which exists mainly for the sake of those who do not belong to it."

The community comes to its highest point of fulfillment in the parish church. There, before the altar, all community concerns are seen in their true light; there, under the judgment of our Lord, the life of our community reaches its deepest expression. Church and community are but two sides of the same coin, where Christian witness and participation are what they should be, and where Christians understand what a community really is. Let no church then be afraid of being a "community" church, in the full sense of that word, for the community belongs to God, as the Church does, and He wills that they shall be one in obedience to His purposes.

PART FOUR

National and International Life

CHAPTER EIGHTEEN

The Churchman and the State

IN AN EARLIER chapter we thought about some of the responsibilities of Christian living in the field of political action. The Churchman or Churchwoman has duties as a citizen in a democracy. They are not necessarily different duties from those of any other citizen. The difference is that to the Churchman they are Christian duties, and part of our ministry as Christians in a democratic society.

This present section will deal not so much with duties as with attitudes—the attitudes of the Churchman toward the state, which underlie and inform his duties. It is perhaps important to point out that the heading of this section is not "Church and State." Our subject is not the theoretical one of the possible relationships between the two entities; it is rather the practical question of the working attitudes of the Christian citizen toward the political body of which he is a member.

This book is content to accept the general American tradition of "the separation of church and state." This subject has no doubt been debated from the beginning of time; and doubtless there is no one, theoretical answer to it which would be satisfactory to everybody. Certainly our American tradition has never reached or attempted to reach a solution in the sense of an absolute and final answer. The American tradition has been, in the main, simply an attempt to find a practical way of getting along with what is admittedly a difficult problem. That practical way is the way of keeping any organized religion separate from the organized political life of the nation. The separation is by no means complete; the doctrine has been established by a long series of small steps—court decisions, laws, provisions of the Constitution—which have, little by little (and sometimes in contradictory directions), built up certain habits of mind and action which we lump together in the phrase "the American tradition of separation."

However, it is important to note that, even though most of us would readily accept this tradition, the tradition actually raises almost as many questions as it solves. At least it does not answer the basic questions which we ask. In particular, it does not answer the question of the place that the state occupies in God's scheme of things.

This is no theoretical problem either. The memory of World War II is still sharp and shocking to us, with its vivid contrast between the idolatry of the state and a different attitude, which was in our blood stream and yet which we found it hard sometimes to put into words. Even today we are aware of a vast range of opinion among our own contemporaries: from those who seem almost as idolatrous of the state as the Nazis were, to mysterious religious sects at the other extreme which appear almost to be anarchists with no opinion of any religious value of the state. What theory can be put forward as the historic Christian attitude toward the state, to guide us in our own attitudes?

THE CHRISTIAN ATTITUDE TOWARD THE STATE

Most Christian thinking would doubtless start with the famous statement by St. Paul in his Epistle to the Romans (13:1-3): *Let every person be subject to the governing authorities. For there is no authority except from God, and those that exist have been instituted by God. Therefore he who resists the authorities resists what God has appointed, and those who resist will incur judgment.*

This Epistle, which represents probably the first attempt at a systematic Christian theology, was written in all likelihood during the reign of Nero who was himself the embodiment of tyranny and of all that St. Paul, as well as we, would call bad government. Nevertheless, the principle is quite clear to St. Paul; all power comes from God and God entrusts that power to and through the legitimate agencies of government, for the punishment of evil and for the establishment of a society within which a peaceful and a just life is possible.

In point of fact, this is a theory of the divine right, or at least the divine appointment, of legitimate government. And while there have been many theories as to *how* God entrusts the power to our rulers (by inheritance, by race, by the agreement of the nobility, by the consent of the governed), the principle would certainly be a central and unvarying one in Christian thought down through the ages—*that all power comes from God and that, therefore, the true and right administration and embodiment of that power has a most fundamental and final claim on the loyalty and obedience of all of us who compose the state.*

In medieval times, Pope and Emperor argued interminably about the "how" of political power, about who had the right to select the authorities and bestow the power of government on them. The political history of western civilization since the Renaissance has been likewise marked by experiment and counter-experiment in theories of legitimate government, from the "divine right of kings" to the "dictatorship of the proletariat." Our American tradition adopted and put into practice still another theory, and a most important one in the history of nations, namely that all just government derives its powers from the consent of the governed. The "governed" do not originate the power; it is God's power. But it is only through the consent of those who are to be ruled by it that this power may be legitimately used. In the Prayer Book, we say this in the beautiful prayer For Our Country (page 36), where we ask that God "endue with the spirit of wisdom those to whom in thy Name we entrust the authority of government."

Yet, under whatever theory, Christian thought would take its start from St. Paul—*There is no authority except from God, and those that exist have been instituted by God.*

This would be a doctrine very comforting to tyrants (and it has been, time and again), except for the fact that there are two sides to it; and Christians never forgot the other side. If there is no power but of God, and if all earthly rulers are ministers of God in their stewardship of this power, then, if that power is abused, God will equally require that the tyrant be deposed and a new ruler chosen in his place. The right, even the duty, of revolution is as true and valid a part of Christian doctrine about the state as is the duty and privilege of obedience.

No less an authority than St. Thomas Aquinas, the central theologian of medieval western Christianity, said as much when he wrote, "Consequently there is no sedition in disturbing a government of this kind (i.e., tyrannical), unless indeed the tyrant's rule be disturbed so inordinately that his subjects suffer greater harm from the consequent disturbance than from the tyrant's government. Indeed it is the tyrant rather who is guilty of sedition, since he encourages discord and sedition among his subjects." (*Summa Theologica,* Part II:2, Q. 42, A. 2.)

The power of God is given to the state to use for the preservation of order and justice, and to make the good life possible. When that power is used rightly, it has the strongest of all earthly claims on our allegiance. When it is used wrongly, then it may be our duty to resist. Whether right or wrong, the state is the agency and the servant of the people, under God.

Part of the trouble is that the state must of necessity have and wield absolute power in this world, if it is to serve its true end. It can have no earthly rival. While the state may, as an act of grace, deliberately limit its power even of life and death, it must be a self-limitation. For if the power were limited, then so would be the ability of the state to fulfill the purpose for which God ordained it.

Therefore the check and discipline on the power of the state, the control of the power, must come from *within the state itself,* from the people who compose the state and direct it. Were it not for this inner check, there would be no way of establishing a higher authority whose servant the state must be.

The problem of establishing that higher authority has been one of the perennially difficult and intricate problems in history. In Western Europe, during the collapse of the classic Roman Empire, where the organized state disintegrated under the invasions and the decay of civil life, the Church was in fact the only organized body which could assume authority and use it legitimately. It is therefore no surprise that in the West, particularly under such strong popes as Hildebrand, the Church became a state, or even a super-state, insisting on the higher authority of God not by the Church influencing the state, but by the Church becoming a super-state.

The principle of the higher authority was sound enough. But most of us, looking back on the medieval experiment, would say that the methods used were heartbreakingly wrong. What resulted was to make political tools out of the very sacraments themselves; the holiest things of the Church and of Christianity became the weapons of secular power; and the end result was the near destruction of the very soul of the Church itself. And the shadow of this experiment is very long, touching us even today in our recurring dislike of any confusion of church and state.

In the Eastern Empire, where the secular state—the Empire—persisted for a far longer time and more realistically and recognizably than it did in the West, the Church was never involved in such a contest and assumption of power. There the Church remained essentially subsidiary to the civil power, even though it was the established church of the Empire and of the nation states which succeeded the Empire. This, too, has cast a long shadow of which we are mindful when we look thoughtfully at the structure and philosophy of the Orthodox Churches and their relationship to the nation states where they are established.

The point of this little detour into history is simply to underline that there is not necessarily any one, historic form of *relationship* between church and state. There is, however, a continuous and consistent *theology* of the state which stems from the attitude in the New Testament church expressed by St. Paul. All power is God's. He entrusts it to governments in order to establish the conditions necessary for the good life of His people. Governments, therefore, have a rightful claim on all of us, save when it is clear that they are not using God's power to serve God's purposes. Then it may well be that the duty of rebellion is the only duty possible to the Christian.

THE CHURCH AND DEMOCRATIC SOCIETY

This is enough about principles. Our concern is with the working attitudes we ought to have, as Christians, in our twentieth-century democracy. What we should learn from history is perhaps no more than this: that man will and should experiment widely with the form of his government, but he will always owe two duties toward it, no matter what form it may take. The duty of what the Articles of Religion call "respectful obedience to the Civil Authority, regularly and legitimately constituted" is the first one (Article XXXVII). The duty of judgment—if that is the right word to use to describe the higher authority which Christians feel must always check and discipline the power of the state—is the other one.

A government like ours presents both unique opportunities and also unique problems in the fulfillment of those duties. Perhaps the supreme opportunity or advantage is the ease with which the power of the state can be checked and disciplined. The misuse of power by a democratically-elected legislature is vastly easier to correct than the same abuse by an entrenched or hereditary ruler or group. We feel that the closer a government can come to the people who hold the true sovereignty, the better it is for all concerned, principally because there is then the greatest freedom and opportunity for opinion and judgment to function.

We have our own problems in this respect, in the dangers of a subservient legislature afraid to develop a policy because of the need of popular favor. Part of the practical art of government is the provision of sufficient stability and independence to our rulers so that they may rule, and not simply hold the office.

Our form of government has recognized the need for judgment and has provided for it. The checks and balances in our constitution are an illustration. The whole system of elective offices is a most vivid illustration. So too is the tradition of the separation of church and state. This tradition is not simply a disagreeable necessity; it is also, and far more importantly, a clear provision for freedom of judgment in our society. Like all our civil liberties, freedom of religion is written into our Constitution in order that the path of judgment may always be free and unimpeded.

Thus it would seem that a government like ours offers a unique opportunity for effective and swift correction. It offers, however, a unique problem when it comes to the other duty of respectful obedience. Personal loyalty to a monarch or a group is a lot clearer to see, and often a lot easier to fulfill, than the same loyal obedience to a democratic republic like ours. A king who inherits power, or an oligarchy or party who legitimately assume power, may indeed be no more legitimate, and have no greater claim on us, than a President and Congress which we ourselves elect. But it is a great deal easier, psychologically, to be loyal to a person or family or group than it is to one's next-door neighbor and several hundred more like him, whom one has elected and who can be fired at the next election. This is part of the spiritual problem of a democracy, and there is no easy answer to it.

The privileges of a democratic state like ours require almost superhuman discipline and responsibility on the part of the citizens— that is our unique problem. There is nothing which can possibly prevent the American State from deifying itself, making a god out of itself, except the vitality, the watchfulness, the dutiful concern

264 ·

and care of its responsible citizens, and the vigor and courage of its religious institutions.

If power is not to be abused, if the power of God is to be used for the end which God intends, then the political responsibilities of the Church, of Church men and women, should have a very high priority on our consciences. To have the imagination which will help us to give intelligent as well as loyal obedience to those to whom we have entrusted authority, and to have the intelligent vigilance and courage in protest to guard against the abuse of that power—these are the urgent necessities of good Christian citizenship.

What part shall the Church then play in a democratic society? We do not wish to see the Church pretend to be a kind of superstate. We do not wish to see the holy things of our religion twisted and distorted into political instruments. No more do we want to see the Church become simply a domestic pet of the state, tolerated and fed because it helps to guarantee docile conformity. In the past, the Church has often seemed to fall into one of those two roles—either to be the state or to be simply the captive of the state. We feel that the Church has a greater part to play than either of these alternatives. It is a part difficult to define neatly or exactly, yet it is clear enough in practice. It is the part suggested by six great Gospel words; and the remainder of this chapter is an attempt to think about those words and the implications of them for Christian citizenship.

THE CHURCH'S DUTY TO DEMOCRATIC SOCIETY

The first great word is *Yeast—the leaven in the lump* (I Cor. 5:6)—*the leaven in the meal* (Matt. 13.33).[1] On our Lord's lips this was a parable of the Kingdom, as so often He portrays the Kingdom as a small and unimpressive quantity—the seed, salt, a little flock—which yet has an effect and a fruit incomparably greater than itself. The little bit of yeast mixed into the great inert mass of the dough penetrates and vivifies so that the whole is leavened and given life.

The parable is all the more suggestive because, in Holy Scripture, leaven is commonly understood with an unfavorable connotation. Because yeast works mysteriously and secretly, it was more often ex-

---

[1] Recall now the earlier discussion of this word, as well as "salt" and "light," in the chapter on community duties.

pressive of a sinister influence—the *leaven of the Pharisees,* or the *leaven of malice and wickedness* of which St. Paul speaks. But it was precisely this element of secret penetration which our Lord was anxious to express, for this is the method of the Kingdom. The Kingdom is not preached nor lived by open show and advertisement. The work of the Kingdom is done by the silent and the inconsiderable, by the quiet word and the unspoken witness, and by the steady, secret growth of the life-giving cell which penetrates and explodes the heavy, unresponsive mass.

Certainly, at the great creative moments of her history, this is an excellent parable of the Church. It was supremely true of the early Church when, under persecution and in quiet, often in secret, the Gospel was preached and lived by little groups scattered throughout the body of the Empire. And the end result was the leavening of the Empire and ultimately the establishment of the Church and the Gospel as the accepted religious institutions of the Empire.

After that time, the image of the yeast needed to be reapplied. The truth of the Kingdom still acted like yeast in the lump, only the lump more often than not was now the Church as well as the world, and the yeast was a minority within the Church. Yet this has not always been true; and within our own memory are times when, under the oppression of totalitarian power, more than a minority within the Church regained for the necessary moment her leavening role.

Perhaps the most significant thing about this leavening process is that the yeast seems to give life not to itself but to the mass surrounding it. The important thing is not that the yeast increases. The important thing is that the yeast changes the character of its host. To transfer this image to the Church and the Empire, the astonishing thing about those early centuries was not simply the growth in numbers of the Church, or its increasing power. It was the way in which the Gospel, preached and lived in the Church, gave life to the old civic duties and virtues which had long lost their initial vitality.

Christianity did not invent new duties; Christianity invested the old duties with a new vitality and a new significance. The responsible use of power; the obligation of civic virtue; the debt that power owed to the weak; the function of the state as serving the freedom and dignity of man—these ancient truths were seen once again as not empty words or inherited institutions, but as living relationships and responsibilities. The way to be a good Christian was to be a good ruler or a good citizen; and this fresh consciousness of living duty was like a blood transfusion in the veins of the dying Empire.

As then, so always. The Church's great gift to secular society, when we are doing our true work and not merely being carried on society's shoulders, is to lead men and women to see the timeless obligations of civilization in a new light and with new eagerness. And this may well be put down as one of the unchanging responsibilities of the Churchman toward the state—*to accept and understand his public duties, and his work as a citizen, as part and parcel of his whole and single ministry as a child of God and a member of Christ.*

We have already talked about some of the implications of this in the life of Christian citizens as voters and in public office. But the word has implications for the congregation as well as the individual. What does a boy or girl learn about good citizenship as he grows up in his Christian education? Does a man's membership in his parish's men's club make any difference in the kind of government his community has? Is the voice of the Church, in convention and synod, clear in pointing out the Christian implications of government policy, and in exploring the areas of life where the power of the state ought be at work to create a fairer society for men and women in which to live and work? These are some of the questions which the word "yeast" suggests, in thinking about the role of the Church in the state.

The second word is *Salt*, as used by our Lord to His disciples in the Sermon on the Mount (St. Matthew 5:13). Like yeast, salt is secret and inconsiderable. It works not for its own sake, but for something quite other than itself. Its vocation is ultimately to disappear, in its own right, in order that something healthy and good may happen in the body that is salted.

It is, of course, of salt as a preservative that our Lord was primarily thinking (although the suggestion of flavor is also legitimately there). Food is made and kept fit to eat by salt. Something like this function was to be served by the disciples and their teaching—it was to be their work to give to the ancient and changeless truths a continuing and vital freshness, precisely as He Himself had done in the Sermon on the Mount in which this saying about salt is embedded. Once again, the function of the Gospel is not primarily the introduction of new truth; the Gospel transforms and purifies old truth, and gives it new life.

Here again the historical application to the Church is obvious enough. Indeed, in the slow rotting-away of the old Empire, the Church was to serve a unique function in history. It was through the Church, and through the Church alone, that the wisdom and virtue of antiquity was preserved and transmitted. The ancient Roman law, that great trophy of classic times, did not disappear under the terrible tide of the barbarian invasions. It persevered and lived, and was passed on to flower again, solely because of the saving life of the Church in Western Europe.

As with the law, so with the virtues which men had painfully and slowly learned. They were not forgotten; they were preserved under Christian names and in Christian dress so that they might continue to enrich the lives of men. And even to this day when boys and girls learn the manly virtues and graces, they are learning lessons that were old in Christ's time, and which have been saved for them because there was a salt at work.

But the image of salt is not simply an historical one. It is still a living image of the work of the Church within the body of secular society. For a large part of the Church's work is that of being the truly conservative body within the state. The Church does not ever forget, in belief or practice, the immutable laws and truths about human behavior and social organization. Fashions in politics change; one generation's meat is another generation's poison. And in this constant fluctuation of values and goals it is well that the Church is there continually to remind mankind of basic meanings and unchanging realities. For instance, obedience can very easily sour into panic, under tyranny, unless it be continually freshened by the remembrance that God has ordained obedience as the other side of freedom. Just so can freedom of thought degenerate into captious opposition, when men forget the common life of humanity and the obligations of charity one to another. These are instances of a central function of the Church and of Churchmen.

The question of civil rights is a pertinent example of an area in a democracy where salt is needed. Any democracy—any government for that matter—is likely to forget the origin of civil liberties, and eventually come to think that they are courtesies which are granted, in easy times, by an indulgent legislature or a kindhearted constitution, and can easily be suspended or revoked in times of stress. The wise architects of our constitution put those liberties where it is hard to tamper with them—in the Constitution itself. It is well that they did so, for our temptation to withhold them or eliminate them is sometimes very great.

In these times, when civil liberties are under very great and searching question and the temptation to tinker with them is strong, the duty of the Church is unmistakable and immediate, to speak for them, to insist on them, to guard them, and to remind the state of where those liberties are born and what they signify. The concern of the Church for these rights is not at all a matter of liberalism. It is a duty imposed on us by our Lord. If we in the Church were not concerned with the stature and dignity of man in human society, we would be, as Christ said, no longer *good for anything except to be thrown out and trodden under foot by men.*

The third word is *Light*—in the same context as the saying about salt, Christ says to His disciples, *you are the light of the world.*

Light is still one more of these suggestive Gospel parables. It is so suggestive and so universal that it hardly needs more than mention. By the way they lived, the disciples were to make the truth about life and the Kingdom visible to men. Yet they were to do it in such a way that God would be glorified and not they themselves. There was to be a kind of unselfish audacity, a bold humility about them and their speech and life.

A more exciting and exact parable of the life and work of the Church in the state could hardly be imagined. For what have people the right to expect of the Church, save that in its teaching and household they may come to see what they most deeply need to see about the true relationships they have to one another. If all they find in the Church is a pale reflection of their own current prejudices, then the Church has failed them. But if people, struggling with the problems of human brotherhood in a divided world, can find in the brotherhood of the altar a deeper and clearer understanding of our common nature under God, then true witness will have been borne. This is light.

So is it light when people hear even uncomfortable and unpleasant truths proclaimed from our pulpits, and accepted by Christians in honest discipline. All men talk of reconciliation, and few dare really believe it; and the greatest service the Church can render to the cause of reconciliation is not simply to talk about it, but to show that we believe it, and mean seriously and at real cost to practice it. This is light.

Social evils do not often exist because people choose them. They exist because we are not really aware of them as evils. Child labor, for example, was not imposed on hard-hearted citizens by wicked employers as a plot against children. It was tolerated and permitted to exist because not enough people saw how horrible it was—most did not see it at all, really. But there came men and women, and Christians in the forefront, who did see the wickedness of it, and the cruelty in which little boys and girls were trapped. They saw it and they told what they saw, standing by their guns until the whole, sluggish body of the state could not help but see what they saw. This is light.

There is always a frontier, where light is needed, and where the adventurous imagination and the stubborn witness of leaders can light the way for the insensitive and unimaginative mass of mankind to follow. This frontier is the place for the Church, and for all the voluntary associations of people; for it is in such free associations as the Church and the innumerable groups who fight for their particular concerns that the health of the state really lies.

This is not said in any sneering tone of judgment on the work of state agencies. We are all under judgment—and the Church under the sharpest judgment of all because of the light which Christ gave us. It is good that God gave us civil government, that we may do together, what, as individuals, we cannot do for ourselves. But it is also good that God set at the heart of the state a light which is not the creature of the state at all, but God's servant. This light shows us what we are really like and what we are really doing and leaving undone, and points the way to a greater truth and a more enduring justice. To bear this light is what we get baptized for.

The fourth word is *Judgment*—the mysterious theme which appears and reappears in the pages of the Gospels. *You who have followed me will also sit on twelve thrones judging the twelve tribes of Israel* (Matt. 19:28). *He who hears you hears me, and he who rejects you rejects me, and he who rejects me rejects him who sent me* (Luke 10:16). *I will give you the keys of the kingdom of heaven, and whatever you bind on earth shall be bound in heaven, and whatever you loose on earth shall be loosed in heaven* (Matt. 16:19).

This is a strange light which suddenly flames up now and again in the Gospels. The truth of God works in secret; it works by love and humble service; it works by persuasion and not by fear. Yet at the heart of the Gospel there is a bright sword which is no symbol of gentle and affectionate secrecy, but of open and uncompromising judgment. There are times when the work of God can only be done by drawing a clear line—in the eyes of God one choice is wrong and another choice is right, and man must not hesitate between those choices.

This judgment may be, and often is, a judgment on the Church as on the world. And the cost of the judgment is one which must be borne with integrity and courage by the Church. For the Church is not the judge; God is the judge. The Church is the place of judgment, and Churchmen are the people under judgment. True Churchmen welcome it and are fearless in accepting it for themselves, and in bearing their witness to it in the world.

This may seem fanciful language, smacking a little of the danger of hypocrisy. For what honorable man likes to pose as a judge and divider? Nor is this what the Gospel requires. Even our Lord Himself disclaimed that role in this world. Judgment is God's, for the truth alone is God's.

But it is our vocation to bear unfailing witness to the absolutes which God has ordained. When those absolutes are disregarded or contradicted by the practice of the state, or in the life of citizens, then the Church has no alternative. If it is to keep its soul, it must speak the truth; there is no more solemn obligation than this; and in the end there is no greater service than this. Church people need not flinch from speaking the truth in love. The Gospel will gain all the more in the respect of the world; and, God helping us, we can do no other, if the truth of the Gospel be really accepted of us, and we mean what we say when we promise, in our confirmation vow, "to follow Jesus Christ as our Lord and Saviour."

This is strong as well as fanciful language. Is the Church, then, to spend its time denouncing the latest acts of Congress? I doubt that such denunciation is generally either necessary or useful. For the real power in a democracy lies in the people. In the long run it is our goals and hopes which our legislatures must know and satisfy; and judgment lies on us citizens, long before it lies on those who need our favor.

Kathleen Bliss said to the Anglican Congress in 1954, "It is no longer a question . . . as it was for so many centuries, of controlling the power of the few over against the helplessness of the many; it is the question of the wills and purposes of the whole citizenry, of the desires of ordinary men and women which shape society and press upon the State—these are the new power. Church and Nation thus becomes as important a relationship as Church and State, and it is not to kings and potentates but to ordinary men and women and the representatives they elect that the Church must speak of the sovereignty of God and its restraint, the only ultimate restraint, upon the people's will. We cannot with impunity say, 'What the people want is right.'" [2]

Legislative decisions need to be scrutinized, and the judgment of God doubtless applies to what governments do. But the first place of judgment is not there; it is in the hearts of plain people, like ourselves. What do we seek? What do we want our government to be and to do? What are the great ends the state exists to serve? What do we think are the important purposes in life? These questions are the primary questions in a democracy. And it is to these questions that the Church must speak with clarity and power, content to bear the judgment of God on our own working desires and ways as well as to proclaim that judgment on those outside the Church.

The fifth word is *Neighbor,* the word for the person to whom we owe the obligation of love, the word illustrated by the story of the Good Samaritan. This parable was discussed earlier, when we were thinking about our community responsibilities, and we need not dwell on the details of the unfortunate traveller beset by thieves, of the callous disregard of the officials, of the overwhelming and unmeasured generosity of the stranger. The point of the parable is to illuminate the universality of neighborliness—every living person is my neighbor. What we need to see is that what really happened on the road from Jerusalem to Jericho is not that the Samaritan creates a beautiful virtue; what happens is that the Samaritan perceives an existing relationship and an obligation which arises out of that relationship. The Samaritan does not meet a neighbor

---

[2] Read her excellent address on "The Church and the Citizen," in the *Report of the Anglican Congress* (New York: Seabury Press, 1954), p. 124.

where none existed before. The Samaritan *recognizes* a neighbor; and in that recognition perceives his duty and fulfills it.

Something like this happens in the life of the Church in the world. The Gospel does not create new duties to add to those man already owes. The Gospel adds a new significance and a new importance to old duties. The Gospel helps us to see forgotten duties. The Gospel is like a searchlight in the dark which enables men to see once again things which had been obliterated by darkness. The Gospel is a stripping naked of mankind, that we may once again see what we really are without the disguise of dress. The Gospel is a lesson in the meaning of words, suddenly illuminating their true sense and leading us to remember forgotten things.

In this, to speak of the Gospel is to speak of the Church. The relationships, the obligations and duties that constitute human society are not created by men. Legislation does not create society; God creates society in the very creation of men themselves. And the laws of society and of the state merely recognize what God has already done. It is this sense of the given character of human society which may indeed be the Church's chief contribution to political theory. Were it not for this sense, it is hard to see what possible limit could ever be set on the absolute power of the state. If the state is simply the creation of men's wills, if the state is simply a device which is adopted by those who have the power and the imagination to devise it, then man has no protection against despotism and an enforced idolatry.

The heart of the Christian insight into the nature of the state is that the state is and can be no more than a reflection of the reality that God has already established. The state can never be the master or molder of that reality; it must always be the creature and the agent of that deeper reality. The society of men, already existing in nature, precedes any state and controls it. We say all this in a somewhat subdued way in our Declaration of Independence, when we speak about those qualities with which God has already endowed humanity—the "inalienable rights." Therefore, in this way, and only in this way, is the state preserved as a servant and not the master of humanity.

The Church is a unique witness to this. Indeed it may be doubted whether there is any other authentic witness except the Church. This is a bold statement; and we will not thereby disregard the valiant witness which many men of good will have borne in all ages in heroic protest against an overweening state. Nevertheless it remains true that this is the unique witness of the Church, through its faith that God has both established and revealed this truth about humanity; that it is God's truth and not ours; that this is the way the universe is. No hypothesis on man's part can ever supplant the certainty of divine revelation; and this is the Church's stock in trade.

Thus, protest by the Church against any arrogance of the state is rooted not only in the fact that such arrogance violates our tradition or is disliked by men of humane and liberal sympathies. The Church's protest is rooted in a reality which alone is greater than the state. And the significance of this protest, at the critical moments in history, is beyond our estimation.

The supremacy of conscience in the individual citizen, for example, is a case in point. If the right of the pacifist and the conscientious objector to freedom from military service were simply a favor granted him by the government, both he and all the rest of us would be on perilous ground. But this is exactly what that right is not. What really happens is that the state recognizes an inherent right, arising out of the obligation of conscience, and a duty which mankind owes to itself to recognize and respect its own nature, as God has created us. If the state were to violate this, the Church would of necessity set itself uncompromisingly against that violation. A higher law is involved—higher because it is given in our creation and not established by some earthly legislature—and our loyalty is always to the highest laws we know.

Nobody is going to pretend that this frontier is clear. It is always cloudy and uncertain because our understanding of conscience and of duties changes as time goes on and experience teaches us more. But perhaps the chief instrument God gives us with which to test such matters is the stubborn, free conflict in which the Church boldly stands for the truth as we see it.

The final word is *Body* (as in I Cor. 12 and Ephesians 4). The Church witnesses to the greatest of all social and political truths, that, in Christ, men are members of a single and universal Body, whose life is that of God Himself—a Body which overrides and supersedes all lesser associations. Because of this Body into which we

274 ·

come through baptism and in which we live in Word and Sacrament alike, it has been given to men to know what their ultimate nature and destiny may be. In the light of this Body, all lesser loyalties and divisions are seen in their true perspective. By this Body, all nations and states are judged. By this Body, every law regulating human society must be appraised. This Body is the ultimate norm and pattern to which all human association must grow if it is to be true and lasting.

This, we suggest, may be the final and most fundamental witness the Church can ever bear, for it is nothing less than a witness to its whole true nature. Human brotherhood is established by God's creation of us; it becomes a final and living truth only in Christ and through His grace and power. To preach and live this Body day in and day out is the greatest service the Church can ever render to the state, for it is to hold up before the state the constant image of what the state itself is designed to establish and serve.

Let these words, then, teach us of the part the Church should play in the life of the state. God expects of us both respect and obedience to the legitimate authority of the state, for the state is His instrument and not simply ours alone. Yet He expects also of His Church and its members that we shall so bear ourselves, as citizens of the state, as He did, in Christ Jesus. It is not for the Church to play at being a state, or to covet worldly power. It is for the Church to be the soul of the state, continually reminding the state of what its true function is and of what its ultimate nature, under God, most truly is. It is the work of the Church to illuminate, to preserve, to vivify. It is the work of the Church to rebuke, to remind, to imagine.

And all these duties fall on the shoulders of loyal citizens like ourselves who rejoice at the privilege of our citizenship and long to fulfill its obligations. We shall have more to say presently of the spirit in which we accept and fulfill those duties. But of the attitudes and duties themselves, let the last word be from the Prayer Book—"that we and all the People, duly considering whose authority they bear, may faithfully and obediently honour them, according to thy blessed Word and ordinance." The "they" and "them" refer, first of all, to the public servants who exercise the power of God for us and for Him. But let it never be forgotten that, in a democracy like ours, every citizen is a ruler, and every citizen a servant. We do well, therefore, to pray for self-respect, and for sober and honorable stewardship of the immense power God has entrusted to us.

CHAPTER NINETEEN

The International Community

IN THE NEXT two chapters, we shall be thinking about the meaning of national and local loyalties in the life of the Churchman. Therefore it is well to spend a few pages on the attitude of Christians toward the whole international community. Here we are thinking not only of existing international bodies and organizations, like the United Nations or NATO, but of the community of people itself which underlies such organizations.

It is certainly true that there is something in the very nature of the Church which predisposes us to a special sense of the reality and importance of the international community. This special concern of ours is not always a congenial one to our fellow citizens. International organizations are suspect to many people. This is probably inevitable in a time of sharp international tension like our own. And any political or economic organization of nations, so far as it is a real meeting place of national interests and ambitions, is bound to be an arena where there are real dangers as well as real advantages.

Indeed the value of such an organization as the United Nations lies precisely in the fact that real issues are at stake and real power is being wielded, even though the safeguards of vetoes and withdrawal rob its decisions of much of their force. If the United Nations were no more than a debating society or a group of fellow idealists, it would hold little interest or meaning for our world. But, in proportion as the issues and the power are realities, so are the dangers to an inherited and established way of life.

THE CHRISTIAN AND INTERNATIONAL COMMUNITY

Congenial or not, the Churchman cannot escape this peculiar, Christian sense of the urgent reality of the international community and of his obligations to it. There are five good reasons for this.

First *he is, as a Churchman, a member of an international community far older and far more widespread than any other in human history.* For many of us Episcopalians our first trip to Canada is an interesting, exciting and somewhat disturbing experience. We have the feeling of being in a strange land, even though the language and the general flavor of life is much the same. Royalty, a different coinage, customs inspections, and a thousand more details combine to give us the sense of strangeness. This is pleasant, for it is a friendly strangeness, yet also sharp enough to remind us of the uncompromising fact of national boundaries.

But, for all that strangeness, an astonishing new sensation comes to us when we worship with our Canadian Anglican brethren in their churches. Despite a few interesting differences in the Prayer Book, it is still our book. The dress of the clergy, the order of public worship, the general pattern of life and teachings are the same. We are gratefully aware of the fact that this is really one body equally established north of the line as well as south, sharing a common life at a deeper level than the more superficial national boundaries can divide.

What is true about our American-Canadian experience is far more radically apparent when we go further afield. The Anglican Communion, this international body of nearly forty million Christians around the world, is a reality which no purely national interests could possibly divide. Those who attended the Anglican Congress in 1954 shared in an unforgettable demonstration of that great single household.

Yet this fellowship itself is only a fraction of a still wider one. The World Council of Churches and its many activities, while less unified at the heart than our Anglican Communion, embraces a vastly greater number of people, and again reveals a unity far deeper than the barriers of speech or color or flag.

Even beyond that is the diffused, yet still real, unity of all Christian people—unorganized, broken by conflicting loyalties and duties, yet still real and unforgettable. In his baptism, that most universal sacrament, the Churchman comes into a world-wide body, international and supra-national. Wherever he goes, he will find that body expressing itself in universal symbols which are greater than any local or national symbol—the Cross, the Altar, the brotherhood in Communion, the written Word of God. His missionary enterprise has taught him to share in the life of other nations. His travels, his military experiences perhaps, have brought him to see this world-wide fellowship at first hand. Once seen and understood, it cannot ever be forgotten. This fact alone would go far to explain the characteristic Christian sense of an international community.

Second, *the Churchman, as a Churchman, is part of an historic community far older than nations, and with a history in which national interests play only a subordinate role.* Not all Churchmen know this. Certainly there are many, especially in the younger sections of the country, whose awareness of Church history goes back only to the beginning of their own parish, or to 1789, or to Henry VIII. This is like saying that the history of the American people began in 1776, as though there had been no Americans before that date, no colonists, no government, no Church, no ships, no farms.

The Churchman is a member of a world-wide body whose continuous and unbroken history covers twenty centuries. His ministers have been fulfilling their duties since the Apostles' time. The prayers he says may have been written a thousand years ago (or yesterday); the laws by which he lives bear the marks of two thousand years of experience; the symbols which aid his worship have been molded in the prayers and lives of a community extending from the Bible itself.[1] It is no wonder, with this long history constantly being impressed on him in every aspect of his daily life, that he develops a different perspective on nationalism than his un-churched neighbor may have.

During most of the history of the Christian community there were no nations in our sense of the word. Most of the basic patterns of the Church's life and teaching were developed long before the modern nation came into existence. The Bible knows nothing of the self-enclosed sovereignty of the modern nation-state. Different peoples there were, and languages, and colors, and traditions, as there have been since time immemorial. Local governments were familiar, either as provinces of a greater empire, or as quasi-autono-

---

[1] Read two of the companion volumes in this series—*Chapters in Church History*, by P. M. Dawley, and *The Worship of the Church*, by M. H. Shepherd—for further elaboration of this point.

mous local units. But the independent, sovereign nation-state with which we are familiar, is hardly more than five hundred years old, if that, enduring for perhaps a quarter of the history of the Church.

The nation-state doubtless fulfilled an imperative need in the world community. To suggest that it is a transitory idea, perhaps already losing some of its usefulness, is to deny nothing of the enrichment of human life which it made possible. But historical perspective is essential, if there is to be understanding and development. Some of us can remember a time, for instance, when passports were unnecessary, and travel to most parts of the world was unlimited. Of late years we have developed very elaborate systems of limiting and reporting on travel, and passports and permits of a hundred varieties are a commonplace need. We are glad we can remember a freer time, for it encourages us to hope for a return to that more relaxed and generous world of our childhood.

Just so we rejoice that the Church can remember a time before the walls of absolute national sovereignty were built, when a man's life was lived in a wider association, when "Christendom" was a reality. It encourages us to hope for the restoration of that greater family which exists despite our national boundaries. "Western Civilization" is a phrase which still has meaning, because it once represented a living reality greater than a collection of separate nations, and may yet point the way to a still greater reality, when even the adjective "western" can be forgotten.

Third, *the Churchman has learned from his Bible and his faith that nothing less than mankind itself is the unit.* In the "new man" of which St. Paul speaks, *there cannot be Greek and Jew, circumcised and uncircumcised, barbarian, Scythian, slave, free man, but Christ is all, and in all* (Colossians 3:11). Differences in tradition, culture, national history we all recognize. But we are also aware that, beneath the differences, man's hungers, dreams, necessities, and hopes are the same everywhere. How eagerly most of us seize every chance for personal relationships with the Russian people— to visit them, or to welcome them in coming to know us, to reach behind the Iron Curtain with radio or balloons or any other means of communication—not because we happen to like them particularly, but because of man's immense impulse to find common ground with his brother man. We feel that if only we can communicate person to person with them, we shall soon discover that identity of need and nature which God has established in our creation. Nothing less than mankind is the unit, in God's creating, redeeming, sanctifying love.

This means interdependence. Few developments in human history have been more sudden and dramatic than the way in which, in one generation, we have rediscovered that no nation and no people can be self-sufficient in this world. Economically, industrially, financially, in natural resources, in political philosophy, in military strategy—where is there any field of human concern left in which any nation can stand alone? The world is one, and the world is very small. Doubtless God understood that when He created us alike, sharing one nature and one hope.

Fourth, *the Churchman is the servant of the Saviour of the world*. To him, the complex decisions of history can never be made or understood simply on the basis of personal or national interest. He will not ignore those interests, for no right or honest decision can be made except by a candid evaluation of them. But he will not forget, as he evaluates his interests, that there is a divine interest superior to them all. The men and women who share his world, whose interests may seem sometimes violently counter to his own, are among those for whom Christ died. Even those who bitterly reject the name of Christ are still among those for whom He "was contented to be betrayed, and given up into the hands of wicked men, and to suffer death upon the cross." And to share the Passion of Christ—the mixed love and pain which together are the marks of Christ—is an inescapable part of the vocation of the Christian.

Therefore the Christian looks at every national interest as, in God's providence, destined to serve a purpose beyond itself. In his eyes God gave nations and nationalism in order that men might better love God and their brother man. That greater purpose must override the selfish calculations of national well-being. This does not simplify his choices by any means. He knows of the constant danger of self-deceit—of twisting selfishness into the appearance of service—and is prepared to make his choices humbly and aware of the pervasive sin of pride. Nobody who remembers the agonizing choices of wartime, when national interests seemed almost to require the annihilation of brother men, has any easy idealism about this. At times of crisis how nearly irresistible is the impulse to see nothing except the necessity of national survival!

Yet even that somber necessity, when it is used by a conscientious people, can in the end be made to serve a greater purpose. England's fight for survival, a matter of national interest, held also the glorious possibility of freedom for enslaved millions. American wealth, once dedicated purely to victory, could and did also mean life and rebuilding and new dignity even for the onetime enemy. These are not examples of the idealism and purity of England or the United States; our choices were very imperfect and shortsighted, and there need be no self-righteousness about them. But in fact, and in spite of man's sin, nations also may serve the wider love of God beyond their own necessities, if thoughtful and humble citizens will have it so.

Fifth, *the Churchman is a servant of the Judge of this world.* However deeply he may cherish and value the gifts that God has given him through his nation and her tradition and resources, he knows that the nation does not have the final, absolute claim on his loyalty. The nation is always subject to judgment herself. "My country, right or wrong," has a strong claim on our emotions; but it has no claim whatever on our reason or our responsible moral sense.

Of course, it is our country, just as inescapably as our family is ours. We are born here; we are a product of the life and tradition precisely as we are born children of a certain family and bearing a certain name. We do not disown our country or desert it because its legislators make stupid mistakes, or because short-sighted citizens dictate a wrong policy.

But it is our country chiefly because it has a conscience, because it acknowledges the operation of laws higher than its codes can contain, because it is under judgment, and can accept that judgment and be nourished by it. We would say this theologically, that the nation exists not only in the order of creation—we are born into a nation—but also in the order of redemption—the nation is a tool in the hands of God. To the extent that our nation, or any, acknowledges no right except that of existence, no law except that of its own necessities, the nation becomes frightening and horrifying to any thoughtful citizen.

Because of God the Judge, mankind is more of a unity than a collection of separate people. Because of Him whose Law governs all people and all nations alike (whether they acknowledge Him or not), His servants, under whatever flag, are bound by one law which transcends all our separate allegiances.

TWO FACTORS SHARED WITH NON-CHRISTIANS

These five factors are specific Christian insights, which predispose us to a certain positive attitude toward the international community. They are, in large measure, peculiar to Christians; and we should not be surprised if non-Christians do not share them. There are other factors, however, which are common to all sensitive and thoughtful people, Christians or not. Two of them ought to be mentioned briefly.

For one thing, *Christians and non-Christians alike share an awareness of a certain kind of unity in mankind,* born out of our common home on this planet and of our common needs and hopes. In Christian eyes, this unity is a given theological fact, established by God in creation. But even to men of no faith, the fact of unity still has powerful appeal—to some it seems to be almost the only thing a reasonable man can believe in at all.

There *is* only one blood in mankind's veins—you don't have to be a Christian to know what every schoolboy ought to know. The world is smaller now than the state of Massachusetts was in 1776— and you don't have to be a Christian to know this. The unity of mankind is no dream. It is a terrible and wonderful fact, open for all people to see.

Our feeling would doubtless be one of sincere thanksgiving that there is at least this much of a common platform for international understanding. We might well go on from that point, and realize with penitence how often we, who should have recognized this unity most clearly and from the outset, are laggard in realizing it at all. Pandit Nehru had this to say in answering a question about our understanding of Indian and Asian problems: "The West has a very good understanding of the economic, social and political changes in Asia, but no awareness of the greatest change of all, which is going on in the hearts of men. Millions of people all over Asia are saying 'the things we have suffered and endured for centuries we will suffer and endure no longer.' This is not a material but a spiritual change and I do not think the West understands either its nature or its extent."

To our shame, we often seem not to understand it. We talk and act in abstractions and generalities, as if the people of Asia were in some strange way entirely different from ourselves, not needing the resources, the dignity, the freedom we need, not wanting the same life, liberty and pursuit of happiness we have. In any human being this callousness would be stupid; in Christians it is close to the unforgivable. Men need the same things and dream of the same things, whatever their flag or tongue; and this unity is there for everyone to see.

In the second place, *we share with all thoughtful people an awareness of the sharp limitations on national sovereignty in a world like ours.* The keystone of sovereignty is the power to protect the nation's good and to enforce the nation's will. When that power does not exist—as it cannot in an age of nuclear warfare—then the claim of absolute national sovereignty has to be re-examined deeply and radically. This re-examination is going on everywhere in the world.

In some cases, as in the new nations of the Orient, a sharp new emphasis on nationalism is to be found, where such a new claim seems to serve people coming out of colonialism, and trying to assert their place in the scheme of things. But even there, for all the keen new pride in national identity, there is also a heightened concern for some form of international community which may guarantee safety and peace for nations which are helpless to guarantee such things themselves, and which will help win for them the elementary necessities of life.

The vast new powers of nuclear weapons have dealt a death-blow to the old idea of absolute national sovereignty. They have done this in two ways. First, they have put into the hands of even a small and militarily weak nation power to work immense and irrevocable damage to other nations. Second, they have taken away from even the greatest nations the ability to protect their citizens and their national life. It is such practical realities as these which bring to every thinking person a realization of the urgent necessity for a more effective organization of humanity's life and resources than the old system of absolute sovereignties could possibly give.

SEVEN FIELDS OF CHRISTIAN ACTION

All that we have said so far is by way of exploring the reasons why Christians are predisposed to take a positive and active and sympathetic attitude toward any legitimate way in which the international community can be made a stronger working reality. As in the case of civil rights or race relations, or in many another area of social and political thought, it is sometimes felt that the concern of the Church and of church people is dictated simply by the fact that we are progressive or liberal in our sympathies—in other words that we are either nice people or fuzzy-minded people, depending on the critic's point of view.

We are no nicer than any other group of people, and we probably have our quota of fuzzy-mindedness. But these are quite irrelevant criticisms. The reasons for the Church's concern about such areas as these are theological reasons, religious reasons. The Christian faith establishes these obligations for us, and they are part of our Christian living.

But attitudes, however generous and thoughtful, will not come to much until they are translated into action. What are the fields of action in which these special international concerns of Christians are worked out? We list seven such areas, not as an exclusive list, but as the areas which are the easiest to get at for the ordinary Christian citizen and which are the most immediately relevant to the world's situation.

The United Nations. Support of the United Nations, and support of every move the government can take to strengthen the United Nations, has been the settled policy of our Church since the United Nations came into existence. The General Convention of 1949 agreed that "it should be a fundamental objective of the foreign policy of the United States of America to support and strengthen the United Nations." This resolution went on to urge the strengthening of the United Nations in order to develop a world government open to all peoples, with defined and limited powers adequate to preserve peace and prevent aggression through the enactment and enforcement of world law.

In 1952, the General Convention again expressed its feeling that "the United Nations is the best political hope of mankind today, and we pledge our support of it." The Convention further urged that the United Nations charter be revised and strengthened, again with a limited world organization in view.

Again at Honolulu, in 1955, the General Convention voted that it should be "a fundamental objective of the foreign policy of our country to support and strengthen the United Nations in every reasonable and feasible manner."

What is at stake here, in Christian eyes, is the urgent necessity for the establishment of order among nations, where there would be anarchy without some effective international organization. Indeed we are close to anarchy, even with the present working United Nations organization. It is the same anarchy, except on a gigantic scale, that we would know in our own neighborhoods were there no police, no courts, no laws. If we are to be free and secure in the world, we must establish the same discipline among free nations that makes order and liberty possible among free individuals. The United Nations, adequately equipped and implemented for that task, is, as our Church has said, "the best political hope of mankind today."

These are all responsible decisions taken by the central legislature of our Church, and beyond doubt they express the mind of the great majority of our people. But resolutions alone do not mean very much. They need to be worked out in parish programs and in individual activity. If the United Nations is to us a form of international organization deserving of every possible support, then we should not only say so, but we should engage ourselves and our parishes in whatever share of the life of the United Nations we can appropriately undertake. In many communities there are associations devoted to knowing more about the United Nations and making it known; and activity in such organizations is certainly one way of expressing our concern.

In communities where there is no such organization, the question ought to be asked about the responsibility of church groups for undertaking such study, not only for our own sake, but as a contribution to the community. The programs in our schools which are designed to familiarize children with the United Nations ought also to be of special concern to church people.

Perhaps the chief value of such participation is to make it clear, to our contemporaries as well as to ourselves, that our concern with the United Nations is part and parcel of our Christian living. The United Nations is not a religious activity; it is not the only Christian solution to the problems of international tension. But it is, now, what our Convention called "the best political hope of mankind today." Because it is this, it is therefore a matter of profound Christian significance.

Atomic energy. The almost incredible possibilities of nuclear energy, for good as well as for ill, have made it a matter of supreme international significance. Both its military uses and its possibilities for peacetime industrial and scientific development present problems which weigh very heavily on the Christian conscience.

As the Anglican Congress of 1954 declared, "we believe that God has created the power of the atom for the furtherance of His purposes. Therefore, it is the duty of the Christian citizen to do his utmost in prayer and influence to the end that the nations of the world use nuclear energy only for God's peaceful and creative purposes." Our Church implemented that world-wide expression of opinion at our 1955 General Convention when a Joint Commission on the Peaceful Use of Atomic Energy was established by the Convention "for the purpose of exploring the ways in which our church can contribute in a positive manner to the development of peaceful and humanitarian uses of atomic energy."

The proposal here is not that all Christians shall become experts in nuclear physics. The point is that nuclear power is a resource of such transcendent possibilities as to represent the number one problem before the nations of the world today. What our government does about it is a matter of concern to every citizen. If this power be of God, then it is essential that it be used aright. If the Church is to give intelligent help to citizens in guiding consciences about the right use of nuclear energy, we have a great deal of collective thinking and exploring to do.

Refugees. The problem of refugees is as old as tyranny. Within the last decade or two it has become, by sheer weight of numbers, one of the gravest of all international problems. Our Church has taken its share, through the World Council of Churches, in trying to meet this problem. Many parishes and individual church people throughout the land have had a part in aiding, and, in some cases, actually resettling refugees.

In many instances the process has been slowed down by the practical difficulties in bringing refugees to this country. The numbers are very great; the practical necessities of weeding out undesirables have been time-consuming. Nevertheless, there are thousands of families who have found new homes and begun new lives thanks to the initiative of concerned Christian people.

Our own Church has a definite part in this program, and the opportunity is open to every parish and family and individual to take a share in that program. There are few better ways of expressing practically our sense of brotherhood with people of other nations than the help we can give to the countless uprooted, despairing refugees of the world.

The actual resettlement of refugees in this country is, of course, only one small aspect of the problem. Depending on what the law permits, we shall wish to do what we can to bring suitable refugee families into our country and integrate them into our life. A much greater challenge is that of giving financial aid to such families and individuals abroad, as through the Presiding Bishop's Fund for World Relief. The millions of uprooted people must, for the most part, be helped to build a new life where they are; and we can help in this with material aid.

Immigration. One of the major expressions of our national policy and national attitude is our immigration practice. Up until the twentieth century, the United States needed immigrants and welcomed them. We have thought earlier about the impact these immigrants made on American life; certainly it should be a matter of thanksgiving for every man and woman of good will that we were in a position to offer that generous welcome to people of other countries. America would not be what it is, had it not been for that flood of new vitality.

The climate has changed profoundly in the last few decades. The Depression sharply limited the labor market and caused us, perhaps for the first time, to doubt the limitless industrial horizon that we had always taken for granted. The war, with its immense disruption and dislocation of the whole world's life, changed radically our attitudes toward many of our sister nations. The rise of communism and its growing influence in the world caused many to feel a fear of strangers and foreigners, on a scale unprecedented in American life.

The result of all this has been a drastic limitation of the welcome America extends. Our present immigration law is more restrictive than any we have ever had; it has been under fire since its adoption; and it may well be hoped that modification will soon be possible, and in the direction of a more generous welcome, in the spirit of the American tradition of opportunity.

Legislation of this type is, quite properly, of particular concern to Christian consciences because it directly affects American relationships with other nations. And the formulation of national policy with respect to other nations ought to be the subject of very searching Christian discussion. It may well be that the days of an unrestricted welcome are past. National security may require some modification, and increasing population has clearly limited the opportunities of earlier days. What should our immigration policy be? How wide a welcome can we give? On what basis should we welcome immigrants? How fearful should we be of traditions and opinions different from our own? To ask these questions, trying to formulate intelligent answers to them, is part of Christian living.

Foreign students. One of the major developments of recent years has been the greatly increased traffic in student exchanges. Our government has provided means whereby our own young men and women can study abroad with far greater facility than ever before. In similar fashion, great numbers of students now come from other lands to study in our own colleges and universities. Most larger communities have organized groups to work with these students. Should not every church within reach of a colony of foreign students have a definite program to help meet their needs and to help open the doors of America to them?

What is required here is not so much physical aid as simple friendliness and an intelligent desire to open real channels of communication to them and for them. These foreign students are, after all, young men and women like our own: they are as eager for companionship; they have the same need to interpret and be interpreted. What will they have learned about America when they go back to their homes? How well will they have learned the lessons of human brotherhood and of the unity of mankind? How great a contribution to world understanding and world peace will these years of their studies be? How much were they able to give us, of their own tradition and experience?

Christians hold in their hands a major share of the answers to those questions. If we mean business by our Christian discipleship, the foreign student is one person who will gain by it.

Public education. How well do our schools and colleges prepare children for informed and sympathetic understanding of international life and problems? One index is the teaching of foreign languages. In many communities in America, students of French or German are now fewer, both relatively and absolutely, than they were ten or twenty years ago. Another index is the amount of study our children make of the history and literature of other nations. Here again, the record in many American communities is discouraging.

Do you know what your own schools do in this respect? Granted that our children ought to know their own culture and tradition well (and better than many of us did), it is hopelessly unwise and unrealistic to train them to live in this tiny world, in ignorance of what their neighbors think and say and do. Some may think that this is a matter of educational rather than religious concern. The answer to this is to ask where the line is drawn. It is hard to imagine any matter of educational concern which is not also, and equally, a primary interest for Christians.

The world-wide Church. Here is perhaps a level of international life which is uniquely close and accessible to every member of the Church. It is impossible to read the Bible, to read Church history or teaching, or even to attend a church service without being caught up into the international fellowship which is the Church. Even if it be nothing more than our own Church's missionary activity, we are necessarily involved in the lives of Christians of other nations.

Multitudes of other opportunities are given. Our Church periodicals keep us informed of Church life in other countries. Visitors come and go regularly. There are great moments, as when the Anglican Congress met in Minneapolis in 1954, or at such world-wide gatherings as the Assembly of the World Council of Churches, when we are privileged to play host to many hundreds of our fellow Christians.

Our reading can be an introduction into this international fellowship. Our prayers ought certainly to be such an introduction. Our contributions, through missionary budgets, through the refugee program, through the ecumenical movement, can all be ways in which we grow more aware of the supra-national body to which we belong.

What is needed here, more than anything else, is the imagination to see and understand what God has already given us in the life of the Church. It is not necessary to construct a new organization, or to try to import some international flavor into our familiar Church life. The whole of the body of Christ is there, if we will only see it.

These are admittedly undramatic and seemingly inconsequential things. We may feel that the international life of the world is not likely to be greatly changed by a prayer or the teaching of German in a high school or a refugee family resettled in our community. Yet the question may fairly be asked whether there is anything more important than these things. It is out of precisely these small things that deep understandings are built. We and our fellow men around the world cannot get much nourishment out of rhetoric. What sustains us is the act of kindness, the flash of mature understanding, the sympathetic interpretation, the willingness of other people to make common cause with us in the central things of life. And out of the steady, untiring witness of a few people in small things, great changes may come.

Perhaps most of all it behooves us to make our tongues and our prayers and our thoughts witness for this world-wide brotherhood. When we encounter the boastful ignorance with which some of our fellow-citizens approach the problems of international life, a quiet word of humble understanding may work miracles. True peace between nations and mutual understanding are not going to be built on boastfulness. If God has been good to America and given us immense resources and incalculable power, it is not for our sakes alone. Let this chapter close with three paragraphs from the Pastoral Letter issued by the House of Bishops from Honolulu in September, 1955:

Since God always speaks to us where we are, He speaks to us here of His lordship over this great area of His one world, of His lordship over East and West; of our inescapable human oneness with all the peoples of the Pacific area and of Asia; of His will for His Church in the fulfillment of her mission in the islands of the Pacific and in the vast continent of Asia.

The God Whom we confess and worship is not our possession. We are His possession. It is His doing that we share our common nature with our fellows of the lands toward which we look, and that we shall rise or fall with them. In Christ He claims us and them for Himself and gives Himself to us and to them. And we can accept His claiming of us as His own and receive His offered life only as we permit Him to break down the barriers our human sin has erected between us and our brethren.

To all who accept Him He gives the command to go into all the world and stake out the claim for the reconciling lordship of Christ in all places of His rightful dominion, not in complacent pride of our human superiority, but in humble witness and service. Standing where we do God speaks to us of His will for His Church in Asia. If we stood in some other place He would speak to us of our mission there.

CHAPTER TWENTY

The Structure of Liberty

PUT IN its boldest terms, the democratic proposition is this: That, in any practical choice which the nation must face, the majority shall have the right to decide. We are very careful to say it this way, and not to say that the majority is right. For in truth, it is no part of this proposition that the majority is necessarily right. Indeed, if they were taken to be necessarily right, then we should not have democracy, but aristocracy or oligarchy. So we say it in the simple, sparse language I have indicated.

The reasoning behind this proposition is familiar enough. Democracy does not rest on any assumption that the majority is necessarily wise. On many practical issues, no doubt the collective mind of the greatest number of people is probably a reliable guide. Yet on the other hand, it is almost certain that, in some new question which has never been asked or answered before, or in some question involving special knowledge, the majority will almost certainly not have adequate information or wisdom. This does not disturb us unduly, because we make it part of our business in a healthy democracy to be sure that the channels of knowledge and wisdom are always kept open, so that in time wiser decisions can be made. Democracy needs to be, and knows it needs to be, very patient with its first decisions. We are not surprised at our second thoughts, and learn to wait for them.

Nor is the theory of democracy based on any idea that it is a more efficient organization of humanity than any other. Indeed, the case is rather to the contrary; we are quite prepared to find that tyranny or despotism may be far more efficient, at least in short-term decisions, than majority rule. This does not disturb us, for we find practical ways around this inefficiency; and at the same time we are quite prepared to accept it as part of the cost of a commodity infinitely more valuable to us than efficiency. It is very easy to exaggerate the supposed "efficiency" of despotism. A despotism can act quickly—more so than a government which needs collective decisions—but that may be even a detriment in the long run.

THE NATURE OF DEMOCRACY

Democracy is not based on any idea of the goodness of the majority. There have been romantic democrats enough, in every age and country, who have tried to reason that there was some mystic, collective goodness about a majority which guaranteed that its decisions would be necessarily right. No working democracy makes this assumption. Certainly the American proposition is not based on it; we are quite prepared to admit that democracies are often stampeded by very wrong fears and hopes which grip a majority and use their power.

Democracy, truly, is very far from any romantic idealization of mankind. What we say is, that in this world, so shadowed by ignorance and by man's common moral failure, the fairest way is to let the majority make the decisions. We say this, even knowing that in many cases the majority will be very far from right. Why?

In our American tradition, the clearest answer to that question is given in the Declaration of Independence, particularly in the three famous sentences which follow:

We hold these truths to be self-evident, that all men are created equal, that they are endowed by their Creator with certain inalienable Rights, that among these are Life, Liberty, and the pursuit of Happiness. That to secure these rights, Governments are instituted among Men, deriving their just powers from the consent of the governed. That whenever any Form of Government becomes destructive of these ends, it is the Right of the People to alter or to abolish it, and to institute new Government, laying its foundations on such principles and organizing its powers in such form, as to them shall seem most likely to effect their Safety and Happiness.

The "self-evident rights" are the ultimate foundation of a democratic system. And of the three—life, liberty, and the pursuit of happiness—liberty is the working right on which our political structure is built. God made us with a right to liberty which cannot be taken away. Because this is so, our government must be designed to respect that right, and to organize our collective liberties in such a way that we shall have the maximum of individual liberty and of life, and the right to seek our own happiness.

Whence come these rights? They come from God. Why are they given to man? Because man is an individual who shares personality with God—who chooses, thinks, hopes, loves, imagines and fashions things, bears and nourishes life, all in the image of God.

To what purpose are these rights given? They are given that individuals in society may have the greatest possible opportunity to make their own choices and to share in the common choices, and to fulfill, through their freedom, the most of what God wills them to be.

It ought never seem eccentric to Americans to find that the answers to our basic political questions are usually theological answers. For democracy itself is at heart a theological proposition, indeed a Christian one. Political democracy is a way of giving constitutional effect to the created dignity of the ordinary individual.

Speaking of the French Revolution, Archbishop Temple once said,

Outraged by Privilege in its most insolent form, they thought Equality was what they wanted. It was not then; it is not now; for it is not a reality. But Liberty they needed and all that hindered it had to go, because Liberty is the political and social expression of the greatest reality in the world—the spiritual personality in man.

Here is the real root of Democracy. We must find some way of recognizing that each individual citizen is no tool to be made use of for the attainment of some prosperity in which he will not share, still less mere cannon-fodder, but is a living personality, with mind and heart and will, who can only be himself so far as he freely thinks and feels and plans. The root of Democracy is respect for individual personality.[1]

It would be saying too much to say that democracy is the only Christian form of government. Most of us would say no more than that it is the best political contrivance man has yet discovered to give effect to our deepest feelings about the dignity of human individuality.

Nor would we say that democracy and Christianity are synonymous. Christianity has much more than this to give to humanity. For even the best of governments is only a reflection of a living

---

[1] William Temple, *Essays in Christian Politics* (New York: Longmans, Green & Co., 1927), p. 73. Used by permission of the publisher.

faith; and the living faith itself, expressed in the community of the Church, is the vital and indestructible element. Yet for all this, there is far more in common between democracy and Christianity than men realize; there are religious duties which men owe to democracy which are part of our Christian living. None of those duties is more sensitive than those which relate to liberty.

Let us add one more thing about the democratic principle before we leave it. So far, all that we have said related to democracy as it is summarized in the symbol of majority rule. Yet this same principle runs through all of the areas of our life. Some of the non-political areas are almost equally as important as the political expression of democracy. Democracy in industrial affairs, for example, is not a principle restricted to whatever legislation we may pass to regulate management or labor. The principle of democracy needs to run all through the body of our society, and to express itself as much in the way we manufacture and market our goods as the way we vote.

So, too, we would feel that democracy needs full expression in our educational process and in our social life. For democracy is far more than a political structure. It is a way of recognizing liberty and enshrining it; and liberty is not simply a political expedient or even a political principle. *Liberty is the dignity which belongs by right to the children of God.*

WHAT CHRISTIANS OWE TO LIBERTY

What, then, are the responsibilities of Christian living toward liberty? In earlier chapters we have thought about the political responsibilities of the Christian—his duty to vote intelligently, and to take his full and rightful share in the political life of the nation. But now we are thinking in wider terms, not simply of political participation as such, but of the spirit and heart with which the Christian man and woman engages himself in the whole enterprise of democracy. As members of a complex social and industrial society, what are the earmarks of participation? Specifically, what does the Christian do about liberty?

The first and clearest responsibility of the Christian citizen, in this matter of liberty, *is his responsibility toward minorities.* The question of the minority is one of the central questions of democracy. If you are going to put into the hands of the majority the right to decide on any issue, then the disappointed minority becomes at once a matter of major spiritual concern. This is so not simply because the liberties of the minority are being affected by the majority decision—that is, after all, part of the bargain of democracy; and a member of one minority knows that in most cases he will be a member of the next majority, and is content.

The minorities which concern us are those of a more fundamental character—the perennial minorities, and the minorities of opinion. A perennial minority may be of many different kinds. One common variety is the racial minority, which can never hope, in most cases, to gain more than a precarious political ascendancy. We pray that such racial or linguistic minorities will soon disappear in the way all such minorities should, by ceasing to find any important interest served by their being a self-conscious minority.

The national minorities in American life are a case in point. There may well have been legitimate place and need for "the Irish vote" in years gone by, when hardship and destitution and the invitation of a new country had brought so many so quickly from Ireland to the United States. But the solution for the Irish was not to maintain a separate Irish vote, nor to become a separate enclave within America, nor to develop a ghetto psychology. The solution for the Irish was to add their virile strength and their warm hearts to the common treasury of American life. This they did; and now they are disappearing as a self-conscious minority.

And this must be the story with every racial or national minority in America, or we shall have failed. We have been enriched by them all; but the way we are enriched is by making common cause with them and having their strength added to the common treasury of the nation. Still, while they are timid and necessitous minorities, they are a task for every Christian conscience.

A different kind of problem is presented by the minorities of opinion. These minorities are rarely rooted in any coherent tradition, national, religious or otherwise. These minorities tend to appear and disappear around specific issues; they are the minorities who disagree in principle with the ruling majority; and they are profoundly valuable social ingredients.

They are valuable because of the essential humility of the democratic proposition. We say that the majority have the right to decide; and in so saying, we recognize that the decision is made, more often than not, by people whose knowledge is very imperfect and whose motives are very impure. We are not at all surprised when, in the event, the minority turn out to have been right and the majority wrong all along. Because of this necessary humility toward majority decisions, there is always in a healthy democracy a profound tolerance and even nourishment of minority opinions. For our own souls' sake, and for the sake of our second thoughts and future decisions, we are watchful to be sure that minority opinion is protected and that full play is given for the interchange of opinion between minority and majority. Washington was right, in the dismal winter at Valley Forge, and the pessimists who wanted to give up the fight were wrong. Lincoln was right, when he foresaw that a nation could not endure half-slave and half-free. If those who had the power had kidnapped and shot such men as these, what would the outcome have been? But, instead, their courage and vision triumphed. Granted that there are not many Washingtons and Lincolns, the example still should command the hearts and wills of the people of a democracy, and remind them that the truth does not necessarily lie with the majority, and that the voice of the few is a vital treasure to be guarded with great respect.

So important is this principle of vigilant protection of minority opinion that the very life of the democracy itself seems to depend on it. A majority that rode roughshod over the liberty of opinion of the minorities would very soon become a despotism of the worst sort. Indeed, a democracy is forever teetering, in moments of stress, on the brink of just this attitude. Certainly there have been moments in the last few years when it seemed a very venturesome thing and required no little courage for a citizen to express a minority opinion.

Because this is so, it may well be that there is a special urgency attaching to a Christian's duty at this point. The Christian knows why there is a certain kind of sacredness about opinions, and perhaps particularly minority opinion. Therefore, it behooves him to be especially sensitive to any threat to the free expression and development of such opinion.

For that matter (and this is a point which merits a good deal of reflection), there are very few true majorities when it comes to opinion. Electoral majorities are commonplace. But when any electoral majority is analyzed, it usually turns out to be a collection of minorities who have agreed, for practical reasons, to vote together. Legislation is commonly a basketful of compromises; and when it is adopted, it is adopted by counting the heads of all the people who are willing to vote for it, no matter how widely different their opinions about parts of it may be. So it is with many of our fancied majorities in a democracy; and this is a safeguard for minorities, and is a practical lesson in liberty about which we shall have more to say presently.

The second great area of particular concern to Christian consciences is that of *civil rights*. By civil rights we mean the constitutional and legal privileges which are accorded to individuals in our democracy. In the main they are enshrined in the Constitution and in the first ten of the amendments. They include freedom of speech and of the press—and that most complicated of freedoms, freedom of religion—they include the rights of free assembly and of jury trial; they include the rights of an accused person not to be required to witness against himself, nor to be deprived of life, liberty or property without due process of law.

These civil rights are very precious in our democracy for a variety of reasons. One reason is that historically they represent rights we asserted in our own fight for independence. For another reason, they come close to the heart of all that we mean by human dignity.

One curious feature about civil rights is that, in many instances, they are not awarded to people because those people have done something to deserve them. The criminal who is arraigned by a grand jury for a capital crime and who claims and uses his civil rights, is not necessarily a person who has any merited claim on the generosity of his fellow citizens. But this is precisely the point. These rights are not given to him because he has deserved them; indeed, it may be questioned whether any civil rights are given to anybody because such rights are earned or deserved. Civil rights are given to people because God created us, whether we are bad or good or deserving or undeserving. Civil rights are the clearest recognition of the dignity of the individual personality under God.

But civil rights present a real problem to many people in a democracy. An instance is the way in which thoughtless people speak about "Fifth-Amendment Communists," as if no decent person would avail himself of a civil right given him by the Constitution. Whatever one's opinion of Communists may be, the issue is

· 299

not whether a particular individual happens to be a Communist. The issue is whether a democracy is going to be prepared to deal with him, or any other individual, remembering that he is a child of God, and as such is given a status which no alleged sin or crime can possibly take away. Civil rights are duties owed by all of us to each one of us, because of the sacredness of human personality.

This is an attitude sometimes difficult to sustain. In times of stress and crisis, it may well be that a majority of Americans would be distrustful of civil rights and tempted to curtail them. Perhaps it is well that they are as deeply embedded in the Constitution as they are. Certainly they represent one of the farthest stretches of the human spirit; and it would not be surprising if many of us fall short of that standard much of the time.

All the more reason, then, for saying that the protection of civil rights is again a peculiar responsibility of the Christian conscience. For civil rights are the necessary consequences of Christian faith in God; and if the people who profess that faith are not zealous to guard those rights, then we have no cause to expect the unbelieving to support them.

The critic who is quick to judge clergymen or laymen for what he calls "liberal sympathies" and an undue preoccupation with civil rights, would do well to think more deeply of the reasons behind that preoccupation. For the Christian, it is a compliment to be called a liberal; because the word may well signify our understanding that liberty is one of the supreme gifts of God. Because the gift is God's, it becomes us Christians to be intent and watchful in our care for our civil rights, and those of our neighbor.

Third, there is a particular responsibility for Christians to maintain *a scrupulous watch over our own use of our liberty*. The whole secret of democracy in practice lies in the patience and self-restraint which men and women show to each other in the way in which they use their liberty. But simply because Christians have a clear insight into the truth of our relationship to one another and our dependence upon one another, we then also have a special responsibility in our behavior.

In quite another connection, St. Paul has something to say to us about this. Speaking of the liberty with which Christians could properly eat food which had been ceremonially offered to idols and blessed by the priests of idolatry, he admonishes us (I Cor. 8:9-13),

Only take care lest this liberty of yours somehow become a stumbling block to the weak. For if any one sees you, a man of knowledge, at table in an idol's temple, might he not be encouraged, if his conscience is weak, to eat food offered to idols? And so by your knowledge this weak man is destroyed, the brother for whom Christ died. Thus, sinning against your brethren and wounding their conscience when it is weak, you sin against Christ. Therefore, if food is a cause of my brother's falling, I will never eat meat, lest I cause my brother to fall.

The occasion is unimportant; the principle is all-important. It is nothing less than the principle of brotherly love, which must govern us in our use even of legitimate liberty, lest our use be a source of offense to another. A tiny example of this might be the way in which we Episcopalians, with our fairly relaxed social disciplines, sometimes unintentionally give offense to others to whom the use of tobacco or alcoholic beverages seems to be forbidden to the Christian conscience. It means little to us; and it is no more than passing courtesy to remember the feelings of others in such things, no matter how petty they may seem.

A far more notable example of the same principle is found in the way in which men and women of standing and prestige in their communities, people of means and of every advantage, sometimes fail to take more than a token interest or share in the common life of their communities. This is a deep and troubling offense to many others who have not a tithe of the advantages, and yet who care, and show that they care, about the needs and freedoms of others. It is tragically true, in many communities, that the Church has been silent when honest protest was called for, and laggard when there was work to be done to purify and strengthen the civic life. There are many exceptions to this; indeed such cases as this may be the exceptions. But much is required of those to whom much has been given; and in no area is this more true than in the area of the use of our liberty.

Nobody has full and complete liberty in a democracy or in any other form of society. All that democracy bargains to give us is the greatest liberty that is consonant with our common life and our interdependence. This means, inescapably, that all individual liberty is limited; and the best kind of limitation is self-limitation. Here the Christian can lead the way in the care and thoughtfulness with which he uses his time and his abilities, and the self-restraint with which he disciplines his own liberty for the sake of his brothers.

A fourth area in which Christians have special concern is that of *education*. One of the great justifications for a democratic society, apart from its one essential justification, is that it can be an educative process beyond compare. Democracy makes no assumption as to the knowledge or wisdom of its rulers; it puts into the hands of the majority immense power, knowing that the use of that power will often be mistaken and even wrong. But democracy also understands that this process of distributing decisions in free discussion is one of the best ways possible for the truth to become known.

We shall have to think more about education in the next chapter, for it plays a peculiarly important role in the American tradition. Let it be understood now, however, that a concern for knowledge and the diffusion of knowledge has an integral connection with the Christian use of liberty.

For freedom—liberty—is meaningless without knowledge. A choice made in the dark by a baby is no choice at all; it is pure chance. So are many choices, made in the light by adults, when they are choices that are based not on knowledge or reflection, but on slogans accepted and prejudices awakened.

Of course, this is a timeless problem and not one for our generation alone. The arts of propaganda, of the unfair influencing of choice, are as old as the hills. What is new is the amazing development in the technique of communication which now exposes humanity to the appeal to prejudice and emotion on every hand at almost every moment.

Man has only two defenses against this unfair pressure. One defense is accurate information. The second is the skill of discriminating judgment, whereby he learns to tell the unimportant from the important, and the false from the true. Both of these twin gifts should be the principal concerns of education. An education which does not teach us how to get at the truth and how to distinguish things that differ is no true education at all.

If we have not these gifts, our liberty is meaningless and can result only in a choice of bad masters and false hopes. Therefore, there is a special Christian concern at this point. For the right use of liberty is not simply desirable to help a democracy flourish; it is the most central and distinguishing gift of God to mankind. How helpful parish study groups on political issues would be, if we could only overcome our phobia about mixing religion and politics!

Finally, it perhaps will hardly need saying that one of the supreme gifts the Christian can bring to a democratic society is *loyal and steady participation in the life of the Church*. A free society, engrossed as our society must necessarily be with the daily claims of its political and social and industrial life, desperately needs the spiritual mirror of itself which the Church provides. It needs to be reminded of the source of its freedom, and of the personal individuality which is its highest prize. It needs to remember that liberty and personality alike are derivative from the God who creates them.

Unless secular democracy can continually see itself in its true nature and its great destiny, it will forget both nature and destiny and become preoccupied entirely with its own day-by-day worldly concerns. There is nothing the matter with the concerns simply because they are worldly. Our life is lived *in* the world; it is not lived *for* the world, but for the God who creates and sustains it. It is this unfailing reminder of God and of the true nature of human society which is the principle function of the Church.

Of course a bishop, writing a book for the Church, may be expected to urge that we be faithful in our church attendance. This is a risk I must take; and so also is the risk of being understood as assuming that church attendance is an end in itself. In one sense, our life in the Church is an end in itself. The worship of Almighty God needs no excuse or apology; we worship Him because it is the noblest act a man or woman can do, and it does not need defense in terms of its social utility or its political value. But in a deeper sense, we accomplish far more by our loyalty to the Church than we commonly understand. For the Church is in the position of no other institution in society: it is able to demonstrate the essential and ultimate nature of mankind and of the liberty with which it is created. And it is of incalculable consequence to the world that we be able, from time to time, to lift our eyes from our daily toil and behold the ultimate and unchanging realities.

To one of us, liberty may mean little more than our right to spend our days in the drudgery of our job. To another, it may seem simply freedom from the harsh disciplines of public duty. To yet another, simply license to spend oneself as one wills. To all of us, involved as we are in the workaday world, liberty tends thus to dwindle and to be taken for granted, unless we are prodded out of that lethargy, awakened to see liberty in its true dimensions. And man has no greater liberty than the freedom to offer himself, and all that he is and has, to the one true God.

The Church can do more than this, too; the Church can awaken that most precious sense in a democracy, *that every liberty implies a corresponding obligation.* The danger of all democracies is the same; it is a danger of which our enemies are quite well aware; it is the heartbreaking peril of losing our liberties simply because we do not care enough or work hard enough to keep them. The surest way to grow careless of our liberties is to take them for granted and forget what they cost those who first won them, to forget what they cost us who have them. The cost, to us at any rate, is the cost of duty and responsibility; and it is the Church's privilege to be able to speak of these duties and responsibilities without self-interest and without cant or prejudice. Therefore, it is incumbent on Christians to look with new eyes at the Church as the great safeguard of liberty that it is, and look anew and with rededication at their own part in her life.

CHAPTER TWENTY-ONE

Christian Patriotism

Finally, my brothers, let me charge you, with all my heart, as I feel myself and every Christian to be charged, to a greater and deeper and more courageous love of country than any we have ever known. God does not mean us to love our country alone, to make it the end and idol of our love. But man has to start somewhere; and in His mercy God gives us a part of the world to be dearer to us than any other and a people to be especially our own. These plains, these green hills, these forests, these men and women are ours; for most of us there is no wider stage than this, and no greater history than to be faithful to our own inheritance. I am not ashamed to love my country, and to be willing to serve her as I am glad to be part of her.[1]

THESE WORDS have only this significance, that they are what almost any Christian would say about patriotism. In a way, there is no such thing as Christian patriotism. Patriotism —love of country—comes pretty close to being a universal sentiment in the hearts of men. Certainly as far back as written history goes, men have felt what we feel for the places and the people which belong to us and to which we belong. It has not seemed to make very much difference what form of political organization there might be, whether tribe or province or king or empire or town or republic. The kind of state that men set up is theirs to choose; but the love of country and of people is a gift from God.

So, at least, the Christian would reflect about these things. And he would very likely say for himself that, as a Christian, he has no other feelings than those which all men share. All he would claim would be a greater assurance that he feels this way because God created him so and that there is a purpose in his feeling this

---

[1] Quoted from the Bishop's Address to the Convention of the Diocese of Olympia, 1954.

way, which has an important place in God's providence. Thus, if we use the phrase "Christian patriotism," it is not to describe a different feeling from that which beats in every heart, but simply to describe the way in which a Christian looks at that common loyalty.

THE CHRISTIAN CONCEPT OF PATRIOTISM

The quotation with which this section begins ought not be taken as careful theology. Yet it describes the first important constituent of patriotism as the Christian sees that quality, namely *that God lets us learn love in small and local things because we must start somewhere, and in His mercy He lets us start with those things which are closest at hand.* Our first community is no more than a baby and a mother. In time, there are more who appear in the community—a father, sisters and brothers, and more remote relatives and friends. School is the next larger community, and then perhaps city or state. Eventually, with many people at least, even the nation and international society become real communities.

And at each stage, it seems to the Christian as if God had been leading him from lesser to greater, from one school of love to a greater one, and then to a greater one still. Doubtless, this is God's way with us.

This is part of patriotism; and so is a somewhat deeper reflection. God does not only lead us from a smaller community to a larger one; it seems to the Christian that the end toward which He is leading us is a kind of universal community and a universal love which taxes our ability even to imagine, much less to encompass. But the curious thing is that all through this process of ever-widening loyalty, God never lets us leave the ground, so to speak. We may begin by loving one person, and end by learning to love many, but at no point do we leave off loving persons and begin to love abstractions. Whether our community consists of a half of a dozen or a half of a million, it is still a community of living persons in a particular place, who require our love and our loyalty in their concrete situation.

To say this is perhaps to say no more than that God works through sacramental means, and supremely through the way of Incarnation. Certainly, at the greatest moments in God's revelation of Himself to us, it is in the most local and particular and immediate ways that He gives Himself to us. For us men and for our salvation,

He came down from Heaven and was made man. So does He come to us and act among us and within us through water and bread and wine. We have learned to expect these things about God, and therefore we have no need to be surprised that our patriotism should be of the same sacramental character. The point of Christian love is not to teach us how to rise above real mankind to some imagined ideal of mankind that has no real existence. The point of Christian love is to lead us to an ever wider and deeper and more profound love of the people who really exist, and with whom we share this world.

And because we are not very wise and not very pure and not very imaginative, God lets us start at least with what is near at hand and easy for us to grasp. A while ago I was writing about General Robert E. Lee, and in the course of it, trying to think myself back inside the pain and struggle of that choice many had to make with him so long ago. We look back on it with the perspective of a hundred years, and wonder that so fine a Christian and Churchman, and so patriotic an American as Lee could have made the choice he did —Lee who despised slavery and longed only to continue his life as a soldier for the country which had given him everything he had. It is hard for any twentieth-century man to see more than symbolic, imagined significance in the issue of 1860. How can we recapture what meant so much to them?

But, in the course of my writing, I had occasion to go by train through the part of the country where the dearest moments and years of my boyhood were spent, which I had not visited in a long time. Riding through that countryside, looking at remembered fields and hills, living over again the adventures of long ago, I suddenly found myself seized with an almost fierce and passionate loyalty—this was *my* country and these were *my* people, where my roots lay and my boyhood and all my early dreams and all my beginning knowledge of life and of mankind. And, suddenly, I felt very close to the men of Virginia a hundred years ago; for it was precisely this same fierce, passionate loyalty which made their choice so incredibly bitter and costly.

The point of this reflection, of course, is neither to grow sentimental nor to try to justify past decisions. The point is simply to illuminate what I am sure is a universal sense, that all of our loyalties begin with the people and the places which are closest and dearest to us, so close and dear that we can say they are "ours," that "we belong to them." And far from feeling that this is a fault or a weakness, the Christian would probably say that this is by God's appointment; that it is God's will that we shall begin all our widest loyalty and our deepest love with a loyalty and a love which may be very small and particular. We do not expect men and women to spend all their lives being homesick for their childhood; but we are concerned for the man who does not have a special place in his heart for his birthplace and his home country, and great pity for those who have been cheated of this birthright because of cruelty and unfairness. We are made to love our native land. That is the starting place of all true patriotism. And where people are driven from their homes by hatred, or lose their homes through hardness of heart, they lose a precious gift of God.

Love of locality, love of the near—these are marks of true love. If we do not learn the lesson which can be taught us by that narrow place and those few people, we shall never learn the wider lessons that life has to teach. Nor shall we ever learn how to serve the wider communities that lie ahead, if we do not know how to respect and serve in our first community.

But this is only one of the Christian attitudes toward patriotism; and the second is almost diametrically opposed to it. The second is the seemingly irresistible logic that God has established, *which urges us continually away from what is immediate and local to an ever-wider allegiance and to the discovery of a greater community.*

Travel, and the acquaintance of people from other places are the principal ways to this experience. Because we Americans are a migratory people, we are familiar with the way this happens. There are few Americans now who do not have a firsthand knowledge of their country, a familiarity that was only a dream for most people a hundred years ago. Years have done their work in annihilating the barrier of time and space for the traveller; and what took thirty days to drive, we can now span between breakfast and dinner. This is a commonplace truth; but it has had a profound part to play in the structuring of American partiotism. The nation has suddenly become a reality to us, most of whose fathers knew only regions and sections, and whose grandfathers knew scarcely more than towns.

This swift transformation helps enormously to make the wider love of country real to us. So also does our reading. Television makes it possible for us to be as familiar with the inside of a Melanesian hut as we are with our own neighbor's house. Thus, it is hard to avoid the fact of the nation and, indeed, of the world community.

Yet it is incredibly easy to avoid the implications of that fact. There is no automatic way in which the knowledge of a wider community can be translated into wider participation. Historians have often commented that after the long isolation of the Middle Ages when mobility and travel were once again restored to Europe, humanity had offered to it a golden opportunity for the establishment of a truly continental unity. Yet the consequence was almost the opposite; instead of the appearance of Europe, a continental unity, there followed a period of the most intense development of nation-states, with a drawing of national boundaries unprecedented in our history.

Somewhat the same comment can perhaps be made about our own times. Despite the growing reality of America, no longer as a political fiction but now as a known and shared reality, sectionalism and regionalism are as strong as perhaps they ever were. Certainly, national boundaries are sharper than any of us now living can remember; and the struggle of humanity to make its world community real is as harsh and thorny as it has ever been.

The wider loves and the wider loyalties do not happen automatically. There are at least two necessary tools, if this growth is to come. One is the tool of *imagination;* the other the tool of *unselfish will.* If we would speak of Christian patriotism, we must remember these two qualities particularly.

Imagination plays its part, as always, in helping us to make other people real to us. It is all very true to say that the nation has shrunk, and the man of Oregon and the man of Texas and the man of New England all know each other far more easily than they ever have before. Indeed, they may know their names and their appearance; but the problem of the reality of man to his neighbor is one of the eternal problems of humanity. You may know all about your neighbor and still find him not at all real. And until he is as real to you as you are to yourself, the Golden Rule has not been accomplished.

Thus it is that information without imagination is an empty accomplishment. For the Northerner to understand the South is not a matter to be accomplished simply by a few trips and a few books. Such knowledge might feed only his own preconceptions about the South; it is desperately easy for us to see only what we are prepared to see and to hear only what we want to hear. Until the Northerner is able to make his own the anguish and division through which his Southern brother must go—and share it—he cannot really make common cause with the South. And this same comment would be as true of the Southerner, who may see his Northern brother only in terms of interference and inquisition.

Here imagination is the necessary tool by which we can relive the experience of others and make it our own. Reading, conversation, thoughtful reflection, and, above all, prayer for one another—these are essential ingredients in patriotism. And the man or woman who is tempted to speak quickly and lightly of patriotism would do well to examine his own armory in this respect.

The other essential tool is the will, the unselfish will. True patriotism is never concerned simply with the past, or with the *status quo*. Let me quote again from a bishop's thoughts:

But, for us children of the Church of Christ, our love of country points always beyond itself. America is for builders; it is for believers; it is for those who are willing to work for what they will never see. America is for those who are content to wait for the second thoughts of a people. Indeed I do not think any man can love or understand America, who is not willing to walk forward with her, to be patient with what has been done because he knows that God wills us to press on to better understanding and a wiser improvising. For in the end it is the purpose of our love for our country to give birth to something far greater and far truer. As a child grows to learn, not always without pain, that there are other good men beside his father, and other and even more satisfying human relationships than those of a child and his family, so does the patriot learn that true love of his land and of his people must irresistibly lead to a wider love and a greater society.

Once again I say that this is not elaborate theologizing. It is no more than the reflection of one American who perceives that a mere emotional attachment to country and people is not enough—that such love points always to what lies ahead, and what can only be accomplished by a resolute will. Patriotism is far more than love of what was or what is; *patriotism is a passionate attachment to what must be.* And if what must be is not to be achieved without pain and conflict, the patriot must learn to accept this cost as the price of his love. There is no evidence in our history that it was ever easy or painless to be a patriotic American. From Washington's time to our own, men have had to fight to be free, and to imagine and fulfill the dreams that were born out of our love.

The third element in patriotism comes closest perhaps to being a peculiarly Christian quality. This element is *the certainty that God's hand is in this whole process*—that both the limited and local love with which we begin, and the wider loyalty to which we are continually being called, are alike the work of God. If it were not for this third element, patriotism might degenerate into nothing more than a barren and tenacious hold on the past.

It is not by accident that there is a pronounced element of the conservative in most patriotic societies. This is not a bad thing, as long as it does not mean a lack of faith in the providence of God and in His call of the nation to serve Him in the years to come. But there is a mood into which we members of patriotic societies sometimes fall, when we love the past with a love approaching idolatry, love the present almost not at all, and fear the future like the plague. When we are in such a mood, the trouble with us is that we have forgotten that God has a hand in all this, and that the nation does not exist for itself but for Him. This is not an argument against patriotic societies; it is simply a recognition that any real patriotism is mainly theological in its roots rather than historical or national. As long as we remember that, then our patriotism is a true and living creative spirit.

It is only within some such assurance that a national community can discipline itself and make the sacrifices which its own true welfare requires. The unselfish will which we thought of as one of the tools of patriotism depends for its very existence on the assurance that local or national welfare are not the final ends to be served. To learn how to submerge local and self-interest for the sake of national life and welfare is no easy task; and the impulse toward it needs the constant assurance that the making of such sacrifices is justified by a law greater than any human necessity. This is even more true when patriotism looks beyond section and nation to the world community.

THE TESTS PATRIOTISM MUST MEET

It may be well to add a few thoughts about the tests and dangers which patriotism must meet. These are days when fear is abroad in many quarters in our land, when the patriotism of many people is under the sharpest question. This book does not share this fear, and has very little sympathy with the carelessness with which rumor and suspicion are sometimes used as tests of a man's national loyalty. Yet there are real tests of patriotism which every Christian ought to know and apply in his own self-examination.

Two of those tests have already been suggested. One is the test of imagination. There are few dangers to true patriotism so deep as that of mere unimaginative and insensitive information. The mark of the patriot is his capacity to convert what he knows into something he feels in his deepest being.

We have suggested also a parallel test—that of the unselfish will, which alone can implement and fulfill the imaginative knowledge we have of our brother men. Here again, there is the danger of letting our true patriotism evaporate in an emotionalism which only sees but does not act.

Two other tests of true patriotism remain to be discussed. One of them is a very homely and pedestrian one—the test of *our knowledge of the meanings of words*. Whenever we discuss patriotism, certain words are bound to come into our conversation. Some of them are "loaded" words; all of them are words that have a place in our thoughts of national and international loyalty; all of them are words which need far clearer definition than is customarily given them.

At least six of these words are key words—*community, country, nation, race, society, state*. Each of them is a useful word, and each of them refers to a reality which, in its place and proper function, plays a major part in God's providence. Some of these words have already been discussed in this book, as for example "community," which is a very precious word in the Christian vocabulary because of its kinship with the Holy Communion. It is also a word slippery and meaningless unless it is given its full meaning and context. Another word we thought about was the word "state." In the Christian scheme of things, the state—man's political organization of his community or his society—has a clear and recognized religious value. It is ordained of God, that men may live in justice and peace.

So too do the other words have a clear place and usefulness. As difficult and ambiguous a word as "race," although now a dangerously misleading word, has had in the past a noble use in describing and transmitting the virtuous qualities of a people.

But words get out of hand in time and often come to signify untruth. For example, the state is an instrument of the nation; it is not the nation nor superior to it, but the servant of the nation. As long as this relationship of mastery and service is remembered, then the state can fulfill its proper duty in God's eyes. But when, in the dark idolatry that we have come to know only too well, the state becomes an object of mystic veneration and even a substitute for God Himself, then it has become a grotesquely evil abuse.

The conception of nation can likewise be a slippery and dangerous one. No thoughtful man ever can forget the part that national unity and national ideals have played and still do play in enriching and deepening the common life of humanity. Whatever one may feel about nationalism as a political theory, the fact is that nationality has brought blessings to the world far beyond any incidental harm. Ideals have got to be incarnated into people and institutions; principles have got to be acted out in a real society of real men and women; and for nearly half a millenium, the corporate life and institutions of nations have been the means whereby the ideals of liberty and civilization have been realized.

Yet, the nation is not the final or deepest unit of human association. We have reached a point in the world's history when we are ready to move on to a larger unit. Absolute national sovereignty was defensible as a theory as long as a separate nation was able to extend protection to its citizens, and to exercise its sovereignty in a meaningful and positive way. Such sovereignty is now anachronistic. There is no nation in the world which can guarantee protection to its people, or whose sovereignty is anything more then a part of the total sovereignty of humanity. Thus it is that we pass through uncomfortable times, not yet knowing what larger unit of association there may be for us, yet uncomfortably conscious that we have in large measure outgrown the nation as our basic form of organization.

The test for Christian partiotism in this is the test of our ability to keep a proper order and value to such words as these. God has made, we believe, "all nations of men for to dwell on the face of the whole earth." Doubtless that universal humanity is an ultimate unit; yet within it God has given us lesser associations, each of which has its part to play in our growth toward what lies at the end. Our local neighborhood and community are second only to our family as the root encounters of our lives. Our country, a larger association, comes by our maturer years to add still one more association to our list, as does the nation. Even the idea of race plays a useful part in at least describing something of the variety of humanity. But in all this process, nothing less than humanity is satisfactory as the final level of unity.

Furthermore, in God's creation, *human society comes first*. It is not a creation of men or laws; it is a given fact. Man is born into society and never knows a time when he is alone; nor can he secede from this society no matter how hard he tries. The universal humanity of our creation is everywhere expressed in a potentially universal society.

The *Church* is this society—this universal community—seen in its truest light, and redeemed.

The state is the organization which mankind, in our regional and racial and linguistic sub-divisions, adopts to make civilized life possible. It is the vehicle of our useful and necessary power, by which we discipline and control ourselves and establish the conditions under which the good life will be possible. Thus, the state is always a practical and changing thing, accommodated to our circumstances and our needs, and never an end in itself.

These are some of the Christian senses of these words. The Christian patriot must know these words well, think long thoughts about them, and learn to examine his patriotism against this background. This is perhaps a clumsy way to say that wherever our patriotism begins, it should end as a real, imaginative, working love of all humanity, born out of the sense of our common kinship and of the single planet which we inhabit, and of the universal God whose providence has made us members of one another.

The last test of Christian patriotism is the test of *a steadfast belief and discipleship in God*. The danger is the danger of idolatry; of letting state, nation, or race usurp the place of God. There is no earthly loyalty which is superior to our final and ultimate loyalty to God. He who has created peoples, nations, and states and who judges them, He alone, has the right to our final loyalty. Most often, we believe, that ultimate loyalty to God is best expressed by true and faithful loyalty to our own country and people; to be faithful in little things is the first requirement of human dignity. But we have always to search our consciences to be sure that our service to our own nation and state is in truth a service to God, and that the state itself is also serving Him. And this searching of conscience is not always a comfortable thing for ourselves, nor satisfying to the idolatrous impulse to set up the state as an end in itself. Such discomfort, no doubt, can be borne by mature and free people; but it is not always easy to bear either the suspicion or critism of others, or indeed our native distrust of ourselves. Yet, this vigilance may be in the end the most precious jewel at the heart of true patriotism.

Epilogue

THESE LAST few pages are not intended to add any new factors to those we have already been thinking about. They are intended simply to bring our thoughts back again to the theme with which we began—freedom, and to Jesus, the Free Man.

Christian living certainly covers an incredible number of things. This book has not even attempted to discuss many of the areas which are involved in Christian living. We have said nothing, for example, about three common moral problems which, in the minds of many Christians, are of very central importance—smoking, drinking, gambling. We have said very little, and that mainly by implication, about many other areas—the issue of pacifism and military service, for example; or of union membership and collective bargaining.

All of us who had any connection with the publishing of this volume agree that there are many things left unsaid in it, and many matters of Christian conscience left undiscussed. This is necessarily so; no single volume could hope to be a complete introduction to all the problems of Christian living.

Yet, even admitting this, the field we have explored is very wide. It has ranged all the way from relationships within a family and attitudes toward our jobs to world citizenship and relationships between nations. How could it be otherwise? The life of mankind in the twentieth century is as broad as that. Therefore the life of the Christian is this broad too, and the implications of Christian living cannot help but carry us to the four corners of the world and beyond.

Were, however, the principles of Christian living as wide and complex as the problems, the task of being a Christian would be an almost impossible one. Our position is that, in contrast to the problems, the principles are quite clear and uncomplicated.

We have tried to express the heart of those principles in terms of freedom, for it is our conviction that this is the most probing and essential term in which to talk about Christian living. As we said at the very beginning, it is by no means the only term. Yet, to think of Christian living as an adventure in freedom seems to us to come closer to the heart of the matter than any other approach.

We think this because the experience of freedom—of choice— is the most general and the most central feeling that any person can have about himself.

It is the most general. When we struggle out of babyhood, the first thing we learn about ourselves is that we have the power and the necessity to choose what we want to do. Everything we learn, everything we see, everything we touch, everything we are aware of, everything we need—all of reality comes to us in terms of *what we want to do about it*. And from then until the day we die, we are never free from this eternal obligation to judge, to want, to choose, to be.

We know that our choices are never perfect ones and many times are poor ones, bad ones. But we also know that at the time there was no help for this, for decisions had to be made, freedom had to be accepted. There is no escaping this, and there is no real humanity without it.

This inescapable element of choice infects everything in life. Our membership in a family, our interdependence with and on other people in our jobs, our citizenship, our participation in the common life of the world—not one of these is optional. There is no way in which a man can dig a hole for himself and pull the hole in after him; there is no way to secede from humanity and its problems and live our own life in isolation. We have the choice only of being either ineffective members of the human race, failing to carry our end of the load, or positive and loyal members, doing our best to take our part in the life of the body. There is no third way.

Thus, the experience of freedom—of choice—is the most general of all human experiences.

It is also the most central; you cannot come closer to the heart of what it is to be human than when you talk and think about freedom. It is through our choices that we first discover ourselves. *What we are is what we choose*. This has two meanings; it means that the "I," my own self, becomes real only in the choices that I have to make; it means also that the real story of my life is the story of my choices, for I have to live with the consequences of my choices, and the way I have used my freedom in the past is one of the cardinal factors in the way I will use my freedom in the future.

Thus it would be hard to come any closer to the center of our knowledge of ourselves and of others than through our freedom. It is for this reason that the doctrine of God's judgment is as central as it is. When we think about the last things—about death and what lies beyond it—the most important element for Christians is not some mystical change in status, or some indescribable merging of our personality into the vast pool of eternity; it is the sober picture of men and women standing before God and giving an accounting of their use of their freedom.

The most important thing, of course, is what our freedom means to God. We tried to say this when we talked first about Christ, the Free Man. God did not simply give us freedom and abandon us. He does not make us responsible—obliged to choose and be judged by our choices—and then leave us to stand alone before His implacable justice. God so loved the world that He came inside our freedom Himself, and showed us how to use it aright.

This is the ultimate significance of Jesus Christ for us. He accepts the same necessity to choose that is forced on us by our creation; He asks and receives no favors; He strides ahead of the rest of us, writing the story of His life in His choices precisely as we do; then He turns and calls us to follow Him along this adventurous road. Thus, freedom is always more than a predicament; it is, most of all, an opportunity. Man can choose God. He can, by the light and power our Lord gives us, make his freedom a way toward maturity and fulfillment and peace and joy.

All these things—the inescapability of freedom, its limitations and its obligations, and the way in which God redeems us through our freedom—we tried to suggest in the first part of this volume. Then we turned to the practical matters of Christian living, in the next three parts. As we went along, we said very little about freedom and its implications. We tried to discuss each of the separate areas more or less on its own terms, suggesting what implications for Christian living there were in our personal and family life, our vocations, our church membership, our participation in local and national communities, and our inescapable share in the international community.

Yet, even though little was said about the great central theme of freedom, we hope that every one of the separate duties and opportunities we talked about was interpreted against the background of freedom and of our selfhood. If we failed in this, then the book has failed of its purpose. If the book was successful, then its readers will have been helped to see that all Christian living, in every area of life from the most personal to the most world-wide, is a matter of personal responsibility and of opportunity to develop the kind of selfhood Christ has taught us.

For what lies at the heart of the adventure of life is something far more than simply the due fulfillment of certain duties for the accomplishment of certain goals. The things we do, the choices we make, are of importance for this world, for this probationary period. But what is happening all the time we are facing and making our choices, is that *we are becoming persons,* fulfilling (if it may be) what God intends for us.

Therefore all of our Christian living is really a personal encounter and dialog with God. Underneath the things we do and the part we play in family and community and world affairs, is our particular, individual, responsible self, working out its own salvation with fear and trembling, and in the steady remembrance and love of God.

The things, the duties, are for the world of time alone. The self, the person, is for eternity. Therefore, eternity keeps breaking through into time, in all Christian living. Therefore, the values and concerns and fears of this world can never be final and determining for Christians. Even now, here in the world of time and space, we are already sharing in God's eternal life, and we are preparing ourselves for that life when it can be lived in its full richness.

This is the "other-worldly" part of Christian living. This is why no Christian duty can ever be interpreted in terms of its results or effectiveness in this world alone. This is why the end and point of Christian living is not merely to produce a paradise on earth. This is why the kingdom is the Kingdom of God and not a utopia in this world. God has a greater purpose than simply to make this world more peaceful and more comfortable.

This, of course, is not to say that our welfare and the welfare of our neighbors in this life is not important. It is of the greatest significance; but its significance comes from the fact that this world is only a tiny fraction of an infinitely greater reality. And Christians live, as indeed all mankind ought to live, for the sake of that greater reality and not simply this fraction of it.

Finally, there is one word and one theme above all others which should be uppermost in Christian minds and hearts. That word is "offering."

As you think about the different areas of Christian living, there are several great themes which seem to run all through them. One is the *inescapable unity* of mankind, given to us by God in our creation and supremely in our redemption. This is truly inescapable; there is no human problem which is only an individual problem. Every sin is a social sin because every sin in some sense affects our relationship to others. Every act is a social act, for there is no such thing as an individual by himself. Mankind is one.

Another great theme is that of *the utter reality and supremacy of God's will.* The moral laws of God are rooted in the way He has created us. There is no alternative to them. God and His will constitute all the reality there is. Therefore, Christian living is built upon a rock, and gains its tranquil assurance and steadfastness from that fact. Christians in their ethical conduct are not nervously attempting to establish a better state of affairs for mankind. They are rather building a world which is true to its own real nature.

Still another great theme running all through the problems of Christian living is the theme of *building*. Part of the essence of Christian living is that it always looks forward to a new relationship and level of life that will transform the old and make it into something better and truer. Another way of saying this would be to say that there is nothing defensive about Christian ethics. They are not a scheme for escaping injustice so much as they are a way of establishing a greater justice. They are not a plan for avoiding pain as much as they are a way of putting love into action and of making something good out of evil.

So too are there other great, common themes which appear and reappear in every phase of Christian living. But incomparably the greatest of these themes is that of *offering*.

God put freedom into His created universe in order that that universe could respond to His love with an answering love of its own. If He had wanted simply obedience, He could have had it. If He had wanted to create in His universe simply a mirror for His own perfection, He could have done so. If He had intended, in the creation of time and space, simply to establish a stage where He could have portrayed His own character, He could have done so. There is no law outside of His own nature to gainsay what He wills.

But He did not do any of these things. He put into the created universe a principle of choice; and He paid a twofold price for that. First, He limited His own freedom to have everything His own way. Second, He committed Himself to having to win out of freedom what He could perfectly easily have commanded as of right.

Why did He do this? This is, of course, the deepest and most searching of all questions. And the answer to it which the Christian faith gives is the supreme answer. Why did He do this? He did it because He is Love; and because Love seeks an answering love, freely given, for Love's own sake.

It is His unconquerable purpose that mankind shall come to love Him for Himself alone. But that love is not an emotion; it is an act. The way in which men and women show their love for God is by the choices they make, and by the way they try to remember Him and serve Him and do His will in those choices. He puts the whole world of nature into our hands, with all its richness and power. He puts into our hands our stewardship of the resources of this world. He puts into our hands the knowledge of the starry universe. He puts into our hands, most of all, the happiness and well-being of our neighbors.

We can use all this power to separate ourselves and our neighbors from Him. It can become a means of defeating love and of building a wall between ourselves and our true nature. But all this immense stewardship can also be the means of restoring the deep comradeship and the loving partnership of God and man, if we will have it so.

The end of all living is to learn how to offer our lives and our world to God and fulfill ourselves in free obedience. In this offering, Christ led the way—in every word and act, and most of all, in the sublime, single offering of Calvary. He invites us to follow Him along this way, in sure and certain hope that the end of the road is right and good and with God. When we were confirmed, we promised to follow Him along that way. *To live as a Christian is then to follow along the way of offering, with Him, in Him, and through Him, Jesus Christ our Lord.*

About the Author

Stephen F. Bayne, Jr., D.D., S.T.D., formerly Bishop of Olympia, became Anglican Executive Officer at Lambeth Palace on January 1, 1960. He also serves as Secretary of both the Consultative Body and the Council on Missionary Strategy; and he is Bishop in Charge of the Convocation of American Churches in Europe. Previously, he taught at the General Theological Seminary, served as rector of Trinity Church, St. Louis, Missouri, and of St. John's Church, Northampton, Massachusetts, and as chaplain of Columbia University. Bishop Bayne is the author of *Gifts of the Spirit* (1943) and *The Optional God* (1953).

MEMBERS OF THE AUTHORS' COMMITTEE

The Very Rev. John B. Coburn, D.D., Dean, Newark Cathedral.

The Rev. Powel M. Dawley, Ph.D., Professor of Ecclesiastical History and Sub-Dean, The General Theological Seminary.

The Rev. Robert C. Dentan, Ph.D., Professor of Old Testament, The General Theological Seminary.

The Rev. Joseph F. Fletcher, S.T.D., Professor of Christian Ethics, Episcopal Theological School.

The Rev. John Heuss, S.T.D., Rector of Trinity Parish, New York City.

The Rev. David R. Hunter, Ed.D., Director, Department of Christian Education.

Leon McCauley, publishing consultant to Authors' Committee.

The Rev. John B. Midworth, S.T.B., Executive Secretary, Laboratories on the Church and Group Life, Department of Christian Education.

The Very Rev. James A. Pike, J.S.D., Dean, New York Cathedral.

The Rev. W. Norman Pittenger, S.T.D., Professor of Christian Apologetics, The General Theological Seminary.

The Rev. Massey H. Shepherd, Jr., S.T.D., Professor of Liturgics, Church Divinity School of the Pacific.

The Rev. Charles W. F. Smith, D.D., Professor of New Testament, Episcopal Theological School.

The Rev. C. William Sydnor, M.A., Executive Secretary, Division of Curriculum Development, Department of Christian Education.

The Rev. Canon T. O. Wedel, Ph.D., Warden, The College of Preachers, Washington, D.C.

The Rev. M. Moran Weston, Ph.D., Executive Secretary, Division of Christian Citizenship, Department of Christian Social Relations.

Books for Reference

GENERAL WORKS ON CHRISTIAN ETHICAL THOUGHT

INTRODUCTORY BOOKS

The Christian Way by Sydney Cave (London: Nisbet, 1949)

Faith and Behavior by Chad Walsh and Eric Montezambert (New York: Morehouse-Gorham, 1954)

Doing the Truth by James A. Pike (Garden City, N. Y.: Doubleday, 1955)

Guide to the Good Life by William A. Spurrier (New York: Scribners, 1955)

Foundations for Reconstruction by Elton Trueblood (New York: Harper, 1946)

Christian Behavior by C. S. Lewis (New York: Macmillan, 1943)

Smoke on the Mountain by Joy Davidman (Philadelphia: Westminster, 1954)

MORE ADVANCED BOOKS

The Destiny of Man by Nicolas Berdyaev (Chicago: Alec R. Allenson, 1954)

Morals and Man in the Social Sciences by J. V. Langmead Casserley (New York: Longmans, Green, 1951)

Religion and the Moral Life by A. Campbell Garnett (New York: Ronald, 1955)

Christian Ethics by Robert Cecil Mortimer (London: Hutchinson, 1951)

Christian Ethics and Moral Philosophy by George F. Thomas (New York: Scribner's, 1955)

The Structure of Christian Ethics by Joseph Sittler (Baton Rouge: Louisiana State University Press, 1958)

The Cost of Discipleship by Dietrich Bonhoeffer (New York: Macmillan, 2nd rev. ed., 1960)

BOOKS FOR STUDENTS AND SCHOLARS

The Divine Imperative by Emil Brunner (Philadelphia: Westminster, 1943)

Conscience and Its Problems by Kenneth E. Kirk (New York: Longmans, Green, 1948)

Some Principles of Moral Theology and Their Application by Kenneth E. Kirk (London: Longmans, Green, 1954)

Basic Christian Ethics by Paul Ramsey (New York: Scribner's, 1950)

Love, Power and Justice by Paul Tillich (New York: Oxford, 1954)

God's Grace and Man's Hope by D. D. Williams (New York: Harper, n. d.)

Christian Ethics by Dietrich von Hildebrand (New York: David McKay, 1953)

Revelation in Jewish Wisdom Literature by G. Coert Rylaarsdam (Univ. of Chicago Press, 1946)

Moral Theology in the Modern World by Lindsay Dewar (London: Mowbray)

A New Introduction to Moral Theology by Herbert Waddams (New York: Seabury, 1965)

Ethics in a Christian Context by Paul Lehmann (New York: Harper & Row, 1963)

Morality and Beyond by Paul Tillich (New York: Harper & Row, 1963)

The Responsible Self by H. Richard Niebuhr (New York: Harper & Row, 1963)

Christ and the Modern Conscience by Jacques Leclercq (New York: Sheed & Ward)

ETHICAL TEACHINGS IN THE BIBLE

In addition to book references in *The Holy Scriptures* by Robert C. Dentan (New York: Seabury, 1949) pp. 191 ff.

THE OLD TESTAMENT

The Relevance of the Prophets by R. B. Y. Scott (New York: Macmillan, 1944)

ALSO:

The Moral Life of the Hebrews by J. M. P. Smith (Univ. of Chicago Press, 1923)

Relevation and Response in the Old Testament by C. A. Simpson (New York: Columbia, 1947)

The Distinctive Ideas of the Old Testament by Norman H. Smith (London: Epworth, 1944)

THE NEW TESTAMENT

The Ethical Teachings of Jesus by Ernest F. Scott (New York: Macmillan, 1925)

Gospel and Law by C. H. Dodd (New York: Columbia, 1951)

The Sermon on the Mount by Martin Dibelius (New York: Scribner's, 1940)

Ethics and the Gospel by T. W. Manson (New York: Scribner's, 1960)

The Ethics of Paul by M. C. Enslin (Nashville, Tenn.: Abingdon, 1962)

The Ethic of Jesus in the Teaching of the Church by John Knox (Nashville, Tenn.: Abingdon, 1961)

Eschatology and Ethics in the Teaching of Jesus by Amos N. Wilder (New York: Harper & Row, 1950)

THE MORAL HERITAGE FROM THE CHRISTIAN CENTURIES

Christian Ethics: Sources of the Living Tradition, Waldo Beach and H. Richard Niebuhr, eds. (New York: Ronald, 1955)

The Vision of God: the Christian Doctrine of the *Summum Bonum* by Kenneth
E. Kirk (London: Longmans, Green, 1931); also an abridged edition (London: Longmans, Green, 1934)

The Idea of Perfection in Christian Spirituality by R. Newton Flew (New
York: Oxford, 1934)

The Sources of Western Morality: from Primitive Society through the Beginning of Christianity by Georgia Harkness (New York: Scribner's, 1954)

Moral Philosophy by Jacques Maritain (New York: Scribner's, 1964)

BOOKS FOR PART I: *FREEDOM AND THE FREE MAN*

GENERAL BOOKS

The Screwtape Letters by C. S. Lewis (New York: Macmillan, 1943)

Real Life Is Meeting by J. H. Oldham (New York: Seabury, 1953)

Life Is Commitment by J. H. Oldham (New York: Harper, 1952)

Beyond Anxiety by James A. Pike (New York: Scribner's, 1953)

Be Not Anxious by Randolph C. Miller (New York: Seabury, 1957)

Christ in the Haunted Wood by W. Norman Pittenger (New York: Seabury, 1953)

The Christianity by Main Street by Theodore Wedel (New York: Macmillan, 1950)

The Optional God by Stephen F. Bayne, Jr. (New York: Oxford, 1953)

Making Sense Out of Life by Charles Duell Kean (Philadelphia: Westminster, 1954)

Authority and Freedom by Robert T. Thouless (New York: Seabury, 1955)

MORE ADVANCED BOOKS

The Christian Doctrine of Man from Committee of the Lambeth Conference
1948 in *Encyclical Letter from the Bishops with Resolutions and Reports*
(London: S.P.C.K., 1948)

The Recovery of Man by F. R. Barry (New York: Scribner's, 1949)

The Nature and Destiny of Man by Reinhold Niebuhr (New York: Scribner's, 1947)

An Interpretation of Christian Ethics by Reinhold Niebuhr (New York: Harper, 1935)

Anxiety and Faith by Charles R. Stinnette (New York: Seabury, 1955)

Pychotherapy and the Christian View of Man by Davjd E. Roberts (New York: Scribner's, 1950)

The Structure of Life by Edgar L. Allen (London: Nisbet, 1945)

I and Thou by Martin Büber (New York: Scribner's, 1937)

Responsibility by Sir Walter Moberly (New York: Seabury, 1956)

Psychotherapy and the Christian Message by A. C. Outler (New York: Harper & Row, 1954)

Christian Morals Today by J. A. T. Robinson (Philadelphia: Westminster, 1964)

Between Man and Man by Martin Büber (New York: Macmillan, 1948)

The Courage to Be by Paul Tillich (New Haven: Yale, 1952)

The Faith of a Moralist by A. E. Taylor (London: Macmillan, 1930; also New York: St. Martin's, 1930)

The Meaning of Existence by Charles Duell Kean (New York: Harpers, 1947)

Man for Himself by Erich Fromm (New York: Rinehart, 1947)

Conscience and Compromise: An Approach to Protestant Casuistry by E. L. Long, Jr. (Philadelphia: Westminster, 1954)

Transformation in Christ by Dietrich von Hildebrand (New York: Longmans, Green, 1948)

Religion and Human Behavior, Simon Doniger, ed. (New York: Association, 1954)

The Secular Meaning of the Gospel by Paul Van Buren (New York: Macmillan, 1963)

The Responsible Self by H. Richard Niebuhr (New York: Harper & Row, 1963)

Morality and Beyond by Paul Tillich (New York: Harper & Row, 1963)

BOOKS FOR PART II: PERSONAL LIFE, FAMILY AND WORK

(These books are in addition to chapters in many of the books listed above under General Works.)

CHAPTER SIX: PERSONAL RELIGIOUS LIFE

INTRODUCTORY

Life, Faith and Prayer by A. Graham Ikin (New York: Oxford, 1954)

The Struggle of the Soul by Lewis J. Sherrill (New York: Macmillan, 1952)

Your God Is Too Small by J. B. Phillips (New York: Macmillan, 1952)

Making Men Whole by J. B. Phillips (New York: Macmillan, 1953)

Rediscovering Prayer by John L. Casteel (New York: Association, 1955)

School of Prayer by Olive Wyon (Chicago: Alec R. Allenson, 1952)

Collected Papers by Evelyn Underhill (New York: Longmans, Green, 1946)

Our Trespasses by Martin Jarrett-Kerr (London: Student Christian Movement, 1948)

Penitence and Forgiveness by Wilfred Knox (New York: Macmillan, 1953)

Know Thyself: An Aid to Self-Examination by James Wareham (New York: Morehouse-Gorham, 1950)

Guilt and Redemption by Lewis J. Sherrill (Rev. ed., John Knox Press, 1956)

Christian Holiness by Stephen Neill (Chicago: Allenson, 1960)

Signposts on the Christian Way by Patrick Hankey (New York: Scribner's, 1962)

Christian Proficiency by Martin Thornton (New York: Morehouse-Barlow, 1959)

ADVANCED

Elements of the Spiritual Life by F. P. Harton (New York: Macmillan, 1932)

Contemplative Prayer by Shirley C. Hughson, O.H.C. (West Park, N. Y.: Holy Cross)

With Christ in God by Shirley C. Hughson, O.H.C. (London: S.P.C.K., 1948)

The Art of Mental Prayer by Bede Frost (London: Philip Alland, 1935. Order from Macmillan)

Anglican Devotion by C. J. Stranks (New York: Seabury, 1961)

The Evelyn Underhill Reader. T. S. Kepler, ed. (Nashville: Abingdon, 1962)

God in Us by Miles Yates (New York: Seabury, 1959)

SELECTED CHRISTIAN CLASSICS OF THE DEVOTIONAL LIFE

Confessions by St. Augustine of Hippo. E. B. Pusey, tr. Everyman's Library. (New York: Dutton, 1910)

On the Love of God by St. Bernard of Clairvaux. Edmund Gardner, tr. (London: Dutton, 1916)

The Little Flowers by St. Francis of Assisi. T. W. Arnold, tr. (London: Temple Classics, 1903)

The Imitation of Christ by Thomas à Kempis. Evelyn Underhill, ed. (London: John Maurice Watkins, 1949)

The Cloud of Unknowing Anon. Evelyn Underhill, ed. (Chicago: Alec R. Allenson, 1950)

Private Devotions by Lancelot Andrewes. J. H. Newman, ed. (New York: Abingdon, 1950)

Sermons by John Donne. L. P. Smith, ed. (New York: Oxford, 1919)

The Golden Grove by Jeremy Taylor. Selected passages, L. P. Smith, ed. (New York: Oxford, 1930)

Introduction to the Devout Life by St. François de Sales. Allan Ross, tr. (London: Burns Oates & Washbourne, 1948) (7th ed.)

The Pocket William Law. A. W. Hopkinson, ed. (London: Latimer House, 1950)

The Practice of the Presence of God by Brother Lawrence (many editions)

Pensèes by Blaise Pascal. W. F. Trotter, tr. (New York: Modern Library, 1941)

Some Fruits of Solitude by William Penn, Pocket classics. (New York: McKay, 1942)

The Pilgrim's Progress by John Bunyan (many editions)

Poems by William Blake. W. B. Yeats, ed. (New York: Dutton, 1901)

Meditations from Kierkegaard by Søren Kierkegaard. T. H. Croxall, ed. (Philadelphia: Westminster, 1955)

The Spear of Gold, Hans Ansgar Reinhold, ed. (London: Burns Oates and Washbourne, 1953)

A Day Book from the Saints and Fathers, John Henry Burn, ed. (London: Methuen, 1950)

The Fellowship of the Saints. T. S. Kepler, ed. (Nashville: Abingdon, 1948)

BOOKS FOR CHAPTERS SEVEN AND EIGHT

The Mystery of Love and Marriage by Derrick S. Bailey (New York: Harpers, 1952)

Sex Life in Marriage by Oliver M. Butterfield (New York: Emerson, n. d.)

A Marriage Manual by Abraham and Hannah Stone (New York: Simon & Schuster, 1952)

The Christian View of Sexual Behavior by W. Norman Pittenger (New York: Seabury, 1954)

If You Marry Outside Your Faith by James A. Pike (New York: Harpers, 1954)

Sex in Christianity and Psychoanalysis by W. G. Cole (New York: Oxford, 1955)

Sex and Religion Today, Simon Doniger, ed. (New York: Association, 1953)

For Better or For Worse by Emile Cammaerts (London: Skeffington, 1948)

The Meaning of Love by Vladimir Soloviev. Jane Marshall, tr. (New York: International University, 1948)

Essay on Human Love by Jean Guitton, Foreword by the Earl of Halifax. Melville Chaning-Pearce, tr. (London: Rockliff, 1951)

Background to Marriage, or the First Twenty Years by Anne Proctor (London: Longmans, Green, 1953)

The Christian Household by Anne Proctor (New York: Longmans, Green, 1950)

The Recovery of Family Life by Elton and Pauline Trueblood (New York: Harpers, 1953)

An Exposition of Christian Sex Ethics by V. A. Demant (London: Hodder & Stoughton)

Talking of Sex by T. R. Milford (London: Christian Frontier Pamphlet)

BOOKS FOR CHAPTER NINE: MONEY AND STEWARDSHIP

Christian Giving by Vedanayakam Samuel Azariah (New York: Association, 1955)

Property: Its Rights and Duties by Charles Gore and Others (London: Macmillan, 1915)

Christianity and Property by Charles L. Taylor and Others. Joseph F. Fletcher, ed. (Philadelphia: Westminster, 1947)

God and the Rich Society by D. L. Munby (New York: Oxford, 1961)

BOOKS FOR CHAPTER TEN: VOCATION AND ITS PROBLEMS

Man at Work in God's World. George E. DeMille, ed. (New York: Longmans, Green, 1956)

God and the Day's Work by Robert L. Calhoun (New York: Association, 1943)

Ethics in a Business Society by Marquis Childs and Douglass Cater (New York: Harper, 1954)

Christian Vocation by William R. Forrester (New York: Scribners, 1953)

Christian Faith and My Job by Alexander Miller (New York: Association, 1946)

A Doctor's Profession. Daniel Jenkins, ed. (London: Student Christian Movement, 1949)

The Ethical Basis of Medical Practice by Willard L. Sperry (New York: Paul B. Hoeber, 1950)

What Is the Priesthood by John V. Butler and W. Norman Pittenger (New York: Morehouse-Gorham, 1954)

Ethics and Business by W. A. Spurrier (New York: Scribner's, 1962)

The Will and the Way by H. Blamires (London: SPCK, 1962)

The Biblical Doctrine of Work by A. Richardson (Chicago: Allenson, 1958)

BOOKS FOR CHAPTER ELEVEN: DEATH

The Great Divorce by C. S. Lewis (New York: Macmillan, 1946)

Death and Life by M. C. D'Arcy (London: Longmans, Green, 1942)

And After This by Harry N. Hancock (New York: Longmans, Green, 1955)

And the Life Everlasting by John Baillie (New York: Scribner's, 1933)

The Christian Hope of Immortality by A. E. Taylor (New York: Macmillan, 1947)

A Grief Observed by C. S. Lewis (New York: Seabury, 1961)

BOOKS FOR PART III: CHURCH, COMMUNITY, AND NATION

The Faith of the Church by James A. Pike and W. Norman Pittenger (New York: Seabury, 1951) and books recommended there pp. 204-5

The Worship of the Church by Massey H. Shepherd, Jr. (New York: Seabury, 1952) and books recommended there pp. 213-26

The Episcopal Church and Its Work by Powel Mills Dawley (New York: Seabury, 1955) and also books recommended there pp. 301 ff.

The Relevance of the Church by F. R. Barry (London: James Nisbet, 1935)

Man's Need and God's Action by Reuel Howe (New York: Seabury, 1953)

Worship by Evelyn Underhill (New York: Harper, 1937)

The Way of Worship, A Study in Ecumenical Recovery by Scott Francis Brenner (New York: Macmillan, 1944)

Ways of Worship. Pehr Ewall, Eric Hayman and William D. Maxwell, eds. The Report of a Theological Commission of Faith and Order (New York: Harper, 1951)

Social Sources of Denominationalism by H. Richard Niebuhr (Hamden: Shoestring Press, 1954)

Religion of the Prayer Book by Powel M. Dawley and Walden Pell (New York: Morehouse-Gorham, 1946)

The Layman in the Church by Michael de la Bodeyer (London: Burns, Oates & Washbourne, 1955)

The Worshipping Community by H. C. L. Heywood (New York: Morehouse-Gorham, 1938)

Liturgy and Personality by Dietrich von Hildebrand (New York: Longmans, Green, 1943)

The Church's Prayers by Henry de Candole (London: Mowbray, 1939)

Worship, Its Social Significance. Lectures at Swanwick. Foreword by P. T. R. Kirk (Toronto: S. J. R. Saunders, 1939)

Christianity and the Social Order by William Temple (New York: Macmillan, 1950)

Foundations of Reconstruction by Elton Trueblood (New York: Harper, 1946)

The Church and Social Responsibility. J. Richard Spann, ed. (New York: Abingdon, 1953)

Christian Ethics and Social Policy by John C. Bennett (New York: Scribner's, 1946)

The Christian as Citizen by John C. Bennett (New York: Association, 1955)

Citizen and Churchman by William Temple (London: Eyre & Spottiswoode, 1941)

Christianity and Justice by O. C. Quick (New York: Macmillan, 1940)

The Bent World by J. V. Langmead Casserley (New York: Oxford University, 1955)

Naught for Your Comfort by Trevor Huddleston, C. R. (New York: Doubleday, 1956)

An American Dilemma by Gunnar Myrdal and others (New York: Harper, 1944)

A Christian Looks at the Jewish Question by Jacques Maritain (New York: Longmans, Green, 1939)

To Secure These Rights by the President's Committee on Civil Rights (New York: Simon and Schuster, 1948)

The Main Types and Causes of Discrimination by The United Nations Commission on Human Rights (New York: United Nations, 1949)

Religion and Economic Responsibility by Walter G. Muelder (New York: Scribners, 1953)

Christian Values and Economic Life by John C. Bennett, Harold R. Bowen and others (New York: Harper, 1954)

Christian Social Ethics; Exerting Christian Influence by A. T. Rasmussen (New York: Prentice-Hall, 1956)

Liturgy and Society by A. G. Hebert, S.S.M. (London: Faber, 1935)

Liturgy Coming to Life by J. A. T. Robinson (Philadelphia: Westminster, 1964)

Liturgy and Education by Massey H. Shepherd (New York: Seabury, 1965)

When Christians Make Political Decisions by J. C. Bennett (New York: Association, 1964)

The Racial Problem in Christian Perspective by K. Haselden (New York: Harper & Row, 1959)

Crisis in Black and White by C. E. Silberman (New York: Random House, 1964)

The Other America by M. Harrington (Baltimore: Penguin)

The Public Philosophy by W. Lippmann (Boston: Little, Brown, 1955)

We Hold These Truths by J. C. Murray (New York: Sheed & Ward, 1961)

The Pastor and the Race Issue by Daisuke Kitagawa (New York: Seabury, 1965)

Race and the Renewal of the Church by W. D. Campbell (Philadelphia: Westminster, 1962)

BOOKS FOR PART IV: NATIONAL AND INTERNATIONAL LIFE

Religion and the Rise of Capitalism by R. H. Tawney (New York: Harcourt, Brace, 1947)

Faith and Society: the Christian Social Movement in Great Britain and the U.S.A. by Maurice B. Reckitt (New York: Longmans, Green, 1932)

War, Peace and the Christian Mind by James Thayer Addison (New York: Seabury, 1953)

The Hope of a New World by William Temple (London: Student Christian Movement, 1940)

The Church and the Atom, A Study of the Moral and Theological Aspects of Peace and War by the Archbishops' Commission on Atomic Power (London: Church Assembly, 1948)

Peace in the Atomic Age by the Catholic Association for International Peace (Washington: Catholic Association for International Peace, 1947)

The Atomic Age and the Christian Faith by the Commission on the Relation of the Church to the War (New York: Federal Council of the Churches of Christ, 1946)

Christians and the State by J. C. Bennett (New York: Scribner's)

The Structure of Nations and Empires by Reinhold Niebuhr (New York: Scribner's, 1959)

Christian Attitudes Toward War and Peace by R. Bainton (Nashville: Abingdon, 1960)

Mater et Magistra and *Pacem in Terris,* the two major social encyclicals of John XXIII: (good inexpensive editions with notes and guides are published by the America Press, 920 Broadway, New York)

Lambeth Conference Reports of 1948 and 1958, particularly the Report on the Family in 1958

Anglican Congress Report of 1963

Material available from the Center for the Study of Democratic Institutions, P.O. Box 4068, Santa Barbara, California

Index

General Index

to

The Church's Teaching

This index includes chiefly those topics and themes that are discussed in more than one volume of the series. Topics of major doctrinal importance, however, are also included although the topic may be treated in only one of the volumes. Where the topic receives its principal treatment the page reference is printed in italics.

Key to symbols used:

I	*The Holy Scriptures*	**S**
II	*Chapters in Church History*	**H**
III	*The Faith of the Church*	**F**
IV	*The Worship of the Church*	**W**
V	*Christian Living*	**L**
VI	*The Episcopal Church and Its Work*	**E**

Absolution: **F** *157-58;* **W** 17, 103, 125-26, 155, 192, 193, 200, 201

Acts, Book of: **S** 119, 126, *150-58,* 159; **H** 5, 30; **W** 49, 141, 146, 170, 172, 173, 184, 191, 200

Adam: **S** 32-33, 86; **F** *66-69*

Anglican Communion: **H** 214, 220, 235, 244; **E** 5-6, *14-18,* 41, 47, 64, 70, 77, 83-84, 97-98, 106, 114, 132, 140, 161, 166, 184, 191, 198, 263 ff.; **W** 68, 93-94, 114, 134, 149, 174, 202

Anglicanism: **H** 91, 92, 102, 132, 134, 160, 171, 175, 185-88, 196, 206, 213, 220, 221, 228-29, 235, 244; **F** 3-6, 16-19, 138-40, 196-97; **E** 6, *10-14,* 16, 19-20, 26, 40, 53, 66-67, 150, 155, 161, 263 ff.

Apostles: **S** 120, *137-38,* 142, 144, 147, 166; **W** 38, 73, 112, 114, 173, 191, 199-200, 205; **H** 38-40

Articles of Religion: **H** 172, *174;* **S** 21; **F** 73, 148; **W** 178

Ascension: **S** 149, 150, 151; **F** *101-04;* **W** 30, 80, 105, 107, 108, 120, 145

Atonement: **S** 111; **F** 14, 22, *70-80,* 152-55, 201-02

Apostolic Succession: **H** 28-29, *38-42,* 141, 175; **F** 138-40

Baptism: **S** 162-63; **F** 128-29, 139, 148-50, 158, 205-06; **W** 14, 39, 51, 62, 70, 73, 75-76, 98, 102, 107, 109-10, 113, 119, 132, 138-39, *166-83,* 195; of Christ: **S** 130-31; **W** 168-69; of infants: **W** 167, 174-77, 180

Benedictus: **S** 129; **W** 118, 131

Bible: definition of, **S** *5-17,* 24; **W** 27, 35-39, 70, 81, 83, 88, 109, 129-32, 153, 203, 204; **F** 16-18, 19, 40

Bishop: **S** 165, 167; **F** 138-40, 157, 160;

Priest: S 113, 114, 119, 167, 178; W 73, 200-05

Priests: E 124-25, 144, 157

Priesthood: F 137-38, 160; of all believers: F 137-38

Presentation: S 126; feast of: W 118

Psalms: S 28, 93, 94, 95-97, 108; W 19, 21, 22, 28, 53, 55, 70, 74, 81, 97, 107, 126-29, 131, 132, 136, 151, 191, 193, 194, 195-96

Purgatory: F 173, see Intermediate State; W 84, 89; L 152

Puritanism: H 148, 150, 173, 184-87, 226

Puritans: W 46-47, 63, 67, 91

Protestant: F 3-4

Protestantism: H 131, 136 ff., 195 ff., 206, 209 ff., 219-30, 251 ff.

"Protestant Episcopal," the name: E 42 n, 114

Protestant Episcopal Church: H 91, 218, 219 ff.; heritage: E 3-23, 78-79, 82, 84; history: E 14-15, 23-72; today: E 67-70; structure and organization: E 73-173; missionary activity: E 57-62, 138-39, 177-220; program and work: E 177-261; ecumenical activity: E 262-76

Quakers: W 52; E 30, 32

Reformation: H 133-88; F 4, 17; W 47, 54, 59, 68, 85, 86-90, 135, 141, 148-49, 178; English: H 151-77, 184-88; E 8-13

Resurrection of Christ: S 119, 121, 128, 147-48, 150, 163, 173, 186; F 99-101, 203; of the body: F 79-80, 164-73, 206-07; L 149-50, 153-55

Revelation: Book of: S 169, 180, 182; Nature of God's: S 5-9, 17, 186; F 40, 43, 48-49, 70, 97-78; W 25, 35-40, 101, 129-30

Sacramental principle: F 144-47, 162-63, 168, 176

Sacraments: W 39, 56, 61-62, 123, 138-39, 178, 183; and sacramental rites: F 144-63, 205, 206

Sacrifice: S 37, 88, 110-11, 114, 116, 171, 178; W 7, 34, 44, 59, 69-70, 144-45, 161, 163, 165, 207-08

Sabbath: S 112, 138, 164; W see Sunday; L 203-06

Salvation: S 34, 104, 161; F see Atonement, Heaven, Justification, Sanctification

Seabury, Samuel: H 220-24; W 92; E 15, 41-43, 45-46, 49, 51

Secularism: F 29, 33, 106-07 (see Agnosticism; Humanism; Marxism; Materialism)

Sex: F 66, 67, 159, 172, 174; L 75-91

Sin: S 18, 19, 32, 33, 34, 85, 86, 103, 104, 111, 116, 148; F 29, 63-64, 71-74; W 32-34, 99, 125, 158, 191, 192

Social Teaching of Bible: S 16, 31, 32, 57-58, 78, 88, 89, 90, 102, 104, 134, 136, 151, 167-69, 179

Spirit, Holy: S 11, 23, 24, 64, 76, 148, 151, 157, 159, 160; F 20, 50, 109-25, 204; W 33, 63-65, 103, 107, 110, 126, 160, 166, 172-73, 177, 178, 184-85, 199, 202, 206, 207; and the Church: F 113-16, 186, 187; secular work of: F 120-25

Sunday: W 8, 19-21, 38, 98, 107, 111-13, 122, 139, 147-50, 179, 201; L 203-06

Thirty-nine Articles: see Articles of Religion

Trinity: doctrine of: S 103, 160; H 32-33; F 22, 97, 119-20, 184-92, 207

Trinity Season: W 121-22; Sunday: W 121

Unction, Holy: F 161-62; W 192-94

Virgin Birth: F 86-87, 96, 203

Wesley, John: H 200, 204-07; W 149

Word of God: S 9-10, 11, 24, 66, 103, 149, 185-87; W 35-40, 52-54, 57, 124, 129-32, 150, 154, 188 (see Bible)

Worship: W 3-94; F 19, 24, 39, 41, 123, 174-75, 192; judgment in: W 25-26, 34, 52, 99, 124, 125, 157-58; social values in: W 12-13, 15, 18, 21-22; L 202-03, 206-10

Zwingli, Huldreich: H 144-45, 146; W 148